EDWARDIAN LIFE AND LEISURE

EDWARDIAN
LIFE AND LEISURE

Ronald Pearsall

ST. MARTIN'S PRESS : NEW YORK

CONTENTS

5

LIST OF ILLUSTRATIONS

7

CHAPTER ONE

POMP AND CIRCUMSTANCE

Death of a Great Queen

AT 6.45 on the evening of 22 January a bulletin was issued by three doctors from Osborne House, one of the homes of Queen Victoria: 'Her Majesty the Queen breathed her last at 6.30 pm surrounded by her children and her grandchildren.'

So opened 1901, and predictably the nation mourned their dead monarch. Lady Battersea, a member of a famous Jewish family, wrote: 'The emptiness of the great city without the feeling of the Queen's living presence in her Empire, and the sensation of universal change haunted me more than any other sensations.' Memorial services proliferated throughout the Empire, and in Europe. Biarritz, one of the fun-loving resorts patronised by the nobility of the time, was ten days late, and among those who attended its memorial service was Mary Gladstone, the daughter of William Gladstone, the now dead Grand Old Man of British politics. She was characteristically brisk about the whole thing: 'Our Mem. Service at 12, crowded, all in deep black. H. read the lesson, by far the most impressive bit of the service, except perhaps the beautiful singing of "Then shall the righteous. . . ." '[1]

Most of Queen Victoria's subjects had never known a time

when she had not been reigning over them. Lytton Strachey looked back with sentimental hindsight in 1921. 'It appeared,' he wrote, 'as if some monstrous reversal of the course of nature was about to take place.'[2] Queen Victoria had become embodied in the national consciousness as the eternal mother figure, even to the ageing once-disreputable poet Swinburne, who declared:

> No braver soul drew bright and queenly breath
> Since England wept upon Elizabeth.

Lady St Helier was one of the many thousands who watched the despatch of the queen's body from Osborne to Windsor via Portsmouth, 'amid all the glories of an unparalleled winter sunset . . . the deeper chords in the heart of a people seem to be reached, and to respond in all their volume to the profounder feelings which play upon them.'[3] The body was escorted by 'Her' fleet—though she was no longer queen; this confusion, this numbness, was felt most strongly by the court. For twenty-four hours after her death everything continued in the name of the queen; and it was twenty-four hours before homage was paid to the new king, homage which was customarily paid immediately upon the monarch's death. Edward was being snubbed again, for the last time and from beyond the grave.

The newspapers vied with each other in tribute. The magazine *The King*, in its column 'Topics of Today', declared that 'One's first feeling is undoubtedly a dazed sense that the impossible has happened'. The *Illustrated London News* had problems: 'Think what it means that we can never again sing the National Anthem in its present wording. The point is rather delicate . . .'

Upon news of her death, the great bell of St Paul's tolled to the 'grief-stricken citizens of London'. There was a wave of warm feeling towards the kaiser, Victoria's nephew, when the public heard that, amidst the chaos and uncertainty surrounding the corpse, he had behaved with manly dignity, unceremoniously ejecting the undertakers from the room and himself placing the body of his aunt in the coffin. The public temporarily ignored the savage tasteless cartoons that were currently running in German newspapers, depicting the queen as a fat woman at a fair being prodded by Kruger (the leader of the Boers, then involved in a protracted war with Britain).

Nevertheless, it appears to us from photographs of the time that the predominant reaction of the crowds who thronged the gates of Buckingham Palace during the last hours of the queen, idly reading the bulletins posted on the metal barriers, was one of curiosity. They were more interested in the cameramen who photographed them; they stand there in top hats, flat caps, and bowlers, inscrutable, hands in pockets, puffing at cigarettes.

The more staid newspapers had had obituaries of the queen ready to print for years, but the 'Yellow Press' was beginning to make its impact, and at Cowes 500 reporters and photographers clamoured for the one extra titbit that would make their journey worthwhile. In spotted bow-ties, with the ubiquitous cigarette poking from the corner of the mouth, the journalists were under no obligation to behave solemnly. There were no shots to be had of the dead queen, so they had to make do with photographs of the various warships riding at respectful anchor or of the kaiser's two detectives, walking, uncomprehended and incomprehensible, in the streets of East Cowes.

After the initial shock, many people found that they were inconvenienced by the queen's death. Theatres and restaurants (including Romano's) were closed, court mourning would persist for a year, and mourning was to be worn by British Army officers for six weeks. But, declared the city columns of the newspapers, 'the year of mourning for the Queen which has been officially ordained can hardly fail to bring enormous profit to Jay's, Limited, and to firms engaged in similar sombre trades'. [ie the provision of mourning wear].

The Stock Exchange closed for a day in tribute. This did not make much difference, for things were slack anyway as it was a time of recession. The moneyed people were holding back their wealth for prices to reach rock bottom. The railway companies had £30 million waiting to be spent when steel dropped below £7 a ton. When the Stock Exchange reopened, little business was done; there was small profit to be made from calamity.

But some profited. Within a few days of the queen's death Cassell's brought out *The Life and Times of Queen Victoria* in weekly parts. Sir Theodore Martin, who had written the life of the Prince Consort, between 1874 and 1880, was confidently expected to be commissioned to write the official biography of the queen (though he was eighty-five and could scarcely be expected to finish it). In the event he was not. Then who would get the prestige-laden job of editing Victoria's letters? The choice eventually fell on A. C. Benson, an Eton schoolmaster.

The air of gloom was interrupted by the proclamation of King Edward VII, read out by town clerks throughout the country. The ceremony at Bradford, accompanied by military and brass bands, encouraged an audience of 30,000; while at Brighton 40,000 turned up. But the festivities were short-lived and the motley was doffed for the mask of tragedy:

On the face of the world in its wideness
Is there sorrow and grief to-day,
For the woman of God has departed—
The Queen that was with us alway.

(words by D. L. A. Jephson;
music by A. H. Behrend)

Or was it? For the eulogising and breast-thumping are in contradiction to the comments of observers who stood aside and watched. 'This morning I saw what I could, over the heads of a vast crowd, of the funeral procession of the queen. The people were not, on the whole, deeply moved, whatever journalists may say, but rather serene and cheerful.' So wrote the novelist Arnold Bennett in his diary, one of the acutest commentators on the social scene. Max Beerbohm was even more outspoken: 'I have never seen such an air of universal jollity. It is a city of ghouls.'[4]

Many watched the funeral procession with secret cynicism. Among the royal mourners was the reprobate king of Belgium, who although nearly seventy had retained the services of a prostitute for his trip to England. There was a jockeying for position between King Edward and Kaiser Wilhelm; Edward had never forgiven the kaiser for his dismemberment of Denmark or the annexation of Hanover. It was believed by many that the king, who had no wish to be outshone in the procession, had conferred on the kaiser the rank of field-marshal in the British Army so as to make him appear ridiculous in full ceremonial dress. Edward liked dressing up and looked well in uniform— despite being called 'the little fat man in red' by the *Pall Mall Gazette.*

In the crowd was A. G. C. Liddell, lawyer and man-about-town. He thought the military tone of the funeral absurd, and the khaki of the guns and gun-carriage carrying the coffin ridiculous. 'The pall was not good,' he wrote in his diary. 'It was white, with the royal arms embroidered on it, but of a small and poor design.' The horses drawing the gun-carriage were ill-trained and had to be replaced. The sensitive saw

BROTHERS IN TRIBULATION.
John Bull: '' Don't you wish we could start the New Century in peace, Sammy ? ''
                                        —*Denver Sunday Post.*

The reign of King Edward VII began in an atmosphere of crisis. This American cartoon shows that this was not confined to Britain

hidden significances: 'There were several strange stories afloat
connected with this event which are worth recalling. In a
material age we regard them as coincidences—but were they?
White birds came and rested on her coffin, and at night a new
star appeared in the sky.'[5]

Things returned to normal with almost indecent haste. The
theatres and restaurants speedily reopened. To those who had
taken the queen's death most to heart it was disgraceful that
people were actually enjoying themselves, or getting married.
In the weekly illustrated papers, pictures of the wedding of
Queen Wilhelmina of Holland faced photographs of elaborate
wreaths in memory of Victoria. The Duke of Westminster
married the daughter of Mrs Cornwallis West, a professional
beauty and a close friend of Edward VII when he was Prince of
Wales.

Abroad, the queen's death had solved no problems. Boer
commandos were still a thorn in the side of the British Army in
South Africa. Another 30,000 mounted men were to be sent to
Lord Kitchener, to be swallowed up in the vast wastes, along
with their officers who regarded the war, said Kitchener, as
being like polo 'with intervals for afternoon tea'. On the
continent, Britain was not loved. Austria had not even paid
lip-service to the late queen, and a meeting of what passed for the
Austrian parliament was broken up by members shouting pro-Boer
slogans. The nations of Europe waited for a realignment of
power; it was well known that the new king was pro-French
and anti-German. Realistic Europeans wondered whether
alliances with Britain were militarily advantageous after the
army's poor showing in South Africa.

What sort of Britain was it in January 1901?

It was a commercially static Britain. She had been surpassed
in coal and iron production by the United States, and in steel
by the United States and Germany, though she was still the
principal exporter of manufactured goods. The last year of the
nineteenth century had seen a boom with £635 million in
exports, but the last year of Victoria had been less impressive,
and a sinister clue to the future was seen in the decline in

To go from west to east London was to encounter 'a new and different race of people, short of stature, and of wretched and beer sodden appearance'

demand for cotton goods. The import of cheap food, especially grain, had helped the urban proletariat at the expense of the farm workers, who in their thousands were leaving the rural areas for the towns. Between 1870 and 1914 acreage under corn went down by 30 per cent, though the overall decline in agriculture was to some extent alleviated by the increase in dairy farming. The introduction of the first petrol-driven tractor in 1902 also reduced the demand for farm workers.

The standstill at home contrasted sharply with the world picture. Between 1884 and 1900 Britain had acquired 3,750,000 square miles of territory, plus 50 million new subjects, demanding to be policed by a massive army that the home country could ill afford. National expenditure on the fighting forces went up from one-third to a half of the total budget. The most hazardous feature of the casual building up of an ill-understood and reluctant Empire was the amount of money invested in far-off places, leaving little capital free for the replacement of obsolete industrial equipment at home, or for the energising of industries whose output had been superseded, or was in the process of being superseded, by other countries.

Industry had had it too easy. Since the 1870s lethargy and self-complacency had reigned. The sons of manufacturers were 'content to follow mechanically the lead given by their fathers. They worked shorter hours, and they exerted themselves less to obtain new practical ideas than their fathers had done, and thus a part of England's leadership was destroyed rapidly'.[6]

For three decades the standard of living had been creeping up; after 1900 it began to decline. The pound sterling of 1895 was worth 18s 5d in 1900 and 16s 3d in 1912. Although between 1893 and 1908 nominal wages went up by 12 per cent, this disguised the real fall in living standards—for the poor, of course. In the same period, profits went up by 29½ per cent. The equation is simple: the rich became richer and the poor became poorer. Edward VII, who worshipped money as much as he did pleasure, was not the man to alter this. He implanted the idea of the respectability of pleasure not only with his peers but with those who could not afford it. In 1901 one-third of the population tried to live as only one-seventeenth could afford to. Of 7 million households, only 400,000 had incomes of more than £400 a year. A third of the population lived in penury. And very few cared.

To go from west to east London was to encounter, wrote Jack London, 'a new and different race of people, short of stature, and of wretched and beer sodden appearance'. The public houses were open from 6 am to 11 pm, and the average working-class family spent 6s a week on drink, a third of its income. A quarter of the people who died in London in 1901 were buried at the expense of the parish.

The respectable were terrified by this submerged class, and of the power it could wield with the advent of socialism, a dirty word since the 1880s. Kenneth Grahame put this terror into symbolic form in *Wind in the Willows*: '[the proletariat] had little evil wedge shaped faces . . . all fixing on him glances of malice and hatred: all hard-eyes and evil and sharp'.

This was in sharp contrast to his heroes, Rat, Toad, and Mole, which were, according to the *Saturday Review of Literature*, 'very human in their behaviour and remind us of undergraduates of sporting proclivities'. Among those who had escaped from the working classes yet did their best to ignore them, was Edgar Wallace: 'As you probably know I hate the British working man; I have no sympathy with him; whether he lives or dies, feeds or starves, is not of the slightest interest to me'. [7]

Few had the courage to put the matter into such uncompromising terms, but many millions shared this sentiment. Apprehension at the way the world was going was combined with dread at the thought of a country where the working classes were in control—a dread brought almost to fever pitch when in 1903 a Labour candidate won Woolwich with a majority of more than 3,000. Fortunately for those who worried most, the bulk of the working class still supported the Liberals.

The poor, it was reckoned, had only themselves to blame, and *The Times* leader of 1 September 1902 voiced the feelings of

Suffragettes tried to change the allegiances of the poor, with scant success

The evening courts of Edward VII provided an opportunity for rich women to demonstrate their sense of occasion

the lower middle classes who felt themselves most menaced by the working classes: 'Their wages would suffice to keep them strong and healthy, but they are thriftless; they drink or bet, or they are ignorant or careless in housekeeping.'

The systematic pursuit of pleasure began as soon as the king was securely on the throne. He named Buckingham Palace 'the Sepulchre' and removed immediately the faded relics of his mother's reign. The task of modernising and smartening up was a difficult one as Queen Alexandra had as little taste—charming as she was—as his mother, and one lot of clutter was replaced with another lot. He detested Osborne House, and as soon as possible gave it to the nation for use as a naval college.

He dropped the venerable institution of the afternoon drawing-rooms, and substituted evening courts. He never tired of pageantry and high living, and at the state opening of Parliament he instructed all peers to use their coaches to the House of Lords. He had a child's delight in dressing up, and expected his court to share his enthusiasm. Woe betide the nobleman who wore an order upside-down, as the Duke of Devonshire did on one occasion.

Following his mother's retirement from a full social life, Edward had given a lead, in morals and attitude, to the aristocracy, and the 'top ten thousand' soon realised that things would go on as before—only more so. There would be no dabbling in the arts or intellectualism, as had been the case during Prince Albert's day. As regards religion, the king's approach was strictly perfunctory; his instructions to Lang, the new Archbishop of York were simple and brisk: 'Keep the parties in the church together and prevent the clergy wearing moustaches'.

It is interesting to speculate upon what would have happened had the king not ascended the throne in 1901, or had been mortally struck down by the illness that in the event merely postponed his coronation. What would have happened had Queen Victoria lived to be ninety-one instead of eighty-one? As it was, life styles did not change abruptly with the accession of King Edward. The repressions and inhibitions, the hypocrisy and double standards of the middle classes had all been less in evidence since the 1880s, despite a number of stern rearguard actions by the *ancien régime*—as in the prosecution and imprisonment of Oscar Wilde for homosexual practices, the hounding of birth control propagandists, and persistent attacks upon the 'licentiousness' of the music hall.

The rumblings of discontent among the working classes, which resulted, in Edward VII's reign, in Labour representation in Parliament and a wave of strikes and industrial disputes, had been felt since the 1870s, when a large number of strikes amazed those to whom the working classes had been dim fugitive figures locked in their East End fastnesses. Cracks had been appearing in the class structure for several decades; if anything, Edward VII succeeded in keeping this structure more or less intact for another ten years.

Whatever his faults, Edward was a strong king. He believed in personal intervention in matters of state, and was responsible for the Entente Cordiale, as well as being instrumental in engineering a rapport with Russia. His worship of wealth had side effects that he could not have foreseen; one of these was the assimilation of rich Jews into society, where they were said to be the only humanising influences. Another was the integration with society of the 'shopocracy'. Typical of society's attitude towards these interlopers was the incident related by T. H. S. Escott in his *London Society in the New Reign* (1904):

> . . . Sir Blundell Maple was doing the honours of his Tottenham Court Road establishment to a stately dowager shopping there in her son's company. 'I think,' naively observed the dealer, 'I had the pleasure of seeing your Ladyship at the Opera last night.' Turning round to her companion, the lady of quality indignantly asked, in an intentionally audible aside, 'What does this man mean?' 'That he will lend you his box whenever you want it, and if I were you I should borrow it like a shot,' came the son's reply.

A lot was expected of the new reign. It was hoped that the liberating forces of the Naughty Nineties would sweep across the board. Edward VII, however, was not only strong, but selfish. Osbert Sitwell summed it up:

'The feast, it was recognised, went to the greediest', wrote Osbert Sitwell

. . . the Rich Man's Banquet, which was to last for a decade, had now begun: the feast, it was recognised, went to the greediest . . . the Edwardians squandered their accumulated riches at the shrine of the strange new goddess Comfort; they spent them on the gilding of pathetic but vulgar dreams from South Africa and the Ghetto, on the installation of bathrooms, electric light, and radiators.[9]

Osbert Sitwell was writing as a member of the landed gentry who resented the intrusion of outsiders into the sacred purlieus of his class. His sentiments were shared by the novelist George Meredith, who wrote of 'folly perpetually sliding into new shapes in a society possessed of wealth and leisure, with many whims, many strange ailments, and strange fancies'. The true aristocracy had a love/hate relationship with the king. He was one of them, as Victoria had never been, in his tastes, his hunting proclivities, his amours, and his life style; but, because of his passion for money and his admiration for those who had it, he had let in the dreaded vulgarians of the middle classes. No longer did the rich middle class slyly emulate their betters; they bought themselves in.

The gentry were cut right out of the picture. They had no place in 'the crowd of smart and moneyed Medes, Persians,

Elamites, and Mesopotamians, New York dandies, Chicago belles, and Hebrew money-brokers . . . [one of the gentry] would find himself in an *entourage* rather less intelligible to him than that thronging the presence-chamber of the grand Lama'.[10]

How one viewed England at this period, therefore, depended on whether one was in the gallery, the stalls or the boxes. In a symposium on Edwardian England published in 1933, its principal features were tabulated as the waning of authority, the fading influence of the middle classes, a lessening of reverence and of hypocrisy, with taboos beginning to lose their hold. The chaperon vanished 'like a ghost at sunrise', prudery was diminished and parental attitudes were more flexible. In social life there was less starch, boredom and pretence. The writers of 1933 were looking back in nostalgia; it is clear that in Edwardian times there were still chaperons, that parental attitudes could be as inflexible as ever (vide the novels of Galsworthy), and that taboos were still in operation, as witness the furore that greeted the writings of Freud and Havelock Ellis.

One feature of the age was the feeling of unease and apprehension. War was never far over the horizon, and many recognised that when it came it would be a new kind of war. Nor, after a few brief flirtations with the kaiser, was there any question that Germany would be the enemy (though some would have preferred to fight the United States, which, like Germany, was stealing all Britain's trade).

This apprehension paralysed the driving force that had propelled the Victorian colossus—Progress and the belief in Progress. In business and industry there was lethargy and indolence, reinforced by cynicism. The underlying philosophy was one of drifting; small wonder that the motto of a typical figure of the time, Asquith, was 'Wait and see'. Small wonder, also, that many of the young men of the age, later to die in World War I, escaped from the brooding nihilism into a life of pleasure.

The years 1901–14 have been called the age of extravagance. It was, to the historian G. M. Young, 'the flash Edwardian epilogue'. When on the eve of the war Sir Edward Grey, the foreign secretary, commented that the lights were going out all over Europe, few could claim that this was unexpected, or—in more cases than might be imagined—altogether unwelcome.

King and Queen

Edward VII had been waiting in the wings longer than any other monarch in English history. He was fifty-nine when he was proclaimed king. Baldness and a long nose had been inherited from the Coburg side of the family, his stoutness and lack of height from his mother. He had heavy-lidded protruding eyes, and his pouting mouth was hidden by neatly clipped beard. His voice was deep and guttural, and he rolled his r's.

The custom of denigrating or patronising past monarchs has produced the image of a kind of stuffed turkey floundering in a world compounded of exuberance, ostentation and vulgarity, of a little fat man who could always get a cheer from the working classes, but who was too passé for the true aristocracy, and surrounded by *nouveau-riche* sycophants. His personality was in fact more complex. His loyalty towards his friends was remarkable, while his affection for his wife and her influence over him had a telling effect.

He was the first cosmopolitan king. An accomplished linguist, he spoke German and French as fluently as he spoke English, and also had a good working knowledge of Italian and Spanish. On his frequent trips abroad he was much better able to gauge the mood of Europe than most of his ministers, who deplored the king's eyeball-to-eyeball diplomacy, preferring more traditional codes of conduct. They distrusted his judgement, which they knew to be based on intuition and feeling rather than thought. They were taking their cue from Queen Victoria, who once wrote to him: 'The country, and all of *us*, would like to see you a little more stationary'.

This view was shared by many of the king's subjects. 'I think the king goes about a damned sight too much,' declared Edgar Wallace, 'and I wish to heaven he would give up processing; one gets very tired of fossicking around after the old cove . . .

after I had got through writing about "lovely consorts", and "kingly presences" and "kindly smiles" I got fed up.'[1] Typical of the import invested in the monarch's visits to Russia, Germany and France was the photograph of the king with Sir Henry Campbell-Bannerman, with the caption 'Is it peace or war?' In fact the king was pondering whether halibut was better baked or boiled.

Edward was ignored by the intellectuals, who deplored his flippancy towards matters which, they considered, he could not understand. The king once said to the scientist Lord Rayleigh, 'Inventing something, I suppose?' commenting to a companion, 'He's always at it.' This was construed as a calculated insult to a clever man, not as a way of putting the scientist at his ease. However, there was less chance of misinterpreting his observation, after a performance of *Arms and the Man*, that Bernard Shaw was 'a damned crank'. Even the most hidebound intellectual, however, must have agreed with the king's reference to 'the trash which the Poet Laureate writes'. The works of Alfred Austin had few admirers.

Some have seen Edward's reign as a mixture of operetta and French farce. It was no accident that *The Merry Widow* was staged in 1907. It reflected all the external signs of the age, in a never-never land in which it was always high summer—gaiety, extravagance and sentimentality. To some observers, Edward's affairs may have indeed appeared farcical, while certain events were reminiscent of a Gilbert and Sullivan opera. At the coronation, for instance, the Archbishop of Canterbury 'blundered sadly, adjuring the king to give his special protection to "widowers", and then with painful conscientiousness substituting "widows"; the efforts to prompt him only seemed to muddle matters further, and he had to be left to stumble through as best he could'. Worse was to come. At the close of his oration the accompanying bishops 'pulled different ways in their efforts to raise him to his feet, and but for the timely assistance of the King, he would have been dragged off his feet by the Bishop of Winchester'.[2]

Matters were not to end there. When it was time to employ

the holy oil, 'the Dean of Westminster narrowly escaped emptying the contents of the chalice upon the Queen', and after the ceremony everyone tried to break through the file of Grenadier Guards drawn up to stop people leaving before the royal procession. The Duchess of Devonshire pressed on, missed her footing, and rolled over on her back at the feet of Sir Michael Hicks Beach, her coronet flying off and striking the stalls with a loud crash.

Such mishaps, it was felt, could not have happened in relation to the dead queen (though in fact Victoria's coronation had its own chain of misadventures). Foreboding looks were cast at the royal favourites incarcerated in the special part of Westminster Abbey known as the 'King's Loose Box'. Here was the raw material of bedroom farce; would the king continue to run after pretty women, or begin to be faithful to his wife?

It was a question admitting of only one answer. The presence

King Edward demanded the presence of pretty women, who were always in evidence at court

*Mrs George Keppel, the last and most
lasting of the king's alliances*

of pretty women acted upon him with the certainty and rapidity of a blood infusion. Nor was he reluctant to admit it. He had his apologists, among them Princess Alice, Countess of Athlone: 'Aunt Alix (Queen Alexandra) was renowned for her beauty, very lovely, with a gracious presence and a disposition which endeared her to the public who worshipped her. But being stone deaf and not mentally very bright, she was not much of a companion for an intelligent man like Uncle Bertie.'[3]

Queen Alexandra was well aware of her husband's infidelities. She could hardly fail to be, when one of his favourite horses was named Ecila (Alice back to front)—Alice being the name of Mrs Keppel, the last and most lasting of the king's alliances. The queen was a woman of tact and discretion, and something more. Her one liaison, when she was Princess of Wales, was with the Honourable Oliver Montagu, and conducted on a lofty plane, though when he died in 1893 she was desolate.

Before her marriage to Edward in 1863 there had been more than a breath of scandal about her. On 15 January 1862 Countess Bluecher wrote to diplomat Augustus Paget:

Bad as human nature is, it is impossible to believe that, out of interested motives, persons of a position in the world can invent histories to injure the reputation of an amiable and unoffending girl! Yet such must be the case in the present instance and I am full of indignation and disgust at it. I cannot say I believed the report which had been spread, and had it only been from one quarter I should never have troubled my head about it, but from vriousa quarters the same thing having come to me and others, all probably emanating from the same source, it became most important to *approfondir*.

Paget's wife took up the story:

I have not yet seen the Princess alone, so I have not found out who spread those wicked stories, but I strongly suspect, from a word she said, and for which the Prince reprimanded her, that it was the Princess of Dessau. If it all goes straight the marriage will be next spring, and I am determined it shall go straight.[4]

Lady Walburga Paget was one of those determined mid-Victorian matrons who exerted considerable influence behind the scenes.

Six children were born of Alexandra's marriage, the last in 1871. By degrees she centred her life on Sandringham and her children, and gave the impression of a docile happy wife unconcerned with what happened outside her immediate circle. Edward's love life encompassed Mrs Greville, the American-born Duchess of Marlborough, Lady Londonderry, Mrs Arthur Sassoon, Mrs Willie James, Lady Troubridge, Lady Lonsdale, and Mrs Cornwallis West. And, of course, the wife of the Honourable George Keppel. There was no question that as Prince of Wales he had slept with others less respectable. When Lillie Langtry had a child, Edward had flipped a coin as to whether or not he was the father (this affair ended in 1881). Then there was Sarah Bernhardt, cold-shouldered by the aristocracy, who had had an illegitimate son when still in her teens.

In the society that centred around Edward it was understood that there were delicate alliances that should be treated with discretion. Bedrooms were allocated accordingly. There were some even more sensitive liaisons which could more conveniently be consummated in private rooms. Rule's, in Maiden Lane, was a favourite rendezvous of Edward's, also Kettner's, where the King Edward Room was said to have a secret passage to the Palace Theatre opposite for the benefit of actresses and others on whom the royal gaze had alighted. Kettner's supplied maids to help undress women who had had the misfortune to leave their own at home.

There were times when even private rooms were too public. Edward's private secretary, Lord Knollys, asked Lord Rosebery for the use of his London house so that the king and his younger brother Alfred could entertain actress friends—a request that met with a refusal. The king was more successful in persuading Sir Ernest Cassel, the financier, to lend his rented villa in Biarritz to accommodate him and Mrs Keppel, together with her children, to whom he was known as 'Kingy'.

The forebearance of Queen Alexandra must be admired. As early as 1870, when she had been married seven years, she had had to watch her husband's affairs paraded in public when he was involved in the Mordaunt divorce case. Shortly after the birth of her first child, Lady Mordaunt told her husband, 'Charlie, you are not the father of that child'. Among the candidates for paternity, Lady Mordaunt admitted, was the Prince of Wales. In due course Edward was served with a subpoena, though he was protected from answering any 'improper questions', the phrase used by Queen Victoria when she was acquainted with her son's predicament.

Edward had written twelve mildly compromising letters, and was cross-examined for seven minutes, an occurrence that was 'painful and lowering' to his mother, while the Prince of Wales had the rare experience of being booed in the street. Though the case was less dangerous to the stability of the monarchy than it might have been, it was perhaps fortunate that Lord Mordaunt lost his divorce suit, on account of his wife's insanity.

There was little that Alexandra could do; to divorce her husband was unthinkable, as unrealistic as returning in humiliation to her native Denmark. She came to terms with her husband's infidelities, the tension was relaxed, and it is not surprising that he humoured her in some of her whims.

Easy-going and amiable as she was in the humdrum business of everyday life, in one respect Alexandra was uncompromising and stern. This was her deep abiding hatred of Germany. Her father was on the throne of Denmark when the Germans invaded and

Alexandra had been resentful that Britain had not done more for her country. Admittedly the British Government had tried to put Alexandra's brother on the throne of Greece, but this had been so mismanaged that the party most concerned had only read of his possible elevation when he opened a newspaper in which his sardine sandwiches had been wrapped. In the event, he only got the Ionian Islands.

Had she had her way Alexandra would have got Victoria to wage war on Germany for what she considered the rape of her country. 'This horrible war will be a stain for ever on Prussian history,' she wrote, 'I think it is very wrong of our Government not to interfere.' After the birth of the first child, the royal couple visited Denmark. Alexandra insisted that the Prussian flag be hauled down from the mast, asserting that she would not move a step until this was done. When the Prince of Wales met his brother-in-law, the Danish Crown Prince, there were more ructions: 'It was not pleasant to see him and his ADC always in Prussian uniform, flaunting before your eyes a most objectionable ribbon which he received for his deeds of valour (? ? ?) against the unhappy Danes'.

The Prussians were stigmatised by Alexandra as 'the Robbers', Prussia as 'the Robber State', and she did not hesitate to declare these sentiments in open telegrams. Victoria was displeased by this attitude. She refused to allow her daughter Princess Helena to marry the Crown Prince of Denmark, though there was no objection to her marrying into the Prussian aristocracy. 'This alliance, of course, cannot be popular to Bertie's wife and family', the queen wrote, 'but that cannot be helped and is of no consequence'.

Not surprisingly the Danish royal family were indignant. King Christian wrote: 'They show us not the slightest consideration and wound our most sacred feelings. That is typically English. They think of nothing but their own advantage, and never consult their heart.' To the Danes there was some satisfaction in the marriage of Alexandra's sister, Thyra, to the Hanoverian Pretender, in 1879, which dismayed the Prussian statesman Bismarck. What did Alexandra want? 'Bismarck's head,' retorted the Princess of Wales briskly.

In the context of the growing hostility towards Germany, Alexandra's hatred fanned the flames. The proposal by Joseph Chamberlain of a race union between Britain, America and Germany seemed an act tantamount to high treason. Occasionally this hatred boiled over, to the surprise of guests. On one occasion when Alexandra, then queen, was brought out on the subject of the kaiser there was 'an explosion of rancour'. He 'has a mania for domineering over everybody and occupying himself with what is no concern of his'. Any entente between Germany and Britain was therefore hampered by the queen's hostility and the king's personal dislike of the kaiser, combined with his partiality for France and all that was French.

Unlike his ministers, the king did not believe in appeasement, but was ready to bury the hatchet if the kaiser would; Wilhelm's exemplary behaviour at the time of Queen Victoria's death had somewhat diluted their mutual distrust. The prime minister, Lord Salisbury, was too old and ineffectual to contribute anything to a rapport. The spokesman for the government seemed to be Joseph Chamberlain, the colonial secretary, who had said at Leicester in November 1899: 'The natural alliance is between ourselves and the German Empire . . . both interest and racial sentiment unite the two peoples. . . .'

This tolerance of the kaiser and all he stood for lasted only a few months. Chamberlain realised that he had stepped out of line, and when the German newspapers attacked the British for their atrocities towards the Boers and their use of concentration camps, he rounded on the Germans, and asserted that the British Army had never been so barbarous as the German Army—or the French or the Russians, thereby creating three possible enemies instead of one.

The first inkling of the coming line-up of powers was sensed by the press. Alfred Harmsworth of the *Daily Mail*, with its circulation of 836,700, and Leo Manxe of the *National Review* did some effective sabre rattling. In 1902 the *National Review* declared that it was necessary to 'combat German anglophobia by working all round for the isolation of Germany'. The tabloid papers were baiting Germany with what that country feared most

Leaving nothing to chance : or preparing for a battue in the Imperial Forest of Hochderkaiser.

The attitude of the press towards the Germans is evident from this 1909 cartoon

—encirclement. In doing so they added a further nail to any prospects of permanent peace.

Throughout the Edwardian period the great powers behaved as though they were playing musical chairs. Statesmen were manipulated by events. It seemed to be a matter of chance who would strike the first blow, and where. After Japan had soundly trounced Russia in a relatively obscure war on the other side of the world, even the languid Arthur Balfour thought that Russia might be worth having a crack at, eventually coming through with the Machiavellian conclusion that 'the most formidable aspect of an Anglo-Russian war is admittedly the difficulty of hitting Russia herself'.[5] The sinking by the Russian Baltic Fleet of a number of British trawlers on the Dogger Bank under the impression that they were Japanese warships was neither here nor there in the context of these comic opera confrontations.

It was quite evident to true blue Englishmen that foreigners could not be trusted. They would have liked to have stopped the clock in the last year of Victoria's reign when Britain had no friends and no irritating alliances, and when there was, in fact, a

After 1907 the king became increasingly depressed and the camera caught him more and more off-guard

comfortable and effete alliance—the Franco-Russian alliance of 1894—unmistakably directed against England.

It was only to be expected that during this game of musical chairs someone would want to shoot the pianist, and amid the confusion the presence of the unflappable king was invaluable. The uneasy atmosphere communicated itself to men of letters and aesthetes who normally did not concern themselves with international matters. Max Beerbohm was more interested in the effect of the Russo-Japanese War on his personal affairs, as is clear from a letter he wrote to his close friend Reginald Turner in March 1904: 'Soon we may be dragged into this beastly war, and then there will be no chance of a sale for any book for a long time to come'.

The king's great asset was his innate honesty. His friend Lord Redesdale put it well:

No diamond could be more purely clear and honest than King Edward, and it was that pellucid truthfulness which made him so powerful in his relations with foreign sovereigns and statesmen; they knew that when they were dealing with him they had to do with a King as honest as Nathanael, a man in whom there was no guile. [6]

After 1907 the king grew increasingly depressed; from 1905 the winter had played more and more havoc with his health, and not even the escape to Biarritz with Alice Keppel could remedy the effects of high living and old age.

It was at Sandringham that the greatest impression of stability was given. Edward had bought Sandringham House from Mr Spencer Cowper in 1861, and it was rebuilt in the High Victorian style between 1869 and 1871. This massive building standing in 7,000 acres was the king's favourite home, where he could relax despite the clutter of bric-à-brac and mementoes of a bygone age. The saloon, with its oak walls and beamed ceiling, was crammed with objects, including two bronze cannon named 'Eugénie' and 'Louis Napoleon', screens, a piano, groups of palms and stands of flowers, while the walls were covered with sketches and paintings. There were curios from India, Japan, Egypt and Turkey; the hoof of King Edward's racehorse, Eclipse; weapons retrieved from the battlefields of the Franco-Prussian War; and under glass cases, set precariously on little tables, a multitude of gold and silver caskets.

Only in the king's preserves was there any semblance of restraint; the bowling-alley 'after the best United States models' was strictly functional, and sketches by the humorous artist John Leech enlivened the walls of the billiard-room. Elsewhere amateurish paintings by the royal daughters hung side by side with stilted full-length glorifications of the king in uniform; life-size white swans were matched with sentimental genre pictures, such as 'Girls Bathing'. In the ante-rooms, there were tiger-skins and tusks and other trophies of the chase in abundance. The queen's boudoir was 'marvellously full of every trivial detail'.

Prince Christopher of Greece observed sardonically:

At Sandringham, royal stability was preserved, a buttress against reality

The Queen's positive genius for collecting trifles of every description and hoarding them long after their origin had been forgotten; books, photos, china, letters, old programmes, odds and ends of ribbons and laces were heaped together indiscriminately anywhere and everywhere, for she never could throw any of them away. Beautiful miniatures and Georgian snuff-boxes occupied a table with Earl's Court china pigs and bog-wood charms from Ireland; she kept the fishing-fly given her by a gillie in Scotland as carefully as she kept a brooch from one of the Indian maharajahs.[7]

In the grounds was a miniature zoo with tigers, elephants, kangaroos and bears; in the kennels were up to a hundred dogs, including the queen's favourite basset hounds.

In such an environment it was easy to forget the troubles and anxieties that lay outside. Sandringham was a buttress against reality—the prospects of war and the social turbulence being whipped up by left-wing agitators. How different were the lives of city workers from those of the labourers on the estate! Every 'village' had its picturesque clubhouse, with billiard and reading rooms, and the men were prevented from squandering their earnings on beer for the simple reason that no pubs were allowed to be built. To Queen Alexandra it was an Arcadia. Bazaars gave the impression that the villages on the estate were *real* villages; at one bazaar a 'fair vendor' was asked by the king for a cup of tea. 'Now the cup of tea is five guineas', said the woman coyly. The king sipped it. 'Will you please give me a clean cup?' he asked. Even the dwellers of this world within a world could be disconcerted.

Marlborough House had had a special place in the affections of Edward and Alexandra, but when Victoria died and they were obliged to move to Buckingham Palace, the house was taken over by the new Prince of Wales, later George V. On Edward's death in 1910, it became the home of Queen Alexandra. During Edward's tenure, guests at Marlborough House were met by a gillie in national costume and two scarlet-coated powdered footmen. Pages wore dark blue coats and black trousers, and for special occasions black velvet breeches, silk stockings, and gold garters. Like Sandringham, Marlborough House was cluttered with objects from Asia and the Orient.

The royal residences were symbols of the old order, and Edward's determination to revive the ceremonial circumstances of the monarchy, that had been in decline since the death of his father, was reflected by the grandeur of his life style. In their hearts the king's circle knew that it could not last, and in early May 1910 the end came. Bronchitis took him off. 'When the black news came a deadly pall fell over the country, and there were many men—some great, some small—who felt that life could never again be quite the same for them'.[8]

The new king, it was felt, would not match his father. The aristocracy distrusted him. What they knew about him they did not care for; he was a Victorian in an Edwardian setting, and had drawn his friends from his own social level. There had been no alliance with continentals or American millionaires. He had carried out his duties as the Prince of Wales, visiting outposts of the Empire, opening this and that, with aplomb, and because his private life had never been open to criticism scandal had to be invented to fit him into the pattern of the Georges. It was widely circulated and believed that during his service with the Mediterranean Fleet he had contracted a marriage in Malta with the daughter of an admiral.

In the inner ring of Edwardian Society malice was not wanting. There were many in or on the fringe of the circle of King Edward who felt that his death was the death-knell of the good times and marked the end of the 'great days' or the 'happy days' of Society. In a narrow sense perhaps they were right.[9]

It was a tradition for lampoons to be devised when a new king took over, but there was a venom about those distributed in 1910. The new court, it was considered, would be drab and vacuous, and the sparkle would go out of society life. The topics that had interested Edward would be barred from polite conversation; and George conspicuously lacked his father's interests in horse-racing.

The country gentry, however, welcomed his accession. He was one of them and had one quality that particularly endeared him to them—he was a crack shot. On one occasion he brought down thirty-nine pheasants with thirty-nine shots. On 18 December 1913, when George V was one of the seven guns, there was a record bag of 3,937 pheasants. Such facts did much to comfort the country squire, who waited with eagerness for the ejection of the moneyed middle classes from their pedestals.

There were a few who realised that towards the end of his life Edward VII had not been the man he was. 'It was well that he died in 1910. He died before his decline had become too conspicuous, and he has left a name which will stand for many generations as a synonym for all that is best in constitutional kingship.'[10]

Although George V had not had the long apprenticeship of his father, he was now forty-five and appeared older. In a wordly sense he was naïve, and diplomacy of the kind Edward had indulged in was clearly not his forte. When in 1911 King George went to India for the Coronation Durbar he was oblivious to the gathering storm in Europe, and when on 18 March 1913 the assassination of the king of Greece pushed the great powers nearer to war, George's sentiments were almost parochial: 'Beloved Uncle Willie has been assassinated at Salonica, while walking in the streets . . . Too horrible, I was devoted to him and he will be a great loss to Greece. Mother dear is fearfully upset by this fresh sorrow'.

In May 1913, King George and Queen Mary, and the Tsar of Russia, were among those present at the wedding of the kaiser's daughter, but the kaiser prevented private conversation between the British and the Russians, and despite the growing European tension no move was made to use the occasion politically. Somewhat relieved, George V returned to England, where he visited the Potteries to meet the people over whom he was somewhat bemusedly ruling. The opening of 1914 saw him doing what he was best at—shooting pheasants.

Events were building up to a climax. Germany and France were unmistakably preparing for war, yet the social life in London—contrary to expectations—continued as before. In May, Prince Henry of Prussia came on a visit to the king, who had great faith in the good sense of the kaiser. Late in the afternoon of 28 June 1914 the king received the news of the Sarajevo murder. Its implications were lost on him, and he merely reported in his diary, 'Terrible shock for the dear old Emperor'. The shock was in fact sufficient to inspire Franz Josef, the 83-year-old Austrian despot, to attack Serbia to avenge his nephew's assassination.

Towards the end of July Prince Henry of Prussia returned home. It was believed in Germany that on 26 July the king and the prince had an interview in which the king stated that in the event of war England would remain neutral. On 29 July Austria declared war on Serbia; on 1 August Germany declared war on Russia, and on 4 August Britain was brought in. 'It is a terrible catastrophe but it is not our fault,' the king committed to his diary. On 10 August the kaiser sent a telegram to President Wilson reporting the alleged statement of the king to Prince Henry. The tone was aggrieved. Of course, the statement was denied. The text of the telegram was quoted in a book by James Garrard, American Ambassador to Germany at the outbreak of war; *My Four Years in Germany* was published in 1917 and serialised in the *Daily Telegraph*. A categorical denial of the story was issued, but the repercussions did not die down. In 1938 Captain Erich von Müller, the German Naval Attaché in London in 1914, repeated the allegations, which brought forth a spirited reply from the Keeper of the King's Archives. And there the matter rested.

Was the British involvement in World War I the result of a chat between royalties, a misunderstanding? King George V was certainly a good deal more out of touch with the time bomb that was 1914 Europe than some of his subjects. Arthur Conan Doyle, for one, brought to the matter an insight that one would expect from the creator of Sherlock Holmes:

> I can never forget, and our descendants can never imagine, the strange effect upon the mind which was produced by seeing the whole European fabric drifting to the edge of the chasm with absolute uncertainty as to what would happen when it toppled over.[11]

Many were glad that the days of unease were over. When asked when war would start one army officer said that it would be on the first pretext after the Kiel Canal was widened—to facilitate the passage of German battle-cruisers. The canal was widened on 14 June. Certain politicians wanted war, to divert interest away from troubles at home, and in Ireland where there was open warfare. There were unscrupulous left-wing politicians who thought that a war would bring down the established society and bring in communism.

And there was the man in the street. 'It will be the most popular war this country ever engaged in', declared Ramsay MacDonald, leader of the Labour Party. 'Look out of your windows now, and you will see the people beginning to go mad.'[12]

The Men at the Top

When Edward VII came to the throne the prime minister was Lord Salisbury, who was over seventy, and clearly due for replacement. Once described by Disraeli as 'a great master of gibes and flouts and jeers', all he now wanted was a quiet life. In the so-called 'khaki' election of 1900, Salisbury's party, the Unionists or Conservatives, had got in with a huge majority and there was no wish for a new broom. Salisbury remained at

A 1908 cartoon of Balfour with Campbell-Bannerman. Balfour, 'an old maid in a frock coat', is on the right

the head of the government throughout the Boer War, and then retired in July 1902.

His successor was his nephew Arthur Balfour, who was 'made prime minister because it is desired by the ruling families that the minimum of change should be made,' wrote J. L. Garvin of *The Observer*.

Balfour was born in 1848, educated at Eton and Trinity College, Cambridge, and entered parliament in 1874, becoming private secretary to Lord Salisbury in 1878. Apart from a brief flirtation with the ebullient Lord Randolph Churchill and his Fourth Party, Balfour's political career was subdued and unsensational. For him politics was a polite game; the House of Commons may have been the best club in London, but to Balfour it was slightly vulgar. He was ethereal and somewhat vague. At school he had been known as 'Pretty Fanny' and the connotation stuck.

> Balfour never reads the newspapers, is as ignorant of popular agitations, demonstrations, and all such vulgar things, as an English judge of a burlesque actress whose name and features stare at him from every hoarding and every printed sheet.[1]

It was suggested that the real prime minister was his secretary, J. S. Sandars, and that Balfour, though not bad in himself, was a typical product of his class, the social function of which was 'the manufacture of old maids in frock coats'. Balfour was a bachelor and lived in Carlton Gardens, with small blue and white pots with ferns on the dining tables, fine furniture and pictures, and the absence of that luxury that was so much a feature of the Edwardian scene. His bedroom was dark and bare, and by the bedside was a lectern. However, it was typical of Balfour that on the lectern was a manual on bridge.

Beatrice Webb, whose left-wing politics were the antithesis of his own, has left in her diaries a summary of Balfour:

> A man of extraordinary grace of mind and body, delighting in all that is beautiful and distinguished, music, literature, religious feeling and moral disinterestedness, aloof from all the greed of common human nature. But a strange paradox as a prime minister!

Balfour was too subtle by half for Edward VII, who complained that 'he is always so vague that probably he is wrong'. On his part, Balfour depreciated and undervalued the king's intuitive soundness of judgement. The two men belonged to different worlds. Balfour had been a member of the group known as 'the Souls', which included the vivacious Margot Tennant (who later married Asquith), Lord Curzon (Viceroy of India 1899–1905), George Wyndham (Chief Secretary for Ireland 1900–5), fragile eccentrics such as the patron of opera and ballet Lady de Grey, so fey that the cry of a cuckoo made her feel ill, and the most literate of the aristocracy. Many of the men who belonged to the Souls found places in Balfour's administration.

The feature that struck everyone about Balfour was his charm; this concealed a vein of ruthlessness, and the 'silk-skinned sybarite, whose rest a crumpled rose leaf would disturb'—as the *Irish Times* had it—could be as savage as the next man, if the occasion arose. The occasion did not often arise, though had the socialist 'menace' been stronger no doubt it would have done. Balfour had no interest in the plight of the working man, and whether or not the question attributed to him, 'What is a trade union?', is apocryphal it is the kind of thing he would have said. He had little time for democracy, and it was a matter of indifference to him that cabinet ministers held directorships and had financial interests that might very well clash with government intent.

The Duke of Devonshire, for instance, the Lord President of the Council, was chairman of a steel company that made armour for British warships at a time when the rebuilding of the Royal Navy was a sore point. Balfour even defended his ministers' involvement in outside affairs, and in a speech in the House of Commons in February 1903 he declared that public life would be poorer if ministers were prevented from holding directorships.

Balfour was unquestionably one of the most intelligent of prime ministers. He was a writer as well as a statesman, and his *Defence of Philosophic Doubt* (1879) and *Foundations of Belief* (1895) were cogent well-written books that were treated with respect. He had his eccentricities. He and his brother Gerald (who was also given a job in government) were obsessively interested in the artificial drying of peat for use as fuel, and between them they lost a quarter of a million pounds.

Balfour did not think the time ripe for democracy, the whole concept of which was under a cloud. In *Democracy and Reaction*, L. T. Hobhouse wrote that 'the golden radiance of [democracy's] morning hopes has long since faded into the light of common day'. Balfour had an aristocratic temperament; his government was languid. He had been forced to inherit some of Salisbury's colleagues, such as the Duke of Devonshire, described by the *National Review* as 'a statesman in the last stage of political ossification', and Lord Lansdowne, who had been secretary of war at the outbreak of the Boer War and held responsible by the press for the army's inept showing. Balfour's main defect was that he was afflicted with that 'specially British curse—the lenity to well-connected muddlers'.[2] And all his muddlers were well connected.

Behind Balfour was the old but immensely energetic Joseph Chamberlain. The stormy petrel of the 1880s was obsessed with the idea of tariff reform. The antithesis of free trade, tariff reform involved financial protection for the products of Britain and the Empire. To Chamberlain the introduction of an entirely new and far-reaching tariff system would protect and inspire British businessmen, and bring the colonies into a close economic union. The supporters of Chamberlain's scheme thought that protection would guarantee employment for the workers, and provide sufficient revenue for social welfare. Chamberlain himself had been interested in the provision of old age pensions since 1892. Although he had retired from industry with a fortune as early as 1874, he had seen the tragedy of the poor when they got too old to work. Acquaintance with the poor was not Balfour's forte. He was grateful to Chamberlain for not offering himself as an alternative premier when Salisbury went, but the crusade for tariff reform was inconvenient; not only did it threaten a split in the Conservative party but if it were implemented there was a good chance of trouble with the United States.

Hemmed in between the rival factions, for and against free

THE SOUTH AFRICAN CAMPAIGN—BIGGER GAME IN SIGHT.
Joe Chamberlain: "Here, I've wasted my powder on that pesky Boer, and look at what's a'comin'!"
—*Minneapolis Journal.*

Joseph Chamberlain had an international reputation as a firebrand, and his frequent discomfiture was noted with glee, particularly by the Americans

trade, Balfour prevaricated, hoping that, like so many topics, the issue would drift away. He admitted in the House of Commons that he had 'no settled convictions on the subject'. His main aim was to keep the party together. If anything he had a slight preference for tariff reform, but he could not understand the venom with which the topic was discussed, and when Chamberlain left the government in 1903, Balfour being too luke-warm for him, open war was waged between the free traders and the protectionists.

To some, tariff reform was the One Simple Answer to all the ills of the age of apprehension. This enthusiasm overflowed into verse:

When wealth and mirth refill the earth,
Let each man tell his neighbour:
All this we owe to Chamberlain.
Hurrah, hurrah, hurrah.[3]

To others, Chamberlain represented all that was worst in modern politics. That he had lived and made his money in Birmingham was an added exasperation. The Bishop of Hereford protested about 'this raging tearing Protectionist propaganda manufactured in Birmingham'; the left-wing former engineer John Burns spoke of 'schemes projected by a political bankrupt in the interests of a distressed bankrupt'; and Frederic Harrison, lawyer, expert on trade unions and a doctrinaire Liberal, resorted to personalities: Chamberlain was 'a tawdry charlatan and impudent demagogue'.

In largely irrelevant debates about the pros and cons of tariff reform the class war erupted, and it was up to the Liberals to make the most of this. Opposition to Chamberlain closed their ranks, and three figures began to emerge as possible Liberal leaders—Herbert Asquith, Lord Haldane and Sir Edward Grey, with Lord Rosebery (Liberal prime minister 1894–5) hovering in the wings. The nominal leader was Sir Henry Campbell-Bannerman, who had somehow acquired this unenviable job in 1898. The joker in the pack was David Lloyd George, as unpopular with his own colleagues as with the Conservatives.

For Balfour there was an ominous sign of the times when, in a by-election at Norwich in January 1904, the Liberals won a seat that they had not even contested in 1900. The same thing happened in Whitby in 1905. Balfour was aware that the Liberals were divided; Asquith, Haldane and Grey being reluctant to serve under Campbell-Bannerman. The Liberals were very busy investigating the conditions of the poor, and exploiting their findings, but how would they shape in office, with the mediocre Campbell-Bannerman having a hard job to put a government together, and with Lloyd George and the envious Rosebery undoubted liabilities? Balfour decided to try them out.

He resigned, anticipating a muddled period of Liberal quasi-rule followed by a general election in 1906, in which the Conservatives would sweep the board and be set for another long period in power. There was also a good chance that Campbell-Bannerman would refuse, in view of the schisms in his own ranks, to take office, throwing the ball back into the

Conservative court. It did not turn out like that. Campbell-Bannerman became prime minister in 1905 and proved a much stronger man than anyone believed, while Asquith, Grey and Haldane showed themselves more anxious for office than principle. Campbell-Bannerman also brought in Lloyd George and John Burns, and Winston Churchill, who had providentially moved to the Liberals from the Conservatives in time to become colonial secretary at the age of thirty-one.

The issues of the general election of 1906 were fuzzy-edged and ambiguous, with both sides speaking of the need for efficiency, greater cohesion in government departments, and the evasion and dishonesty of their opponents. The Liberals shelved the Irish Problem (Home Rule and Catholic v. Protestant)—there was nothing in it for them. To the Independent Labour Party, both Conservatives and Liberals were the same—parties for the rich whose joint aim was to keep the working classes down. All parties were compelled to talk of social reform, old age pensions and compulsory national insurance; the only difference

There was little communication between Members of Parliament and their constituents, and the twenty-nine Labour members who were elected in 1906 did little to alter this

was that when the Liberals got in on a massive land-slide they did something about it. The welfare state dates from 1906.

It was a traumatic year for all those on the right wing of British politics. When the new parliament assembled there were only 157 Conservatives, instead of 402. To the distress of the old order, there were twenty-nine Labour members plus twenty-four 'Lib-Labs'. The *Edinburgh Review* saw ominous signs of socialism even in the Liberal members—'the spirit of socialism pervades the whole House'. In 1906 Joseph Chamberlain retired from politics on grounds of ill-health.

The most important thing about Campbell-Bannerman, it was said, was his taste for French novels. He was heartily in favour of a closer relationship with France, and did a good deal to bring nearer Franco-British military co-operation. He distrusted the Germans. The kaiser, he said at the end of 1905, was 'a dangerous, restless, mischief-making man'. Campbell-Bannerman was deceptive. Generally thought third rate, he proved to be good second rate. He was the man without a face, whom everyone expected to find boring and whose astute guilelessness would appear crude after Balfour's savoir faire. Edward VII was one of those who dreaded the thought of meeting Campbell-Bannerman, expecting him to be even more trying than Balfour. To his surprise, he found him companionable and much to his taste. And so did the military people. The Duke of Cambridge, who had been commander-in-chief of the British Army, 1856–95, thought him 'very nice, calm and pleasant'.

Without the subtlety of Balfour, Campbell-Bannerman nevertheless fitted in with the pattern of Edwardian prime ministers. If anything untoward arose, he would rather do nothing. Like Balfour he would have approved of Lord Melbourne's dictum, 'Why not leave it alone?' He was 'easygoing to the point of laziness', commented Margot Asquith, but no doubt Campbell-Bannerman thought that there was enough energy being employed by Lloyd George. Campbell-Bannerman paid lip service to the common man. England, he declared when coming to power, would be 'less of a pleasure ground for the rich and more of a treasure house for the poor'. Lloyd George

Insult to Injury

Miss B-LL-NGT-N: "Free! but I don't want to be free—besides, I'm fearfully dangerous—and determined—and—oh! you *are* mean!"

Asquith was suave and civilised, and even the suffragettes found him difficult to cope with

was more committed and more vehement: 'There are conditions of poverty, destitution and squalor that would make the rocks weep'. On one occasion Campbell-Bannerman asked Lloyd George, 'Are you feeling cooler now?'[4]

In 1908 Campbell-Bannerman died, and Herbert Asquith, as the new prime minister, had to take on the task of governing the country and coping with Lloyd George. Asquith had many of the qualities of Balfour; he was suave and civilised, and moved amongst the same people. Born in 1852, Asquith's first memory was walking with a Sunday school procession to celebrate peace after the Crimean War. At school he won all the prizes, and at Balliol College, Oxford, was nurtured by the benign Master, Benjamin Jowett, along with his parliamentary contemporaries Sir Edward Grey and Lord Curzon. Jowett saw the successes of his famous pupils as college trophies, and Asquith was one of his best buys: 'Asquith is the one pupil of mine for whom I can most confidently predict success in life . . . he is so direct'.[5] Jowettism might be summed up as the philosophy of getting on; as his pupils were scholars and gentlemen the worship of the main chance was robbed of its grossness and materialism.

Asquith was President of the Union, and took a first in classics. Called to the bar in 1876, he became a QC in 1890, four years after he had entered politics. Between 1892 and 1895 he was Home Secretary under Gladstone and Rosebery, and Chancellor of the Exchequer under Campbell-Bannerman between 1905 and 1908. He and Lloyd George were a good team, though in 1916 Lloyd George unsaddled him, holding the premiership until 1922. Lloyd George was the power house, Asquith was the dynamo, and between them they upheld free trade, inaugurated national insurance and old age pensions, payment of MPs, and a Parliament Act that cut the power of the House of Lords.

Asquith usually escaped the torrent of abuse that was directed against Lloyd George and his sensational 'People's Budgets'. He went placidly along with Lloyd George's frenetic crusade against drink. The nation's liquor bill was £200 million, twice that of the United States, more than the National Budget. There were 160,000 convictions a year for drunkenness.

Rabble-rousing in the East End became a recognised sport. Fortunately for the parties in power, it was greeted with apathy

A nation that is suckled on alcohol is doomed . . . as long as Drink is allowed a free hand on the hearth the result will be that although you may convert your slums into garden cities, your garden cities will in a short time be reduced to slums.[6]

Lloyd George was given a free hand to rabble-rouse in Limehouse. 'Why should I put burdens on the people?' he asked. 'I am one of the children of the people.' And he proved it by trying to put the burdens on the rich, with increased death duties, duties on undeveloped land and minerals, a levy on unearned increment, and a supertax on incomes above £5,000. Not surprisingly the rich wished to throw Lloyd George to their hounds.

It might be supposed that a rapport would be made between the working classes and the rejuvenated Liberal Party, that with Lloyd George the existence of a Labour Party was unnecessary. But Lloyd George was not altogether trusted. He was Welsh for one thing, but more important was the fact that, although he claimed to be a man of the people, he was not. John Burns was; he scorned Lloyd George, and spoke sardonically of the housemaid's knee that the Welshman had acquired from a too frequent kowtowing to royalty.

David Lloyd George, born in 1863, was the son of a schoolmaster, and had started life as a solicitor. Nothing could be more middle-class than his background. Despite his enthusiasm for improving the lot of the poor, he was alien to them, nor did his crusade against drink help his image in the back streets of the East End. Insurance, old age pensions, these only scraped at the paintwork of poverty. In 1908 there was a higher level of unemployment among the wage-earning population than there had been in any year since 1886. Dividends were flowing into the rich man's coffers, but prices continued to rise proportionately to wage increases. Trade union membership rose; these were different unions to the defensive cringing unions of the nineteenth century. The members were harsh and aggressive, and contemptuous of those who sported the Labour label in parliament, and there was a growing militancy in the ranks.

Against this background Asquith was an irrelevancy, even though he

> had in his character every traditional virtue—dignity, honour, courage and a fine selflessness. In temperament he was equable and generous. He was a most competent head of a traditional Government and a brilliant leader of a traditional party.[7]

He was impercipient, his mind was not open to new ideas, and he had no overall scheme. His motto was 'wait and see'. General elections in 1910 had not altered the parliamentary picture very much, though middle-class people sighed with relief when it was found that Labour representation in parliament was slightly down. The Liberals seemed to be set for a long spell in office. Balfour stepped down as leader of the opposition and his place was taken by Bonar Law, another honourable man, upright, straight, uncomplicated, of whom it was said: 'The construction of his mind has no shadows, or ingle-nooks, or cosy corners'.[8] It was also said that he had a hot head and cold feet. It needed more than efficiency and a cool common sense to set a spark to the chill opposition benches. With his pessimism and Scots Presbyterian ancestry, Bonar Law reminded Lord Beaverbrook of a sombre raven among the glittering birds of paradise. Bonar Law, who eventually became prime minister in 1922, was one of the few politicians who saw things coldly. Lloyd George, he thought, was 'the most dangerous little man that ever lived'.

Lloyd George, who had never been abroad before, went to Carlsbad and Berlin, and laid down the law on foreign policy. Edward VII watched his antics with alarm. Clemenceau, wrote the king, had been amazed 'by the *crass ignorance* which L. George displayed concerning foreign politics'.[9] Winston Churchill was also causing problems. He was canvassing methods for reaching a naval understanding with Germany. On such matters the king considered that no one except the prime minister and the foreign secretary was qualified to speak, and resolved to consult Asquith about it. The king's secretary, Lord Knollys, said that Churchill and Lloyd George did not behave like gentlemen, were disloyal to their colleagues, and spent most of their time in unprincipled intrigue.

Fortunately Lloyd George had formed a friendship with King Edward's mistress, Mrs Keppel, and the king had a soft spot for Churchill, as he liked Mrs Churchill. There was also some excuse for the two offenders in that Asquith and Sir Edward Grey were only too pleased not to talk of foreign policy.

Grey was a good deal younger than most of his colleagues, but the energy associated with youth was never much in evidence. He was in his early forties when he was given the job of foreign secretary, and carried out his work in a conscientious manner, proud of being an amateur, an aristocrat in politics who played by the rules. When he took over in 1905 he promised that he would pursue the policy laid down by the previous administration under the conservative Balfour. This involved friendship with the United States, the alliance with Japan, and the Entente with France. 'He had no prejudices, class or otherwise, and always approached every problem of public or private life with the question "what is right?" and having decided on his answer he held unswervingly to his convictions'.[10] But this was hardly enough.

Grey handled small things well, but lack of imagination prevented him grasping the enormity of what would happen if things went wrong. His inflexibility meant that he was misunderstood, not least by the Germans, whom he appeased and conciliated, who referred to him as 'Liar Grey'. Many of his colleagues thought that he could have avoided the war by concession; others thought that he should have been bolder. In any event, he was perfectly set up as a scapegoat for both factions.

It was held that no man could be so wise as Grey looked. His prestige was bound up with his Roman profile, his aloof manner, and his economy of speech. His attempts to reach an accommodation with the Germans was looked upon as half-promises to betray France or Russia. The German statesmen took him to be a subtle conniving man, for they could not believe that anyone so scrupulously honest could be the spearhead of British diplomacy.

For a foreign secretary he was astonishingly naïve. He did not
even trouble to read up foreign countries and did not go abroad,
preferring to fish (he has a book on fly-fishing to his credit).
The only language he understood was French, and that imper-
fectly. He did not believe that Britain was immune from attack
or strife; he knew it. He was a Victorian of the old school, and
any suspicions of Germany were lulled by the honest and
straightforward attitude of the German ambassador in London,
Prince Lichnowsky, who, as it happened, was not in the
confidence of his own government.

Right up to the outbreak of war, there was no concerted
foreign policy. Actions were taken on an *ad hoc* basis. Things
would get better if they were left alone. But Europe sidled into
war in 1914, and though Grey displayed an unusual energy in
trying to avert it at the last minute, the combination of circumstances was too much for him. He was not a Palmerston, ready
to make off-the-cuff decisions. Today he is known by one
epigram: 'The lamps are going out all over Europe; we shall
not see them lit again in our lifetime.' The date: 3 August 1914.

Notes to this chapter are on page 292.

CHAPTER TWO

LONDON—THE GREAT SPRAWL

DURING THE nineteenth century London had spread out
alarmingly, and this expansion accelerated during the dozen
years preceding the First World War. The rising young novelist
Frank Swinnerton idly wondered if the growth would spread
across the whole of the southern counties, leading to the
ultimate disappearance of rural England. He saw no cure except
the demolition of all the tall houses near the heart of London
and the erection in their stead of enormous blocks of flats and
dwellings 'built with some beauty'.

The paradox was that, although the 8-per-cent unemployment
rate was reaching a height that would today shatter the nation,
there was an increasing demand for male and female workers
in factories, shops and offices. The amazing industrial development
of the city's outskirts called for skilled and semi-skilled labour
which could not be found in the stock of unemployed, compounded of the work-shy, of rural labourers unadapted to
industrial life, and elderly men programmed for a different age.
London industry wooed Birmingham, Coventry and the north,
and the provincial engineers and artisans flocked into the city in
their thousands.

Hotels and restaurants were springing up to cater for the

Edwardian London was rich in hotels and restaurants. It was the age of the Piccadilly Hotel and the Ritz

wealthy. It was the age of the Piccadilly Hotel and the Ritz, and the great West End emporiums, the most famous of which was perhaps Selfridge's. Gordon Selfridge had learned his trade in Chicago and had assimilated American promotional methods, spending £36,000 on advertising before the store was opened in 1909 with stock of more than £100,000 and a staff of 1,800. It was boasted that it was not a shop, but a social centre. Victorian shopping habits had been based on the small store, usually undercapitalised. The shopocracy, Maple, Heal, Selfridge, altered all that, pouring thousands into advertising and lavish window displays, made into fairylands by the wonders of the electric light. Although Paris was creaming away some of the custom, London was rich in dress shops, milliners, and all those pandering to conspicuous consumption.

Hustle, bustle and confusion characterised the life of central London. Motor buses, horse buses, motor cars, horse cabs, taxis, bicycles, and private carriages, all vied for road space, and the air was redolent with exhaust fumes and the smell of horses. The congestion was partly relieved by the underground railway. The switch to electricity made the tube train a viable proposition, and when the Bakerloo Line was opened in 1906 37,000 passengers used it on the first day, making nonsense of the *Railway Engineer*'s statement that 'this tube railway may now be regarded as a beautiful failure'. It took only seven minutes from Piccadilly Circus to Baker Street, whereas an omnibus took twenty minutes and a horse cab a quarter of an hour. The tube train was phenomenally cheap—all fares were twopence, though this was later altered. The movement of passengers was facilitated by the introduction of the escalator, only possible with the invention of the electric motor. This was initially alarming, and at Earls Court a man with a wooden leg was employed to show how safe and easy it was to use.

There were no junctions between the underground railway and the overhead system until 1913, when the Bakerloo Line was connected with the Great Western Railway. The railway companies resented the new rival, realising that their own great age was departing; between 1900 and 1913 only 1,200 miles of track were laid, and the last major station in London,

There was great congestion in London, and accidents of this nature were bound to happen

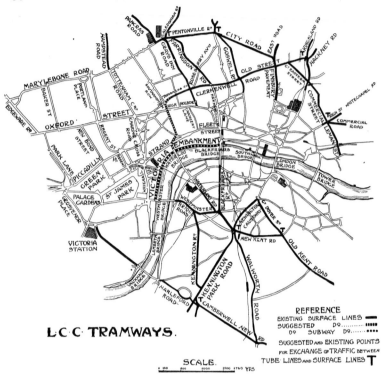

The electric tram revolutionised London transport. This map of 1902 depicts existing and projected routes

Marylebone, built in 1899, had an air of obsolescence almost as soon as it was opened.

The build-up of suburbia might appear to have been the answer to the railway dream of fresh custom, but transport between the outskirts and the centres of London was catered for by electric tram. The electric tramcar speedily eliminated the steam tram, first run in London in 1873 along Vauxhall Bridge Road; the compressed air tram, an abortive 1883 venture along the Caledonian Road, and the short-lived gas tram of 1896. The tram ran on rails or by means of overhead wires (the trolley bus). In 1900 340 million tram passengers were carried in London, and in 1903 the 8½-mile route from Westminster Bridge to Tooting was opened. In the same year Hampton Court was incorporated into the tramway system; in 1904 it reached Uxbridge, followed in 1906–7 by Kingston and Wimbledon, Lewisham, Dulwich and Peckham; in 1909–10 by Hampstead, Highgate and Norwood, and 1911–12 by Parliament Hill Fields and Herne Hill. Eventually the railways regained the custom when the tramways and the trolley buses ceased to run, but although the tram lines were a hazard to cyclists and motorists, something was lost when these clanking monsters were withdrawn from the London streets. Impervious to fog and the elements, the trams kept running when the rest of London's road transport was at a standstill.

The tramway system was democratic, used by the occupiers of aesthetic Hampstead and the jerry-built terrace houses of Tooting and Peckham. Where the tramway reached, ribbon development followed, untrammelled by planning considerations. Lovers of London were aghast at what they considered the vandalism of the speculators, with acres of the old city being replaced by huge stores and commercial buildings. The

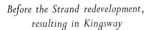
Before the Strand redevelopment, resulting in Kingsway

After the Strand redevelopment

most startling 'improvement' was carried out near the Strand, where the new thoroughfares of Kingsway and Aldwych, arguably two of the most uninteresting streets in London, were thrust through a maze of mean but picturesque streets and alleys. Holywell Street, the centre of the pornographic book trade, was one of the streets to disappear completely in this £4.5 million project. Quaint riverside London was also disfigured by a new stretch of embankment between the Houses of Parliament and Lambeth Bridge. Tunnels under the Thames at Rotherhithe and Woolwich proved an admirable answer to the bottlenecks of its bridges, and the contemporary byelaws governing their operation have their own period charm: 'No person shall take into the tunnel any loaded fire-arm, gunpowder, dynamite, nitro-glycerine, gun-cotton, Nobel's explosive or other explosive . . . No person shall drive or conduct into the tunnel any cattle or any animal forming part of a menagerie, or any wild animal'.

Surprisingly, despite the tram, the trolley bus and the tube

train, horse-drawn vehicles remained strong contenders as public transport. In 1912 there were still 567 hansom cabs on the London streets, and 576 horse omnibuses. In the more exclusive residential quarters of London there was a concerted refusal to let motorised public transport run. Small traders continued to use horsepower, and livery stables throughout London saw little diminution in their trade. The breweries in particular were reluctant to change over to the motor, and their shire horses were for many years to remain features of the London scene.

The good living of the fashionable suburbs and the gaiety of the West End depended on the prosperity of the City. Extravagant life styles were based on trade, banking, shipping and overseas investment—investment that, had it been used to benefit British industry, might have increased home production and halted the decline in the living standards of the less well-to-do by holding the pound steady and keeping prices down. The various facets of London were more distinct than they had been in Victorian

Despite the motor-car and the tram, the trolley bus and the tube train, the horse cab remained very popular until the outbreak of World War I

times, when boundaries tended to blur, when rich residential areas rubbed against centuries-old rookeries. This can be seen in the gradual supremacy of Oxford Street over the Strand; in the Strand all types and classes met, and the shops of instrument-makers abutted upon chop-houses and public houses of dubious reputation.

It has become traditional to look upon Edwardian London as gay and uninhibited. John Buchan thought it 'dull and mer-cantile' after Oxford, Max Beerbohm declared that it was 'too awful—fogs—depression—inanimation', and D. H. Lawrence wrote: 'London seems to me like some hoary massive underword, a hoary ponderous inferno. The traffic flows through the rigid grey streets like the rivers of hell through the banks of rocky-ash'.

The 'banks of rocky-ash' were the buildings that were being erected, which, like the age, were flatulent and intended to impress. The Ritz hotel, built in 1904, with a steel frame covered with Portland stone, emulated a French château; the Royal Automobile Club in Pall Mall (1909) seemed to reflect ennui rather than the dash and abandon that characterised contemporary

Houses for the rich were built regardless of expense, (left) 12 Hill Street, Berkeley Square, with its monstrous facade

(right) a more sedate house in Chelsea

motoring; the redesigned front of the Piccadilly Hotel was an insult to nearby Burlington House, and a new low was reached in the cavernous and gloomy design of London County Hall (1908).

The public buildings of the period were products of lazy thinking; the styles used were consciously 'English Renaissance' (the London County Hall), 'Classical', or what Osbert Lancaster termed 'Pont Street Dutch', favoured also for dwellings of the *nouveaux riches*. As the editor of *The Builder* wrote at the time: 'Many of the new residential streets in the west end of London present a really picturesque *ensemble*. . . .' Houses in Pont Street Dutch in Buckingham Gate, and Georgian Revival (with extra sculpture flung at the façade) in Margaret Street, strove for status, along with Harrods, a terra cotta monstrosity with dome of 1901, and Selfridge's. At the same time, the Edwardians were doing their best to destroy the Nash curve of Regent Street, a continual act of vandalism dating from 1910.

Perhaps the common denominator of Edwardian public building was a vaunting of tastelessness; whereas life was trivial and ephemeral, architecture was joyless and sombre, appropriate perhaps for the Old Bailey of 1902 but hardly for the new music halls, the architects of which were as devoted to red brick and terra cotta as the speculative builders of suburban terrace houses. There were few attempts to make use of the techniques or motifs of *art nouveau*, and when architects did try their hand they were a good deal more timid than their contemporaries on the continent. The Horniman Museum in Forest Hill was one of the architectural successes in the *art nouveau* style.

In ecclesiastical and commemorative architecture the Edwardians were at their most aimless and lazy, and, although an eye-stopper, the Central Hall, Westminster, has few religious connotations. The Victorians managed to do something new in their revival of Gothic styles, but Edwardian Gothic plumbs the depths of insipidity. Not surprisingly the death of Victoria called for a quantity of statues, the most grandiose of which is the one set in front of Buckingham Palace, and now rightly treated as nothing more than a traffic island.

The trouble with Edwardian architects was that they tried to be artistic. Their heads were full of unassimilated styles. They were much better when they got off their dignity or were faced with eccentric projects. They were obliged to be monumental in carving out Kingsway or Millbank, but when it came to designing cinemas with names such as the Olympia, the Bijou, the Jewel or the Picturedrome, then they were able to use their talents in an uninhibited way. John Belcher was a typical architect of the period, responsible both for the deadly dull Holy Trinity church in Kingsway (1909) and the exotic fantasies built to house the Franco-British Exhibition of 1908—the White City in Shepherd's Bush, a virtuoso performance only fragments of which survive; this vast complex of buildings was an early example of built-in obsolescence, being constructed of fibrous plaster. In the illustrated review of the exhibition it was stated that 'every building is white without shade, and under the ardent sun it has looked like some brilliant Oriental fantasy—a dream of a virgin

The movement of the Victorian rich from the immediate environs of the City accelerated with the Edwardians. This photograph shows horse-drawn omnibuses, soon to be replaced by trams and motor buses

city bathed in light'. It is a pity that the enthusiasm that permeated the concept and construction of the White City did not infiltrate into the drab world of public buildings. Great chunks of Edwardiana still remain in central London, and no doubt will be with us for many years to come, for they are functional and well-constructed, and with their steel frames and massive foundations they are not so vulnerable to the developers' bulldozers as their Victorian predecessors.

There were parts of London that the Edwardian improvers left untouched. The exodus of the Victorian rich from the immediate environs of the City had meant that the Georgian houses left vacant were taken over by the poor, turned into lodging houses, filleted for apartments and flats (a word, surprisingly, dating from 1824), and filled to bursting point. Nineteenth-century philanthropists, such as Angela Burdett-Coutts and George Peabody, had done something to relieve the congestion of these slums by financing model working-men's dwellings, but they were only scratching at the surface. Nothing was so out of fashion in the early years of the twentieth century as disinterested philanthropy, and the anticipated rent from such dwellings did not warrant their erection. The squalid seedy areas of London were left much as they were, and although there was a building boom between 1901 and 1910 the products were concentrated in the newly accessible suburbs, fashionable districts such as Chelsea and Kensington, and the business and trade areas.

But at least old London was alive. 'The West, like all things of fashion, is but a corpse electrified'.[1] Kings and queens came and went and no one in the East End bothered, and the 'unfortunate classes' fought out their lives in filth and decay without realising that things had changed, that they were now living in the age of extravagance and ostentation. In Limehouse the Chinese were still in their ghettos, and not all the opium dens had been replaced by fish and chip shops. Few London County Council inspectors visited the Asiatics' Home, where there were stone beds, caged cubicles, and no bathrooms.

The unimproved parts of London were still villages, each

The unimproved parts of London were still villages, with their own atmosphere. This snapshot of Whitechapel was taken early in the reign

with its own character and inhabitants. The Jews were scattered over London in fiercely antipathetic cliques; the French Jews were in Soho, the German Jews in Great Charlotte Street, the Italian Jews in Clerkenwell, while those in Whitechapel were Russian emigrés or were long established. It was customary for the Whitechapel Jews to move to Highbury, Maida Vale and, especially, Golders Green, when they had made their money. The Irish settled around Southwark and Bermondsey, areas with the highest unemployment. Journalists considered that the two worst streets in London were Dorset Street and Hoxton Street, though others chose Duval Street, Spitalfields, full of common lodging houses and which held an unenviable record for the number of suicides occurring there.

The most self-contained of the villages was Soho, with its restaurants catering for suburban pleasure-seekers; with the exception of Maxim's, most of the snob restaurants were outside the area. Soho posed as the Bohemian quarter of London, and was dominated by the French. There were stories of Parisians who had left their native city, had come to Soho, and had never afterwards left that square mile, whose world ended at Piccadilly Circus. Shadwell, today an indeterminate district edging on the Thames, was populated by Danes, Norwegians, and Swedes, as well as Mr Jamrach, London's leading dealer in wild animals who had his menagerie there. Shadwell contained what had been the most notorious street of early Victorian London, the Ratcliffe Highway, though the name had been changed. The speciality of Shadwell was providing girl prostitutes for the Scandinavian seamen, a trade that had been publicised in the nineteenth century but which the Edwardians were keen to keep covered up.

Street musicians were very much a feature of Edwardian London. A large number of these were Italians centred in Clerkenwell, who hired out their barrel-pianos from mini-tycoons. The Italians lived mainly in the huge blocks of Victorian tenements that still stud the district, and vendettas were commonplace. Clerkenwell had a faded air of once being of importance, an air that was totally lacking in Hoxton, a place of fish and chip shops, cast-off clothing stalls, and beer-houses. Hoxton contained one of the last of the old-time music-halls, the Britannia, a world apart from the vast new music-halls raised by syndicates. Hoxton was a no-man's-land to the Edwardian spirit, a place beyond reformation that one would sooner forget. The Edwardians did not systematically try to improve such areas as Hoxton or Stepney as their fathers and grandfathers had done, and the projected new city of Eastminster was an idle pipe dream. They looked with indifference on the spectre of the demon drink, the providers of which were everywhere in evidence (London had more than 30 per cent more pubs then than today). Willing to lavish huge sums of money on prestige projects such as Kingsway and Aldwych, they stemmed any financial aid to the slums; to do the Edwardians justice, no one else bothered for forty years.

Notes to this chapter are on page 292.

CHAPTER THREE

EDWARDIAN LIFE

Society in Jeopardy

MANY MEMBERS of the landed gentry cordially disliked King Edward, whom they found as uncongenial as his mother. His concept of what constituted society was not theirs. The king's friend and confidant, Lord Esher, asked:

> . . . what is called 'society'? Too much attention is paid to the word, which is really an anachronism now, and rather common! In fact, there is no such thing. Society is dead and died with d'Orsay and Lady Blessington. There are people 'who give dinners' and people 'who give balls.' That is all. It is open to you to choose whether you will go or not, as you please. This was not the case when society existed. Then, you could no more refuse than you could now refuse to dine with your Colonel. Either you were 'in society'—and in that case you kept its rules, quite simply—or, you were not in society, in which case (if you were anybody out of the ruck) you were generally considered to be some sort of swindler; or to have disgraced yourself.[1]

Nevertheless many people disagreed with Lord Esher. The social round continued, with tennis and garden parties, days on the river, presentation at court, the Eton and Harrow match at Lord's, and all the extravagances of the London Season. The rules of the game were frequently involved and intricate, and some were so obscure that they perplexed even the upper

The subtleties of society etiquette could precipitate disaster. A 1908 cartoon of a party to which no one came

echelons of society. At one dinner Arthur Conan Doyle took in Lady Curzon, simply because he was nearest the door. He had no presentiments of anything out of the way, until she said to him: 'Do you know that you have established a precedent and solved one of the more difficult and debatable matters of etiquette that has ever caused ill-feeling in British Society?'

Why was this? Lady Curzon was the wife of the Viceroy of India. She went on: 'There has never been so vexed a question as to whether a Vice-reine when she is away from the country where she represents royalty shall take precedence over a Duchess. There was a Duchess in the room, but you by your decided action have settled the matter for ever'.[2]

Medieval sophistry as to how many angels can dance on a pin-head was nothing to the subtleties of society etiquette.

At one great country house a footman kept a meticulous record of all the bad English and 'ignorance' he heard while waiting at table, and related the choicer items, with names and dates, to the servants of later visitors. Weekend visits and dinner parties could be, observed H. G. Wells, 'as unbracing mentally and as pleasant as going to a flower show and seeing what space and care can do with favourite strains of some familiar species',[3] but they could also be extremely daunting especially when members of the old order were intent on proving to newcomers that they could snub and patronise as expertly as in the old days.

Licensed eccentrics were still at large in the great country houses of the aristocracy. When one of them slid with abandon down the whole length of the banisters, Sir George Sitwell reproved his son Osbert with the words, 'Don't laugh! These Great Men have their Little Idiosyncrasies'. Sir George himself was not free from eccentricity—'if he *must* meet the living, to him as insubstantial as were the dead to others, he preferred them to be in a trance-like condition of subservience and astonishment'.[4]

But he did not compare in oddity with the Scotsman George Thomas, who carried with him a strap to chastise the children of any friends or relations who happened to be near at hand, and who fined his domestics—and the cat Sambo—if they displeased him. When he died he was buried in a wicker coffin, as this, he considered, was more convenient for the resurrection.

Arrogance and irritability marked many of the old gentry in both town or country. It was as if they were aware that they were a dying breed. Arnold Bennett commented on this in his diaries: 'In Bond Street this morning the main thing to be seen was the well-groomed, physically fit, male animal: a sort of physical arrogance with it'.[5] In the women there was a note of petulance when confronted with the changed conditions. 'The lavish expenditure and the feverish pursuit of pleasure that constitute Society do not appeal to me any more than the restaurant life, which did not exist in my day . . . Nowadays money shouts, and birth and breeding whisper!'[6] So declared the Countess of Cardigan and Lancastre. Lady Dorothy Nevill was at one with her:

> Society to-day and Society as I formerly knew it are two entirely different things; indeed, it may be questioned whether Society, as the word used to be understood, now exists at all . . . Society as it used to be—a somewhat exclusive body of people, all of them distinguished either for their rank, their intellect, or their wit—is no more.[7]

Lady Dorothy commented acidly that in the old days the desire of the *nouveaux riches* was to get into society; now they bitterly complained that they could not keep out of it. All was changed. Society was on the make. Lady Dorothy thought that money was the root of the trouble. In the old days £10,000 a year was considered a decent income; now the millionaires who were buying themselves into the favoured circles would spend as much on a picture. Not that £10,000 a year was to be despised; it was still 'a snug fortune, sufficient to have a little shooting, some hunting, a modest house in the country, and a small *pied-à-terre* in town'.

The keynote of Edwardian high life was enjoyment, the pleasures of the flesh rather than those of the mind. There was a great emphasis on food. Breakfast went on until half past ten, a solid luncheon was followed a few hours later by a substantial

There was a great emphasis on food, well illustrated by this early cartoon by H. M. Bateman, the poet of social embarrassment

tea, and then there was dinner which, even without guests, seldom consisted of fewer than twelve courses.

Notwithstanding the regular meals, one of which would have provided sufficient sustenance for a working family for a week, well-off Edwardians were great nibblers, and in some households dinner was capped by massive suppers (Edward VII thought that for supper nothing could beat oysters). On the piano in the drawing-room there would be a bowl full of crystallised violets, and for any activity calling for extra energy there were snacks at a minute's notice. King Edward favoured a lobster salad or cold chicken to fill in the hours between breakfast and lunch.

Elizabeth Robins-Pennell wrote a weekly column on cookery in the *Pall Mall Gazette*; she was on the side of the gourmet and not the glutton. 'Dish follows dish, conceit is piled upon conceit; and with what result? Before dinner is half over, palates are jaded, "fine shades" can no more be appreciated, every new course awakens fear of the morrow's indigestion'. It was not surprising that at regular intervals the indulgent paid visits to Marienbad or Ems to 'take the waters' and try and restore some order to their bloated and ill-used stomachs. At these fashionable spa towns they underwent the rigours demanded—mile walks from pump to hotel, mud baths, bed at ten—knowing that soon they would be back at their troughs. There were compensations; the spa towns were ideal places for picking up women and offered uninhibited entertainment. The fact of Maud Allan dancing before King Edward VII wearing only two oyster shells and a five franc piece was not news-worthy; it only became so when it was decided to bring her to London for her performance.

Newsreels of the period give the impression that the Edwardians were constantly jigging about, moving in sharp strutting actions. The difficulty in matching the film speeds of the early 1900s with modern projection speeds has made the denizens of the period look a good deal smarter on their feet than was the case. Too often, the Edwardian rich were slow in thought and action, and their intellectual demands were too few to admit of ennui. They encouraged those about them who provided easy entertainment.

Frank Lawley of the *Daily Telegraph* was welcomed in royal circles, because there was cockfighting at his house in Mayfair; the Marquis de Soveral, Portugese Minister in London, blue-chinned and known as the 'blue monkey', because he was a dashing roué; the marine artist Eduardo de Martino, because he was amusing and agreeably sycophantic. There were other hangers-on, such as Sir Herbert Maxwell, who had a habit of entering rooms 'like an elastic ball gently propelled by some invisible hand'; and the gossip Herbert Gardner, 'pleasant of face, agreeable of manner, with a pretty turn for small talk, and good connections'.

The relative inactivity of the men contrasted sharply with the energy of their wives, who flew from boredom with dash and vigour. A new variety of women emerged, termed enigmatically 'the married bachelors of the fair sex', who frequented clubs for women only, such as the Ladies' Army & Navy in Cork

The hall of the Lyceum Club, sacred to women

Street, the Empress in Dover Street, and the Empire, presided over by Lady Jersey. Here they indulged their passion for the in-game of the period, auction bridge. For many leisured women this game became an obsession; by three o'clock they would be waiting impatiently to begin; they would play throughout tea, eat a light club dinner talking bridge all the time, and were back in the card room immediately they had choked down their food, eventually leaving in the early hours of the morning.

The days of the rich women, whether or not they were in society, were spent in passing time, with a languid obeisance to 'duty' in the form of running, or rather being distantly associated with, whist drives and jumble sales. Afternoon calls would take up some of the hours, and when the time was hanging rather more tediously than ever they would pop in at the Law Courts and savour the latest juicy divorce case.

A good many hours were spent in dressing and undressing; there were tweeds for being sporty in, a frock for luncheon, diaphanous tea-gowns, long dresses with trains for dinner. Officially cosmetics were 'fast' though many women used them. As a different dinner gown was considered essential for each evening, a weekend in the country could not be undertaken without a mountain of clothes. The new sport of motoring obliged women to supplement their wardrobes with heavy sealskin coats, goggles, veils, and appropriate hats.

A great deal of time was spent in having their hair done. Extravagant coiffures were built up on pads and with the aid of wire frames. Consequently tall women looked grotesque and short women top-heavy. The ideal woman was shaped like a swan, but crowned with their outrageous hats many ladies gave the impression of being dolls that had been put together in an odd sort of way.

The energy which society women had in abundance, an often desperate attempt to escape from a meaningless round, could result in indiscretions, and adultery was indulged in to enliven an otherwise insignificant existence. Victorian country house gatherings were notorious for the way in which bedrooms were allotted for the convenience of the various occupants, and this trend gathered momentum during the Edwardian years. Adultery in society was made easier by the motor-car revolution, and the tendency of the rich to escape to the riverside or the seaside at weekends, where opportunities for misbehaviour, with or without the tacit consent of married partners, were legion.

There was a dichotomy in Edwardian high society that had been lacking in the Victorian. King Edward VII had strengthened the ceremonial of the court, and the etiquette and decorum in the externals of society had been kept up, and even augmented. Yet the fabric was cracking. The fashion scene offers an indication

The motor-car revolution made it possible for the well-off to escape to the seaside, where opportunities for misbehaviour were legion. Southend, as shown in this photograph, was not yet downgraded

of this. Although nudity was not accepted, and the décolletage in evening dress was less sensational than in Victorian times, the use of lace and chiffon reached new heights of suggestion. There was a completely new attitude towards underclothing. Victorian underclothing had been functional, and even the most expensive prostitutes wore flannel drawers. Edwardian underwear was renamed lingerie, and its basic function was to attract and tantalise the men. Garments that previously no one had seen except the wearer and the dressmaker were now openly labelled 'seductive', drawers were replaced by knickers, the shift had passed through the late Victorian phase of chemise to a slip, and petticoats became frillies. It was the age of frou-frou from the knees down. The most sensational new undergarment was the brassière introduced in 1912. In late Victorian times the cult of the breast had been sly and seemingly accidental; the breasts had been pushed up by tight-lacing. The brassière concentrated attention on the breasts, and combined with the 'temptatious teagown which absolutely defines the figure in a manner which is insinuating' unquestionably set men's pulses racing. The 'pneumonia blouse' was another innovation, a transparent promise of muslin and lace. Everything was in pastel colours, later ridiculed as 'nuances of nymph's thigh, lilacs, swooning mauves, tender blue hortensias . . . all that was soft, washed-out, and insipid'.[9]

The rich could spend a good deal of money in conspicuous display; a petticoat could cost as much as £50, 'evening confections' were priced at £200. The rich brocades, velvets and satins of the Victorian dresses did not cost so much as the lace fripperies of the Edwardian age, in which detail was picked out with a precision and a delicacy that reflect great credit on the dressmaker's art.

Edwardian beauties there were in abundance, and their appeal was brought out by the elaborate dresses of the period, so pointedly that, as Cecil Beaton wrote, 'there was an intriguing perversity about such excessive prettiness'. The demarcation

The house of Worth, favoured by the rich

A rational dress had arisen for sporty women. A surrealist drawing of Princess Victoria with her Beeston-Humber bicycle

line between the professional beauty and the society lady was nearly lost. In Victorian times, wrote one cynical observer, 'the natural goal of professional beautydom proved to be the stage; that of the she-gambler and turfite of the twentieth century is quite as inevitably the divorce court'.[10]

The women treated the men with an affectation of indifference notwithstanding the incessant teasing implied by the new attitude towards underwear. There was a conflict between the introduction of see-through blouses and dresses, and frilly knickers, and the continuation of the long floor-sweeping skirt and high neck-line. The high neck-line was influenced by the decision of Queen Alexandra to always wear such. The reason for this has been maliciously assigned to the debatable fact that the queen contracted syphilis from her husband, and needed a high neck-line to cover scars (vide the unexpurgated version of T. E. Lawrence's

The Mint). Others maintained that these were scars resulting from small-pox.

Looking at the wide picture, it might be postulated that the sex appeal of high Edwardian dress arose instinctively from the demands of mother Nature that the nation must breed, to counteract the falling birth rate due to the increasing use of birth control methods, though perhaps it would be too extravagant to say that women were instinctively preparing their organisms for replacing the casualties of World War I.

There was a clash also between femininity and function. A rational dress had arisen for sporty women, and though still cumbersome by present-day standards the costumes worn for fashionable sports such as tennis and cycling were reasonably suitable. Yet these costumes, outlandish as they were to the reactionaries, were derived from the ordinary clothes of the period, and this cannot be said of the sudden switch in fashion design that followed the introduction of the Russian ballet to western Europe. Many women were more interested in the décor and costumes of the Russian ballet than in the music. *Modernisme oriental* threw a few buckets of bright paint over the pastel shades that had dominated fashion, and the French houses siphoned off the custom of Jay's and Liberty's. One of the leading couturiers was Poiret, who hobbled the acquiescent English-women in harem skirts, hung them with fox furs, draped them in pearls, and enveloped them in wired tunics and jewel-laden capes. 'It was strange', wrote a reporter from *The Queen* in 1910, 'to find oneself wafted into a world of beauty, ease and luxury, and for a moment or two the Puritan in me rebelled'. But not for long. Oriental and Russian barbarism was more amusing than pastel seductivity.

The harem skirt was laughed into obscurity but the hobble skirt caught on to an amazing extent, and the frilly under-petticoats were abolished. 'The narrow skirt of 1910 was an astonishing change from the flowing skirts which had prevailed for the last fifteen years', wrote James Laver in *Taste and Fashion* (1937). 'No longer was it necessary or even possible to lift the skirts when crossing the streets'. The hobble skirt, superbly

With the prevailing fashions, it was often difficult for a woman to lift her skirts when crossing a street. In this illustration to a magazine serial, it even seems painful to walk

named, was as anachronistic in the Edwardian environment as the crinoline had been in 1850 or the bustle in its day. It was anti-sexual, inconvenient, and meaningless; it was said that a staircase called for gymnastics and that it was impossible to stoop without disaster.

It may be that the crying out for novelty, for something different, resulted in these curious phenomena; it may be that society, ashamed by its voluptuousness, was wearing apparel as near as could be got to the hair-shirt, that the hobble skirt was symbolic. Its one sexual charm was that it permitted only little tripping steps. The hobble skirt was harsh and realistic, and to some fashion experts the dissolving fairyland of frillies and chiffon was being replaced by a more masculine spirit in response to the shadow of approaching war. Apprehension was beginning to have its effect on clothes, and when towards the end of 1913 the neck-line began to drop as if to start another age of breast-orientation it was treated as scandalous. Society might be immoral but it was never permissive.

Suburban Life

The Edwardian age was the period of the garden city, the small country house, and artistic suburbia. It saw the coming of Port Sunlight (1905), Bournville (1908), Hampstead Garden Suburb (1907), and Letchworth Garden City (1903), and anticipated Welwyn Garden City (1920) of which Dailymail model village, sponsored by the newspaper of that name, was part.

The nostalgia for the past, the flight from the anxiety that pervaded the era, found expression in the re-creation of village life. As John Betjeman put it, 'Each garden village had houses graded carefully to income—but no rich man's palace nor poor man's hovel—a leafy, happy medium instead, with communal grass and clubs and institutes and a choice of churches'.[1] The gaunt reality of Victorian town life was thrust into the background, and the chilling symmetry of council housing estates was still in the future. The garden cities and newly discovered suburbs brought into action by improved urban transport—the

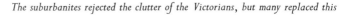

The suburbanites rejected the clutter of the Victorians, but many replaced this

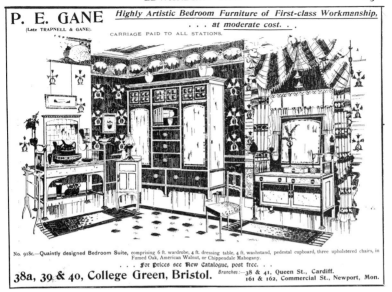
By this!

tram, the trolley-bus, the motor omnibus, and the tube train—reflected the new life.

Snug, seemly, practical, the houses in the commuter belt were machines not exactly for living in but for being cosy in. The clutter and profusion of objects that marked the Victorian home were rejected out of hand. A few acute observers recognised the implications of suburbia. In his book *Democracy and Reaction* (1904), L. T. Hobhouse wrote: 'Suburban villadom is a political and social portent the meaning of which has never yet been analysed . . . Politically it is a greater burden than the slums'.

Suburban cultural life was replete with operatic and dramatic societies, madrigal singing, and folk song; suburban sports were golf, cricket and tennis. The suburbanites adored the gramophone and phonograph, and played intellectual games such as Styles, Epigrams, Consequences. The more class-conscious changed for dinner, and the more emancipated invented a vocabulary in which teagowns were 'teagies', nightdresses were 'nighties', in which 'deevie' meant divine and 'diskie' disgusting. There was a fad for Italianate endings (partnerina, dansares, dinnare) and

The rich suggestive life of Wimbledon

10.30 whisky replaced the end-of-day cup of tea. The houses were too small to boast a billiards room, and apart from card games the favourite indoor sport was ping-pong, yet to be christened table-tennis. C. F. G. Masterman wrote about suburbia's 'vicarious sports and trivial amusements', but in the cause of middle-class unity the suburbanites managed to encompass a great many participant sports and pastimes.

Those who lived in the suburbs did not go much for religion. The Church of England was still confusedly grappling with the problems of modern life, and the only sector where it was holding its own was in High Church, now renamed Anglo-Catholicism. A fillip to fundamentalism was given by the arrival in Britain in 1905 of two American revivalists, Torrey and Alexander, who tried to recapture the successes of Sankey and Moody of a previous generation. Would Edwardians, they asked, like to have Christ find them in a ballroom, or at the card table, or playing ping-pong on a Sunday? Initially their audience answered with a cowed 'No', but the impact of the American revivalists rapidly wore off.

Mr Kensit, a draper's assistant, also came forward to tackle godlessness. Torrey and Alexander were at least positive; Kensit and his followers were negative, and they saw it as their principal role to create scenes in Anglo-Catholic churches, by brawling and shouting. Kensit's vogue was short-lived, for while carrying out his duties in Liverpool a fellow-Christian threw a chisel at him and killed him.

The hold of Anglo-Catholicism was disturbing to the establishment, and in 1906 a Royal Commission on Ecclesiastical Discipline produced a bulky report predictably casting scorn on Popish ritual and threatening retaliation. The suburbs were not interested. Although they still married in churches rather than registry offices, many suburbanites indignantly rejected anything that interfered with their week-ends, those week-ends consecrated to what G. K. Chesterton termed 'the rich suggestive life of Wimbledon'.

The upsurge of Edwardian suburbia has probably never received the attention it deserves. For the first time the middle classes were branching out without taking a lead from the upper classes.

The suburban husbands were basically white-collar workers. Between 1900 and 1911 the demand for office workers had

The middle-class picture of the working man, given to drink, sport, and lewd pursuits

gone up 50 per cent in the public services, 33 per cent in commerce, and 17 per cent in the professions. Although they did not earn much more than the manual workers, their attitude towards those whom they considered their inferiors was harsh and patronising, and although they did not have much more money to spend, they knew how to spread it around, and the necessity of a fairly frugal and austere life style was made a virtue. They indulged in respectable but inexpensive pursuits, and as their new homes were labour-saving (with dining-nooks instead of dining-rooms) there was no need to employ domestic help. By and large they were fairly gregarious, and in the summer they went on cycling holidays—very few of them owned cars.

Their common factor was a fear of the working classes and democracy, which they considered synonymous. Their collective image of the working man was, considered C. F. G. Masterman, 'a loud voiced, independent, arrogant figure, with a thirst for drink and imperfect standards of decency, and a determination to be supported at some one else's expense'. When Lloyd George produced his 'People's Budgets' he became the most hated man in the canon, the person who would take their money from them and turf them out of Eden.

The image of the working man was mixed with that of the 'man in the street':

> He knows already all about any appeal you can make to the better side of him, and he has long ago chopped it up in his mill of small talk and catch phrases and reduced it to such a meaningless patter that the words which must be used have acquired trivial and lowering associations. [2]

The white-collared classes moved self-consciously away from any identification with the man in the street and, aided and abetted by their wives, lived lives of overpowering gentility. The living-room was renamed the hall, and had much of the Spartan qualities associated with such a room, and the bedroom was renamed the bower or the boudoir. The houses were furnished in two styles: reproduction, especially sham-Georgian and Regency, and debased 'Arts & Crafts', deriving from William Morris, with *art nouveau* graftings. Sometimes the *art nouveau* element predominated, sometimes the cottagey and hand-made.

An art nouveau interior by the firm of Goodyers

Art nouveau was the perfect background for the artistic and genteel life of suburbia, and, like the reproduction styles of furnishing and décor, suburbia got it second-hand, for by the time it reached England from France the momentum had run out of the movement. *Art nouveau* in Britain centred around the store of Liberty's in Regent Street, and so prominent was this firm that the style itself was called the Liberty style even in the country that instigated *art nouveau*.

The style itself was stigmatised by a cynic as the concentrated essence of a wriggle; an art critic spoke of it as abounding in squirming lines and blobs, and said the source of *art nouveau* inspiration had been found in entrails. There were no hard and fast rules, and supporters found in the movement beauty of line, grace of form, and freedom. T. G. Jackson, an artist, thought that the main motive of the designs was a conscious striving after novelty and eccentricity, that the forms of the objects obscured and ignored the lines of the construction, that the natural quality of material was not respected, and that throughout there was a fidgety vulgar obtrusiveness. 'Perhaps I am old fashioned', began Alfred Gilbert, a sculptor best known for Eros in Piccadilly Circus, but *art nouveau* struck him as decadent and nonsensical. The architect C. F. A. Voysey thought that the movement demonstrated atheism, conceit and imitation.

None of these opinions prevented the march of *art nouveau* to commercial acceptance, and the twisting swirling furniture on which was grafted motifs of lilies and other appropriately decadent plants, the 'art pewter' and copper banged out in a variety of shapes and sizes, all fitted in remarkably well with the products of the arts and crafts movement, the angular furniture and the general air of rusticity. The smaller *art nouveau* objects fitted in equally well with perhaps the only piece of furniture invented by the Edwardians, the cosy corner, which combined settee, screen, bookcase and cabinet, all in one. 'Much advertised in ladies' fashion papers, and recommended in journals which profess to give advice and instruction to the enquiring housewife, it is a type of unstable and ill-balanced structure which, so far from conveying any sense of cosiness or comfort, to my mind always seems to be threatening to topple about one's ears'.[3]

The products of the movement also merged into the new houses of the period, in which the round window was a particular feature and there were innumerable artistic nooks and crannies. The trend of décor also facilitated the introduction of what some saw as monstrosities but others as reflections of a new spirit; there was an emphasis in décor on white paint and waxed unpainted or unvarnished wood with designs in low relief, and on fabrics that were self-coloured or gave the impression of being hand-woven.

Many observers saw the fad as the pursuit of novelty for its own sake, and the more acute as a commercial gimmick. George Haité, President of the Society of Designers, drew attention to 'the insatiable desire of our manufacturers for novelty at any cost, and the facilities offered through the illustrated journals for flattering personal vanity by the reproduction and publication of immature efforts'.[4] This last point is important. For the first time modern advertising methods were being used to promote a style; this had not been done for the arts and crafts style, and the aesthetic movement of the last quarter of the nineteenth century, with its emphasis on flimsy pseudo-Oriental furniture and blue-and-white china, had come too soon for the full exploitation treatment. The 1880s had seen a revolution in illustrated magazine techniques, and photographs of the latest consumer goods were widely circulated via the illustrated press and the quality women's papers.

AIDS TO ART.

Reuben: "WHAT YER DOIN' WID DAT OLD DRAIN-PIPE?"
Phil: "SELLIN' IT TO DE DECORATIVE ART SOCIETY FER UMBRELLA STANDS!"

It was easy to be original if beauty was no object, declared Gilbert Scott in 1903. This 1907 cartoon shows this admirably

The suburban market, though not specifically rich, was a wide one. But other people were buying *art nouveau*, especially those who were made wealthy by the upsurge in profits and dividends that marked the Edwardian period. Although the poor were getting marginally poorer by the lowering of real wages, the middling rich had never had it so good and could afford to spend a great deal of money in quality *art nouveau*, the kind promoted by Liberty's, Goodyer's, and Story & Co, who set out rooms in the style for the edification of their customers. The suburbanites had too often to be content with the trade versions, which were either ludicrous or timid. The purists resented the bedroom suite, a fairly new term, in which a motif, quite acceptable initially, became overbearing and monotonous when repeated *ad nauseam*.

It was fortunate that metal-work was ideally suited to *art nouveau* decoration, and with items that had not existed before in the private home—such as electric light fittings—the designers could really indulge themselves with hammered brass and hand-wrought copper. The results were novel and interesting, though, as Gilbert Scott, the architect, remarked in 1903, it was very easy to be original if beauty is no object.

The establishment was set against *art nouveau*, which lent itself to ready wit. Gerald Moira, the artist, thought there should be a law against people perpetrating 'such abortions as the kidney and the squirm for a wall decoration, or the dining table with legs that start in the corners of the room, and terminates some eighteen inches above the board in a thing that is half a muffin and something of a quoit. The embroidery, the design of which consists of telegraph wires, at one end an emaciated head, and ending in caterpillar wriggles at the other, the motive of such a design being "A Lost Soul's Thoughts Finding No Resting Place" or something of that sort'.[5] Professor Moira, indeed, put his finger on the crux of *art nouveau*. It was inclined to be intellectually pretentious. Its devotees liked mottoes on beams and over fireplaces, preferably high sounding, not altogether legible, and perhaps in a foreign language; they were the logical replacement of the religious mottoes that had for so long hung above bed-heads;

'God is Love' was no longer the message that the suburbanites wanted to see.

The astonishing acceptance of *art nouveau* by perhaps the only new social class to arise for more than half a century is understandable only if one sees it as the aftermath of the aestheticism that flourished around 1880, when women clad in the long shapeless dresses of the movement asked their escorts, 'Are you *intense*?' The trial of Oscar Wilde gave the thumbs down to the movement, but the mood of the fin-de-siècle infiltrated into respectable life in suburbia. If a sociologist had asked that same question again, the answer in a thousand twee, mullion-windowed homes would have been 'yes'.

The main difference between the aestheticism of 1880 and the suburbanism of 1905 was that aestheticism was certain of itself, and the suburbanites were not. The sinuous lines of their furniture, the freakish metalwork, objects 'in which solid forms disappeared in amazing twists and contortions, ornaments of glass dripped cloudy tears, ashtrays looked like spent dum-dum bullets',[6] all these were directly relevant to their possessors. The one attribute of *art nouveau* that by chance no one mentioned was spinelessness. This was a strong characteristic of suburbia, no matter how the men tried to demonstrate their masculinity on the golf course or at the tennis net, or the women their forward-looking tastes in buying from Liberty's. They had souls to let, and no amount of ping-pong or intellectual word games detracted from this. The triviality could be interpreted by some as an amiable philosophy; as is seen in the 'little man' heroes of H. G. Wells' Edwardian novels, such as *Kipps* or *The History of Mr Polly*. The thwarted desire for romance and the escape from being the insignificant creature who was something, but not much, in the City, these elements play a vital part in the emergence of the Edwardian suburbanite.

Crouched up in their cosy corners, striving to forget the anxieties that pressed down upon them—the falling value of money, the unpleasantness of the working classes, talk of wars and the threats of wars—the occupants of neat houses in Surbiton or Harrow-on-the-Hill read, if they were women, Ella Wheeler

"I SUPPOSE, LIKE ME, YOU HAVE YOUR TROUBLES?"
"OH, YES, MUM; JUST LIKE YOU."

(*Drawn by* JOHN HASSALL.)

A variety of household aids had reduced the need for servants, while those servants who were available belonged to a numerically decreasing species

Wilcox's *Poems of Passion* ('favourites with all cultured persons')
or Florence Barclay's *The Rosary*, the best-seller of 1909. The
men read A. E. W. Mason's *The Four Feathers* (best-seller of 1902)
or Edgar Wallace's *The Four Just Men* (1905). One of the most
prolific writers of the period was Nat Gould: by 1909 his
healthy extravert novels had sold more than six million copies.

The inner uncertainty was reflected by an uneasiness about
one's role. The new woman, emancipated and hard-drinking,
pedalled from point A to point B like a mad thing, occasionally
flirting with the suffragette movement, enlivening an afternoon
by throwing half a brick through a cabinet minister's window.
Yet femininity erupted in great billowing dresses and elaborate
corsages, and waists of the utmost waspness were achieved by
rigorous tight-lacing that harked back to Victorian days.

It may be that things were moving too fast in the early 1900s
for anyone to comprehend; the internal combustion engine had
revolutionised passenger transport, the electric motor had
brought the vacuum cleaner and other household gadgets into
the home, reducing the need for a servant, and the wireless
telegraph and the first fluttering indications of cinematography—
the first London cinema was in Bishopsgate in 1906—promised a
revolution in life styles, a challenge that many were reluctant
to meet. Such a challenge had been offered nearly a century
earlier by the Industrial Revolution, and had been met by a
reversion to pre-industrial modes of living, which in its literary
form was known as the romantic revival.

Some writers have claimed that the dabbling in *art nouveau*
by suburbia was ephemeral, but it is equally arguable that this
strange movement, culled from the fag-ends of aestheticism and
various outlandish continental movements (especially the odd
style known as the 'Vienna Secession' movement), was ready-
made for the apprehensive and self-conscious denizens of outer
London and the garden cities. It is curious that socialism found
an audience there; but it was socialism with a small 's', the easy-
going version of the Fabian Society and their high-minded
supporters who were as shocked by the brusque attitude of the
workers as any timid member of the middle class.

*Sir Ambrose Heal tried to emancipate the suburbanite from the 'pretentious stuffiness' of
the villa. This advertisement for Heal & Son's 'toilet wares' dates from 1906*

Another feature of Edwardian suburban villadom was that it
was inconsequential. The inhabitants thought that they had
something to contribute, but deep down they knew that they
had not. They were a ready market for any new entertainment or
diversion, and could be unmercifully snubbed by their tradesmen,
especially those representatives of the new shopocracy who,
thanks to the patronage of King Edward VII, were being assimilated into society. Ambrose Heal, who had entered the
family business in 1893, considered that it was his patriotic duty
to emancipate the suburban dwellers from their childish adherence

to the gaudy and meretricious absurdities of *art nouveau*, which he made sound sillier by anglicising it.

In the Heal catalogue of 1909, promotion of his own sane no-nonsense products co-exists with a crusade against the style which he hoped to supplant: '. . . all the pretentious stuffiness of the suburban villa, the "new art" overmantel smothered in rococo photograph frames, ineffable green grotesques of cats and other depressing forms of pottery'. Whatever its merits, the Heal furniture of the period is certainly of less interest today than the products of *art nouveau* at its most 'ineffable'.

It was easier to escape, both metaphorically and physically, in the first decade of the present century than it had been. The bicycle had given all but the very poor personalised transport. Escapist literature was abundant; readers could identify readily with one of the best-known fictional detectives of the time, Trent, created by E. C. Bentley:

> A man not yet thirty, with an air of irresponsible good humour, and an easy, unceremonious carriage of his loose-knit figure that struck his visitor as pleasing in general . . . His features were regular; his short, curling hair and a moustache, and, indeed, his whole appearance, suggested a slight but not defiant carelessness about externals.[7]

There was, and is, no better way of escape from the trivial and

Typical of Edwardian crime fiction heroes was E. A. Freeman's John Thorndyke

the incomprehensible than in deliberately allowing oneself to be lured into a doom-laden atmosphere, and this was supplied by a number of skilled practitioners of fiction. Algernon Blackwood in 1908: 'Forces rose all about him, transforming the normal into the horrible, and the spirit of craven fear ran through all his being, bringing him to the verge of collapse'.[8]

E. F. Benson in 1912:

An awful shuddering and nausea of the spirit rather than of the flesh had seized me, and more than once he had to place my feet upon the steps, while every now and then he cast glances of terror and apprehension up the stairs.[9]

The haunted and the macabre could even be modelled to suit the woman reader, as is evident from Ford Madox Ford's *Riesenberg*, published in the *English Review* in 1911:

He caught her in his arms. She screamed, a shrill and violent sound like the cry of an eagle, that dissipated itself in the tenuous and desolate air. 'Do not touch me', she cried out. 'I am mad. I have gone mad. Do not touch me! Look down! What do you see?'

The awful and the occult always appeals to a readership that is out of tune with the times, and there is no surer way to gauge the mood of an era than to sift through the tales of mystery and horror that were served up in the weekly magazines of the time (*Strand Magazine*, the most typical of these, sold 400,000 a month). It was significant that when the topic was too near reality even the most accomplished cliff-hanger did not receive its due—this happened to the novelist William le Queux when he described the 'horrid and thrilling invasion' of London by the Germans in 1910, driving home the message by having the book advertised by sandwich-board men dressed in the uniform of the Prussian infantry.

Escape through fiction was highlighted by the increased use made of public libraries. Between 1901 and 1914 library stocks doubled. It is interesting to note that the most popular novelists were those who wrote for the women's market. The number of books per library written by M. E. Braddon (1837–1915), the author of *Lady Audley's Secret* (1862), was 109 in 1907, and she was followed by Mrs Henry Wood, ninety-one, and Emma Jane Worboise, seventy-seven.

To cater for the self-conscious literary suburbs, there was an upsurge in the reprinting of the classics, and the firms involved in this laudable trade must strike chords in all those who haunt second-hand bookshops. World's Classics, originally published by Grant Richards and taken over by the Oxford University Press in 1909, date from 1901; Collins' classics from 1903; Everyman's Library from 1906, and Cassell's People's Library from 1909. The important thing about all these books is that they were cheap. The large sales of these reprints demonstrate that the demands by the suburbs for quality literature was more than skin deep, and that to some extent the literary pretensions were justified.

It is easy to patronise suburbia and all that that implies, but Wimbledon and Surbiton produced a simulacrum of the civilized society that was in welcome contrast to the self-indulgent lives of many rich people. The inhabitants of the custom-built villages that were neither town nor country did not rage and bemoan their condition, and their eagerness to create their own modes of living and culture, shallow and superficial as they may have been, can be seen in retrospect to be pathetic rather than irritating.

It is certainly true that without the patronage of suburbia and the professional middle classes, Edwardian 'culture' would have been very thin indeed. One of the greatest achievements of the suburbanites was to hand down their not undistinguished ethos to their children.

Many of those desperate to acquire a veneer of culture took their text from Edward Carpenter, an apostle of the refined life:

Life is an art, and a very fine art. One of its first necessities is that you should not have *more* material in it—more chairs, and tables, sevants, houses, lands, bank-shares, friends, acquaintances, and so forth, than you can really handle . . . It is so much better to be rude to needless acquaintances than to feign you like them, and so muddle up both their lives and yours with a fraud.[10]

The desire for the intellectual life was fed not only by
Carpenter, but by the Book Club and the subsidising of the
Encyclopaedia Britannica by Lord Northcliffe; not only by the
cheap reprint of the classics but by the fad for folk dancing and
singing, and the resurrection of ancient music under the aegis of
the Dolmetsch family. A. C. Benson gave an amusing picture of a
concert in Cambridge, with Dolmetsch saying, 'What I am going
to play to you is awfully beautiful, awfully simple, but really
beyond the reach of the modern people'.

> Then some odd tinkling things were played on virginals and lute—sounds as
> if one had shaken up a cage of mice and canaries together . . . The collection
> of people listening with grotesque earnestness to these very odd sounds,
> the deliberate antiquity of it all, the sweeping aside all the progress of
> the art . . . [11]

Garden-city life tried to approximate to that of a university
town with rustic trappings, but no matter how strenuously the
intellectual ideal was pursued there was a lack of depth, and
although externals were grasped there was a superficiality about
the appreciation. It was the idea of ancient music that appealed,
not the music itself. Suburban interest in philosophy was in the
idea of philosophy rather than in the meat and substance, and
for every dozen persons who professed an acquaintance with
G. E. Moore, the fashionable philosopher of the period, hardly
one would have been able to be more specific. They were at one
with the auctioneer of George Eliot's *The Mill on the Floss*, who
brought with him from school 'a sense of understanding Latin
generally, though his comprehension of any particular Latin was
not ready'.

Fortunately the Edwardian arts readily gave up their secrets
without any great intellectual effort, and the writers consciously
or subconsciously wrote for middlebrows who saw themselves
as highbrows. Pseudo-classics such as Edward FitzGerald's
Rubáiyát of Omar Khayyám were gift-wrapped and presented in an
overwrought frenzied manner and left lying on coffee-tables,
tokens of membership of the elect. Although G. K. Chesterton
betrayed a talent for close analysis in his journalism, it was his

essay-writing, light and whimsical, that was enjoyed, and his slim volumes of *pensées* rubbed shoulders with equally quaint books of essays by E. V. Lucas, Hilaire Belloc and Robert Lynd.

This literature was cosy and flattering, and politely shut out the horrid world outside; if one wanted to peer into this outside world, one preferred to go to the fashionable commentators. George Bernard Shaw explained it to one in a simple jovial manner and even made socialism sound friendly. There was no lack of filters or the makers of filters against reality.

This was true also of art. Until 1910 painting was comfortable and comforting, and techniques had altered little over the last twenty years, though if anything paint was being handled in a freer manner by such artists as Wilson Steer, Sickert, and Charles Sims. Subject matter had changed little, and historical scenes were still being churned out by the academic professionals. The 1905 Royal Academy exhibition included *St Agnes in Prison receives from Heaven the Shining White Garment* by Frank C. Cowper and *For He Had Spoken Lightly of a Woman's Name* by John Lomax, works that would have found a place in exhibitions of forty years earlier. *The Cheat* by John Collier was a typical Victorian genre scene; the only contemporary characteristic was the Edwardian dress.

These pictures would not find wall space in the suburbs, which had little money to spend on such luxuries. The Royal Academy catered for the rich for whom expensive pictures were frequently status symbols and not life enhancers. More to the taste of the middlebrows were the products of the New English Art Club, first given an airing in 1906, though there was never much enthusiasm for fine art as such; applied art was another matter altogether. The lack of interest was reflected in the small number of private galleries in the West End.

The suburbanites scorned the affection that the rich had for portraits. The new rich were desperately anxious to get hold of portraits that they could specify as being of their ancestors. In 1903 a Raeburn portrait fetched 14,000 guineas, and a Romney 9,400 guineas (in 1877, forty-nine Raeburn portraits sold for a total of £4,707). In garden city and suburb, artistic products were valued more than art works, and there was a big market for aesthetically designed book-plates. This mood was fostered by the first numbers of the new magazine *The Studio* which sponsored *art nouveau*, and if the intellectual suburbs did buy pictures they were inclined to choose those by artists of that persuasion (artists who have only recently begun to be evaluated and whose work now sells at high prices).

The Studio did much to bolster up the garden city ethos. It gave support to the devotees of the arts and crafts movements and imitation rusticity, and piloted art into the perspective enjoyed by its readers. Lack of confidence was the prevailing malaise of suburbandom, and directly relates to the apprehension that was ever present. It can be seen now that their fears relating to the coming dominance of the working classes were unjustified; working-class leaders doffed their aggression with miraculous ease when they became members of the establishment, when they took their seats in parliament, and the bureaucracy set up by the pioneers of the welfare state proved less damaging than the middle classes dreaded.

This self-consciousness made the suburban middle classes an easy prey to the communication media. One of the key men in the principal medium—newspapers—was Kennedy Jones of the *Daily Mail*. His personal motto was 'Nothing really matters', but in the interests of mass circulation Jones was prepared to play on the nascent anxieties of the newspaper readers (it is worth mentioning that the story by William le Queux of the German invasion of London was serialised in the *Daily Mail*, with the technical details supplied by Lord 'Bobs' Roberts, hero of the Boer War). Lord Northcliffe, the owner of both the *Daily Mail* and *The Times*, was directly involved in creating middle-class worry about world events. When he bought *The Times* Northcliffe stated: 'I shall leave the Editor unrestricted control unless he should—which is quite impossible—fail to warn the British People of the coming German Peril'.[12]

The German Peril and the bogey of socialism—these were the two factors that prevented the apotheosis of the Good Life in the suburbs as expounded by Mrs Miniver in H. G. Wells's

Ann Veronica (1909): 'Everything was "working up", everything was "coming on"—the Higher Thought, the Simple Life . . .'

In retrospect it can be seen that suburban apprehension was not justified. Its loose-limbed culture was interrupted but not destroyed by the war, and in 1918 garden citydom continued where it left off. As a class they suffered less during the war; the upper classes provided the officers and the lower classes the cannon fodder. Suburbia provided the new bureaucracy of the war machine. In the evenings the white-collared hordes returned to their artistic homes, to their cards and their reading and the crackle of the gramophone. Socialism had been averted and the peril was not so bad as they had anticipated. Furthermore, life now had a purpose and was even exciting what with Zeppelins and Russian soldiers with snow on their boots. Whatever confidence the suburban dwellers had gained they had not lost their gullibility.

The Condition of the People

The years preceding World War I were strong in consumer spending and conspicuous display, and notably short on compassion. The poor were getting poorer and the rich were getting richer, but, as T. H. S. Escott, under the pseudonym of 'a Foreign Resident', wrote in his *London Society in the New Reign* (1904), 'Nothing is so out of fashion today as genuine emotion of any kind'. The poor, it was considered, were poor because they deserved to be, and were largely made up of idlers and scroungers who could get jobs if they were less work-shy. Their existence was ignored as much as possible, and the danger of a rising of the submerged classes was repressed despite the warnings of H. G. Wells, who said that Great Britain was in a dangerous state of social disturbance, and that the discontent of the labouring mass of the community was deep and increasing. In 1912 Wells prophesied that 'we are in the opening phase of a real and irreparable class war'. C. F. G. Masterman was even more explicit: 'That vast portion of the working-class which, raw and half developed, has long been half hidden amid its

The existence of the poor was ignored as much as possible, but this was sometimes difficult, such as during the 1912 troubles. A photograph of East End children waiting for food

poverty and squalor, is now issuing forth from its hiding place to assert an Englishman's heaven-born privilege of doing as he likes, meeting where it likes, breaking what it likes'.[1]

Fortunately for the well-being of the rich and the passably well-off, the poor were deliberately kept under, and their apathy was unscrupulously worked on. From the evidence of Poor Law reports and Parliamentary Commissions, there is no question that they were kept below the poverty line by the establishment, and made to wallow in degradation. At its most Machiavellian this can be seen in the organisation and running of the workhouses.

The workhouse, or 'union', was run by a Board of Guardians. These boards were frequently corrupt. They had as their agents relieving officers, men of no training or necessary ability, who doled out money as they thought fit. The goal of the relieving officer was to have an easy life, and this involved dispersing the money with as little inconvenience to himself as possible. The Guardians looked on their terms of office with Public Assistance Authorities as a necessary step to more significant employment in local government. In 1909 there was a commission of inquiry to look into the whole operation of the Poor Law, and its members attended numbers of meetings of Boards of Guardians. At one meeting 'the relieving officers and the chairman stated the cases so confusedly and so incompletely that it was almost impossible to form any opinion as to the methods on which out-relief is distributed . . . There was practically no enquiry as to the resources of the applicants, and with the old people the amount of relief was determined solely by age'.[2]

Relief was distributed without principle or knowledge of the facts. Applicants were bullied and roughly treated according to the mood of the Guardians or the relieving officers, and amid the babel, the slamming of doors and the general air of inquisition, the commission found it difficult to understand what was going on. On one occasion:

> The Board, as a whole, seemed slack, uninterested and unintelligent . . . In one case where the woman was reported dirty and the man given to drink, one of the Guardians mentioned having seen him at the public-house that morning. Relief was, however, granted at the instance of the Guardian of the parish, *who was also the publican whose house the man frequented*.[3]

Blame for the poor quality of the whole machinery for distributing relief was laid at the doors of the general public, who were not interested in the plight of the poor and could not be bothered to elect suitable Guardians. The people who put Guardians in office were the very ones who would benefit from the selection of some particular men. One of the Guardians was quite open about it: 'We are sent here to give outdoor relief to our relations, our fathers, and our mothers, and our sisters and our cousins, and our uncles, and our aunts, and if we did not do it we should soon be sent about our business'.[4]

With this degree of corruption, almost rivalling that of the old Metropolitan Board of Works in the days before the formation

Itinerant workers were always on the verge of the workhouse. A young billposter photographed about 1914

of the London County Council, it is not surprising that those
who deserved help failed to get it. The poverty of Edwardian
England was no whit less than that of Victorian England; if
anything it was more pronounced, for the rich philanthropists
who had done much to relieve poverty were now replaced by the
money-grubbers.

No one seemed astonished that Boards of Guardians were
made up of estate-agents, owners of slum property, and publicans.
On one board there were thirty-five members; seven of whom
were publicans. The common denominators Boards of Guardians were meanness (the money came out of the rates and low
rates would guarantee their success in local government) and
discrimination (the money was given to friends and relations,
those who spent money at Guardians' pubs, and those who were
inclined to cause trouble if they did not receive their beer-
money). Occasionally such Guardians were prosecuted for
fraud and 'conspiracy to defraud the ratepayers', and although
strictly speaking the Guardians were only supposed to serve
three-year terms, when they were making money out of their
position they were happy, and indeed eager, to stay on. This
was also true of workhouse masters and matrons.

The workhouses were no better than their nineteenth-century
counterparts. Women and girls were huddled together in filthy
dormitories, with aged prostitutes and twelve-year-old orphans
sharing beds. The worst conditions were in the infirmaries,
essential sections of every workhouse, where beds were pushed
close together, clothing and utensils lay about anywhere, and
where the inmates themselves had to drive nails into the walls
to hang their paltry possessions on. In the infirmaries there was
usually only one nurse, and when she had a day off the inmates
were left to their own devices; it was rare for a doctor to be in
attendance.

The existence of workhouses can be seen as the failure of
civilisation. They were the repositories of the old, the infirm, and
the unwanted. The 'union' was, to many of the poor, the ultimate
in degradation. In 1906 Ellen Regan, who was starving, cut her
own throat and died rather than go into the workhouse, and one

The workhouse was, to many, the ultimate in degradation, and many of the poor struggled to hold down jobs for which they were physically ill-equipped

of the jurors at the inquest commented 'Oh, what a shocking thing in this country!' In the same year Andrew Mullen jumped on a wall of Regent's Park canal, and spun a penny, saying to a witness, 'Heads I drown myself; tails I don't'. It turned up heads; he threw his cap to a witness, and jumped. Even suicide was preferable to the workhouse.

Reliable statistics about the poor were hard to obtain, for there was always a certain amount of perambulating poverty. Summer pauperism was always considerably lower than the winter, but averaging out the figures, the paupers of 1907 numbered 793,519—2.27 per cent of the population of England and Wales. These were the people right at the bottom of the heap. The number of people who received relief was 1,706,592, 4.7 per cent; a third of these were in workhouses, two-thirds received what was called out-door relief. Poverty was more pressing in the towns than the country. Rural labourers had fled from the country to London and the big cities, only to discover numbers of unemployed already there. Rural poverty was less obtrusive, for although there was just as much it revolved mainly around the old and the infirm.

London had the big problem, maintaining 15,800 more paupers in 1907 than in the 1880s. In the East End, and in such boroughs as Southwark and Walworth, there existed a residuum of people doomed to perpetual unemployment. The poor married too young, had large families, were riddled with venereal disease, and drank. They were also hindered rather than helped by indiscriminate charity, the donors of which salved their conscience by dealing out money to those who were most insistent—the idlers and the drinkers. The demon drink was used as an excuse for doing little—the poor must take their punishment for giving in to the temptation. In some workhouses nearly half the inmates were there because of intemperance.

The incidence of venereal disease amongst the poor was high. In the Leeds workhouse infirmary between sixteen and twenty inmates were always under treatment. The disease was non-notifiable, and rarely cured. 'Syphilis once, syphilis ever' a British surgeon had said, and this epigram was respected by

Casual labour was a prime cause of basic poverty, and street traders and coster-mongers often barely scraped a living

those whose duty it was to administer treatment to the workhouse population. Venereal disease was considered a just reward for immoral behaviour. The treatment usually consisted of mercury pills, and the recommendation to live a simple life without alcohol was usually rejected by the patients.

Tuberculosis brought many to the workhouse, and although it was known to be contagious the authorities persisted in crowding people together, the fit and the sick, emulating the conditions of the slums and lodging houses. Some lodging houses contained 200–300 beds, often let out in eight-hour shifts.

Many observers saw the prevalence of casual labour as a contributory cause of basic poverty. In the days before labour exchanges, supply and demand of workers was haphazard, and employers used the uncertainty as a means of utilising a cheap work-force. For the most part, work at the docks was carried out by casual labourers, taken on 'by the day, half-day, quarter-day, hour, or job'. The example set by the London and India Docks Company, which employed 72 per cent of its labour force on regular weekly wage, was not followed. Port employers considered that the poor were there to be profitably used.

On every side the poor were battened on by employers desirous of cheap labour, by do-gooders who relieved their own minds by indiscriminate charity, by nepotism in office, by patronising relieving officers operating under the aegis of the Boards of Guardians, and by the clergy. The relieving officers, going from slum to slum, dished out their sixpences and shillings with scant regard to need. 'Cases are seldom discussed with reference to their needs. "She will be content with that", or "That is what the other old women are getting", or "She is over eighty, give her another sixpence", were the sort of considerations brought forward'.[5]

A typical case was the widow living alone who received 3s 6d a week, out of which she paid 1s to a girl to attend to her room, as she was helpless. Coal and rent cost her 1s 4d, leaving her 1s 2d a week to live on. The relieving officers considered themselves both judge and jury; if there was any suspicion that there were what was termed 'undisclosed resources' they withheld their shillings. One observer stated: 'There is no doubt whatever that a large number of the outdoor paupers are living in an environment of filth and immorality, and in many cases I fear they are participants in, and abettors of, these foul, insanitary, and degrading conditions'.[6]

In the slums, cleanliness and ventilation were not considered important, furniture consisted of straw palliasses and orange boxes, and the inhabitants defecated in passageways or in corners of rooms as there were no lavatories. A typical slum in the East End of London was described as not a room, but a den. Measuring 8 ft by 7 ft, it contained a sagging couch with ragged coverlets, a rickety table, a chair and two boxes. On the walls were blood marks, the remains of bugs and other insects. Even the respectable poor lived in similar conditions, though their standards of cleanliness were higher. Many did the best they could in atrocious circumstances. In Bermondsey in 1900 one water closet and one stand pipe served twenty-five houses; water was switched on for two hours a day, but never on a

A slum interior of 1912. All the food in the house is on the table

Sunday. In Manchester lavatories had not been introduced until 1898, and in Blackburn and Wigan less than half the houses had them.

The poor were also badly treated by the capitalists of their own class, the small shopkeepers. At its simplest level, 'the poor buy their food in small quantities and thus pay a higher price for it'.[7] They also bought their food 'on tick' and thus had no opportunity to shop around for bargains.

In 1903 21s 8d was considered the minimum living wage for a family of five. Yet in 1914 nearly a quarter of male wage earners earned less than 25s a week. With unemployment averaging about 8 per cent, there was no choice but to work for a pittance. It was either that or the dreaded workhouse. The most ghastly conditions were found in the 'sweated industries'. Jack London in his overwritten but sincere *The People of the Abyss* (1903) tells of the old woman, dying and broken, who supported herself and four children making match boxes at 2¼d per gross. In her

Many slums did not have their own water supply. Water was obtained from stand pipes in the street or alley

98-hour week she made 7,066 match boxes, earning 4s 10¼d.
Out of this she had to pay for her own paste and thread. At one
sweat shop, little girls were employed licking adhesive labels
from early in the morning to late at night, and in the Nottingham
lace trade children's eyesight was remorselessly destroyed and
few of the juvenile work-force lived past thirty. Outworkers
were just as badly off. In Leicester old women did glove stitching;
their earnings for a full week averaged 1s 4d. The benevolent
authorities supplemented this by 3s 6d all round. A London
widow aged 79 working from 5 am until 10 pm at steel-covering
earned 2s 11d a week, plus 4s from the parish and a loaf of
bread from the local clergyman. In Glasgow an old woman
worked ten hours a day at shirt-finishing, and earned 1s 10d
a week.

The better off did not want to know about the condition of the
poor. One attempt to bring the matter to their attention was
made by the Fabian Society and its associates, though most of
them had no idea of the plight of those whom they were
supporting. Among these do-gooders was Lady Warwick,
described by H. G. Wells as 'that remarkable intruder into the
class conflict' and who always appeared too well-dressed for the
gatherings of 'dingy earnest people'. Many people were appalled
by the awful conditions of the poor when they happened by
chance to come across them. When Winston Churchill visited
Manchester, he commented to his secretary, Edward Marsh,
'Fancy living in one of these streets, never seeing anything
beautiful, never eating anything savoury, never saying anything
clever.'

The poor did not want to help themselves, nor did they
particularly want their betters interfering. They did not want to
be cleaned, enlightened or inspected. They did not want their
drink regulated or their intimate organs examined for venereal
disease. They wanted their rights. They were contemptuous of
the well-meaning efforts of the paper socialists, and ignored such
attempts to help them as that given to nursing and expectant
mothers by the School for Mothers in St Pancras where 1½d
dinners could be obtained.

Foreigners were shocked by the spectacle of the poor sleeping in London parks. This drawing of vagabonds sleeping in St James's Park was done by a visiting French artist

It was impossible for the rich to visualise the depths of squalor that existed east of St Paul's, and the moral turpitude that resulted from hideous living conditions. Occasionally the well-off were brought face to face with the denizens of this other nation, when the workers came 'up west' to demonstrate in Hyde Park, or in the persons of the homeless who slept rough. In most cases their reaction was indignation, not against the authorities particularly, but against the poor who dared to bring themselves to their attention.

The London parks were shut at night, but Green Park had the reputation of closing its gates earlier than most. 'It was Sunday afternoon, the sun was fitfully appearing, and the well-dressed West Enders, with their wives and progeny, were out by thousands, taking the air. It was not a pleasant sight for them, those horrible, unkempt, sleeping vagabonds . . .'[8]

To the rich, socialism was equated with the supremacy of the poor. To Lord Rosebery, it was 'the end of all—the negation of Faith, of Family, of Monarchy, of Empire'. The People's Budget introduced by the Liberals in 1909 to alleviate the condition of the aged poor was treated as creeping socialism, not least of all by *The Times*. The budget was 'a chaotic welter of half-ascertained facts, half-thought-out arguments, half-sincere sentimentalism'. The paranoia that surrounded the first tentative gropings of the welfare state reflect a strange attitude of mind, a cynical selfishness. The poor were not only poor because they deserved to be, but the old were indigent because they had not scraped any savings together from their miserable past earnings. A cartoon in *Punch*, on 5 August 1908, was decidedly ambiguous. Lloyd George, the chancellor of the exchequer, was depicted as a highwayman at a cross roads, holding a pistol in one hand and clutching a box on which was inscribed 'Old Age Pension Fund'. The caption read, Mr Lloyd George: 'I'll make 'em pity the aged poor!'

In his peroration in the House of Commons, Lloyd George said:

> This is a War Budget. It is for raising money to wage implacable warfare against poverty and squalidness. I cannot help believing that before this generation has passed away, we shall have advanced a great step towards that good time when poverty, and the wretchedness and human degradation which always followed in its camp, will be as remote to the people of this country as the wolves which once infested its forests.[9]

The old age pension thus introduced was more of a token than a bonanza, and the small Labour Party representation in parliament was more concerned with the tax on cigarettes. The pension was 5s a week for those with less than £21 per annum, and this reduced by 1s for every 2½ guineas. The result was not gratefulness on the part of the working classes, but a wave of strikes. These were alarming not only to the Conservatives and the Liberals, but also to the Labour contingent, who reluctantly shelved their abhorrence that twenty-five Wild Woodbine cigarettes were likely to cost more than 5d.

Strikes did more than anything to convince the timid that their inchoate anxieties had a basis in fact. As early as 1905 the Welsh miners had struck, followed by railwaymen, cotton spinners and engineers. In 1911 there was a seamen's strike, starting in

Southampton and spreading to Liverpool and Cardiff. At Hull, dock labourers joined in; there was looting and rioting, and warehouses were burned. Shortly afterwards Manchester dockers and carters came out, and the trouble spread to London where there was danger of bringing in the military to clear the docks. While the strike raged in London, an unofficial strike in the north erupted into a general rail strike. A mob attacked the police, many of whom were injured, and the troops were called out. They opened fire, killing two of the rioters. The incident was given wide publicity by the press, and an analogy with the Peterloo massacre was drawn.

Trouble at power stations plunged cities into darkness, and gangs of hooligans taking advantage of the labour troubles roamed the streets. There was active support from the intelligentsia which had for so long confined itself to the lecture hall. The London dock strike led to a procession of 100,000 through the City, joined by women workers in Bermondsey. In Liverpool,

Poverty in Wales was acerbated by strikes and lock-outs in the mines

Tom Mann, a firebrand with ominous attachments to the syndicalist movement of the United States, was pressing for a general strike. Some measure of the reaction to these manifestations of organised labour can be gauged by the rise in membership of the trade unions from 2,369,067 in 1910 to 3,918,809 in 1914.

The potential of organised labour had been seen in 1893 in the mining industry. The owners had demanded a 10-per-cent reduction in wages, and their employees had retaliated by withdrawing their labour for fifteen weeks. Not all mines were involved, those in South Wales being kept open. It was here that the most ominous events happened, so far as the general public were concerned. The Miners' Federation, under whose auspices the strike was held, tried to close the South Wales pits by provoking a hauliers' strike. 'Marching gangs' of hauliers moved from pit to pit, intimidating and beating up the Welsh miners, and were only stopped when 2,000 miners at Ebbw Vale fought a pitched battle with the gangs.

At Featherstone, near Pontefract, when troops were brought in following a mob riot, two miners were killed; trade union officials never let the government forget this incident.

More comforting to the middle classes and the employers had been the result of a strike by the Amalgamated Society of Engineers in 1897–8. The engineers wanted a working day of eight hours, and their strike was countered by the employers banding together to form a solid front. The Amalgamated Society of Engineers was the most powerful union in the country but against the forces of organised capitalism it was ineffective, and the strike ground to a humiliating halt. Employers hoped that their defeat of the engineering union would register with organised labour.

Capital knew that the law was on its side. In 1898 a court judgement laid down that picketing was lawful only if confined to 'communicating information', and that picketing to 'persuade', for example, others to strike was actionable. No one could say how a strike could be conducted lawfully. The employers seemed to have all the cards on their side, and could hardly contain their jubilation when in 1901 the manager of the Taff

Valley Railway determined to sue the Amalgamated Society of
Railway Servants for loss suffered by his company as the result of
a 'wrongful strike'. The trade unions thought that they were
protected by the 1871 Trade Union Act. They were wrong.
The Taff Valley Railway was awarded £23,000 damages against
the union, plus costs, and what has since been known as the
Taff Vale Judgement cast a gloom over all unions, who now
knew that their funds could be sequestered by a hostile court.

The Taff Vale Judgement encouraged the high command of the
Trades Union Congress into politics. Only by representation in
the House of Commons could the unions be protected, or,
indeed, survive. Fortunately there were many in the Liberal
camp who were disturbed by the implications of the Taff Vale
Judgement, and the Miners' Federation succeeded in 1906 in
returning twelve MPs to Parliament, some of them without
Liberal opposition. The representation of Labour in Parliament
was largely by courtesy of the Liberals, and the Conservatives
have never wholly forgiven them for it.

Unfortunately for the militants of the trade union movement,
as soon as their candidates became MPs they seemed eager to
join the establishment, to ignore their brief, to emulate their
betters, and the waves of strikes that marked the Edwardian
age illustrate the failure of capital and labour to come together—
a failure that, with rare exceptions, has persisted until this day.

The strikes and associated violence mirrored the feelings
of hysteria that prevailed in the years leading up to the war.
They can also be seen as an indication that the traditionally
submerged classes were breaking surface. They were still poor,
but now, goaded and exhorted by larger, more powerful unions
with spokesmen in parliament, they wanted to know why.

The Rural Exodus

In terms of the picturesque the countryside was at its best during
the period, and townees sought succour and inspiration amidst
flora and fauna, the artistic recording the gently decaying villages
in water-colour and prose poems. 'A sunset of quite extra-

Inspiration was sought in the countryside by amateur artists, and this cartoon of 1908 cannot have been far from the truth

The countryside was at its best
during the Edwardian years,
though the suburbs of the big
towns were encroaching on it

ordinary beauty', wrote A. C. Benson in his diary on 10 December
1905, 'the leafless trees, seen over bare fields, the hamlet roofs,
the world beyond, and the sun sinking orange into smoky wisps
of cloud, which he seemed to draw with him. We watched the
crimson orb slip behind the hill'.

The countryside was treated as a phenomenon especially laid
on by the almighty for the edification of town-dwellers, who
were somewhat indignant that many country people could not
see the beauty and the charm of rural Britain, and much preferred
the towns. 'Nature has little meaning for most of them, and no
charms; but they love a gas lamp. Nature, in my opinion, only
appears to the truly educated'.[1] The rustics, in fact, were in
flight from the countryside, where the easily-discerned come-
liness of village and hamlet directly related to the stagnation of
rural life.

Throughout the nineteenth century agriculture had slowly
been losing ground, and in the last thirty years acreage set aside
for wheat had fallen by half, following imports of large quantities
of cheap grain from America. In 1894 wheat prices were at their

lowest point for more than a century and a half. Between 1891
and 1913, about 45,000 acres per annum went out of cultivation
in Great Britain, of which half was lost to rough grazing and
half to non-agricultural uses.

The 1880s and 1890s were locust years, and although the
position became somewhat stabilised by 1900, the impact of those
two decades had reduced agriculture to a chronic state of
depression. A 700-acre farm in Wiltshire that sold for £27,000
in 1812 came on the market again in 1892, when it fetched
£7,000. In 1874 one farmer rented his land at £600 per annum,
and paid tithes of £196; in 1901 he paid £250 rental, while the
landlord paid the tithes. The farmer stated that he made much
more money when he was paying nearly £800 a year than in 1901.
In the same county, a 1,600-acre farm had warranted a rent of
£2,100 per annum in 1870, but in 1901 this had decreased to
£825.

This pattern was repeated throughout the country, and the
average fall in rental of land between 1875 and 1901 was 33 per
cent. A number of factors contributed to this trend. The great
future that had been forecast when steam power was applied to
agriculture was never realised, and many farmers almost bank-
rupted themselves by buying the new-fangled machinery. In 1877
herds were decimated by cattle plague (rinderpest) and although
this was the last year that farming was hit by this disease its
financial effect was felt for a decade. Even more disastrous was
1879, when persistent rains and a sunless summer ruined the
crops and reduced many farmers to destitution; the floods led
to an outbreak of liver-rot in sheep, which for a time crippled
sheep-rearing. A royal commission was appointed to look into
agricultural distress; it took three years for the report to come
out, and then merely stated the obvious—that landlords, yeoman
farmers, and tenants had all suffered, and that rents would continue
to drop. No policy was framed for helping agriculture; and
farmers became disillusioned. Grain was pouring in from abroad,
and now that there was refrigeration in ships it was cheaper to
import beef and mutton from Australia and New Zealand than
produce it at home.

*At harvest times women and children were able to contribute towards the family income,
and in real terms agricultural labourers were probably better off than town workers*

Many farmers turned to dairy farming, but the sequence of
bad seasons ruined the hay, and early experimentation into
methods of preserving green fodder (ensilage) only partly
relieved the situation. In 1883 there was a particularly virulent
outbreak of foot-and-mouth disease. Towards the end of the
1880s, farming prospects seemed to improve slightly, but any
alleviation was cancelled by the drought of 1893. Another
commission of inquiry was appointed, but by the time their
report came out, a sequence of droughts had confirmed their
view that agriculture was in a bad way.

These years were the yesterdays of the Edwardian farmer, who
took the vicissitudes of nature with characteristic British phlegm.
Their greatest problem was labour. Before 1871 the supply of
farm labourers had always exceeded the demand, but from then
on they began leaving the land for the mills and factories of the
industrial towns. By 1901 the shortage of farm labour was
desperate. In the old days, a farm hand was usually sure of a roof

over his head, but with the decline of agriculture landlords could not afford to replace cottages that had fallen into ruin. A cottage cost £550 to build, and with a rent at £10 a year this represented a profit of 2 per cent per annum; with other pressing demands on capital it is not surprising that few were built. Some labourers who kept to the land found themselves living in derelict shacks which were often no better than city slums.

In 1850 the average weekly wage of the agricultural labourer was 9s 3½d; in 1903 it was 14s 7d. These wages were low compared with those obtainable in the city, but there were additional perquisites, such as farm produce, free beer or cider, tied cottages, plus extra earnings at harvest time, when wives and children would also contribute towards the family income. In real terms the agricultural labourer was probably better off than the town worker. Leaving the country for the town, 'he does not think of the rent of the squalid rooms, of the cost of the tramcars, and the music hall'.[2]

A Sussex farmer in 1901 speculated that if he could afford to pay his workers 50 per cent more he could keep them. But most farmers could not, or felt that they could not. They were conditioned into taking what labour they could. Country boys could now read and write, and even when they did not go to the cities they preferred to be shop-boys rather than work on the farms. Hedgers, ditchers and thatchers were dying out and most of those engaged in this essential work were over fifty years of age. Farm labourers in the mid-Victorian period had been happy to work seven days a week, knowing no different, but now they demanded, as their right, a six-day week. On dairy farms it was found almost impossible to get the cows milked on a Sunday, and many farmers were forced to turn their land over to beef cattle (Guernseys fetched between £17–£20 and calves £1). Between the wars, with mechanical milking, the position reversed. In 1937 the dairy herd in England was 36 per cent higher than in 1913.

There were few gilt-edged propositions for Edwardian farmers. Hops in the past had been a reliable produce, but in 1901 they cost £60 an acre, and on this £10 an acre profit was

Many landowners suffered from the agricultural depression, and some of them sold their land to the nouveaux riches who turned farmland into hunting and shooting territory

realised. One Kent farmer was philosophical: 'Hop growing is just like a rubber of whist. I have lost £1,000 a year at it, and have made £1,000 a year'. Fortunately the hop-growing counties were within easy reach of London, and every year by tradition the East Enders left the city to pick the hops. Farm labourers in the home counties had sampled the delights of London and found them wanting. Thankfully they reverted to the land and were willing to put up with conditions that farm labourers further afield would not countenance. In Essex in particular, the absence of cottages forced some farm hands to live in shacks made of orange boxes.

Tenant farmers were in some way compensated for their lower incomes by paying less rent than they had been paying, but landowners suffered unceasingly from the agricultural depression. They were, as one of them cynically mentioned, 'like the eels which are said to grow accustomed to being skinned'. Many were forced to sell up, and thankfully relinquished their heritage to the *nouveaux riches* who turned good farm-land into hunting or shooting territory and fancied playing the squire. The shopocracy, made wealthy by trade, were prominent in this field, and increased the labour problems by hiving off the more useful rustics for service in their retinue.

The decline of agriculture was watched with complacency by successive governments and, although there seemed a future in smallholdings, nothing of moment was done until 1906. By 1914 some 14,000 holdings covering 200,000 acres were created, but these did not alter the general downward trend. Co-operative ventures foundered because of the doggedness and independence of farmers. One such typical experiment was inaugurated near Northampton, where Earl Spencer provided 300 acres for co-operative farming, backing this generous gesture with £3,000 at 3 per cent. For two years the community lost heavily; the next year a profit of £30 was made, and then a run of ill luck finished the project, into which Lord Spencer did not feel inclined to inject any more money.

One curious venture in co-operative farming was carried out by Edward Carpenter. He arrived in the north of England with great ideals, glorying in the environment he found: 'It was all in the old rural style—the leisurely long day with its varied occupations and interests, the life of the open air and the fields, the cattle and the crops, the barn and the public-house'.[3] The only snag was that when Carpenter mentioned the Land Question to the locals their eyes glazed over and their conversation reverted to pigs and potatoes.

Nevertheless Carpenter did see that the great drawback of country folk was their want of initiative, for which he blamed the incubus of landlord and parson. Certainly the farmers did little to rethink their operations, and preferred to place the blame on shortage of labour, the inactivity of the government, and the high price of transport of their produce. In Kings Lynn it cost £400 per annum to send £1,200 worth of market-garden produce to London. Farmers looked back to the good old days when farm labourers were eager to work for a pittance, instead of reappraising the whole pattern of farming.

Village life, which depended on the prosperity of agriculture,

HIGH STREET, WEST MALLING.

*With the agricultural situation many country towns, such as West Malling, in Kent,
fell into decline*

languished with the departure of so many young men to the
towns. There were few of the old festivals, and social life became
unenthusiastic and drab. Village inns lost much of their trade,
but to some extent were kept going by the passion of suburbia
for the country life and by the cycling boom. Rural activities
were pepped up by injections of arty-crafty culture. The widow
of the bursar at Eton collected a village chorus together in
Stanhoe, and claimed that the whole life of the place had been
quickened, or, more guardedly, that decadence and dullness
had been arrested. Some communities became self-conscious
and trivialised for the benefit of the tourist interest; villages
were seen as 'quaint' and pretty, and were benevolently defended
by the clergy together with a way of life that no longer existed.
Wrote one clergyman: 'It is easy to pick holes in the theory of
Squire, Parson, and Tenants, but when you have the right people
on the spot it is found to be the best society of the kind yet
devised by man'.[4]

Creaking attempts were made to keep the old order going, to
pretend that village life was flourishing as it had done fifty years
before. Bemused and apathetic, villagers were dragooned into

acting out their predestined roles. At Mayfield in Sussex an attempt was made to revive the old mummers. Kenneth Grahame, author of *Wind in the Willows*, watched the charade cynically: 'Hardly any of the good old "St George and the Dragon" play left. Instead cheap comic songs from the London music halls'.[5]

It was easy to wax lyrical about the English countryside—'The sedged river, with the fragrant smell of the river-water bubbling, through the sluices, into a pool where a teal was diving, made up for me a scene of great sweetness—so English, so serene, so utterly unaffected'.[6] The writers of *belles lettres* and slim volumes of verse could always be turned on by village and country life, where it seemed that nothing was altered except the replacement of the blacksmith by the garage. The Edwardian essayists echoed with Wordsworth their appreciation of 'splendour in the grass, of glory in the flower', and believed that it was all for them. The countryman's sardonic wit and underlying pessimism they considered quaint, and not the expression of defeat. Nor did they enter these so picturesque cottages, in which were conditions more akin to those of the Middle Ages than those of the twentieth century, where rags and sacks did duty as bedding and straw was used as floor covering.

And what did the occupants of these cottages want with a wage well below the primary poverty level announced by sociologists when they had fresh air and a beautiful view from the window (admittedly the window measured 2 ft square, the glass was broken and replaced by cardboard, and the landlord did not have the money or the inclination to replace it)? Lack of communication between town and country was never so evident as during the golden years of Edward's reign.

Notes to this chapter are on pages 293–4.

CHAPTER FOUR

THE COMING OF THE MOTOR CAR

THE MOTOR car was the supreme status symbol of the Edwardians, .and in 1909 *Punch* printed a humorous article on this theme which begins: 'I was tired of pedestrianism and being poor, so I waved imperiously to the passing taxicab. "I will now," I said to myself, "be rich. To be properly rich I must be in a motor".' When the taxi is flagged down, the driver is suspicious of his fare, and asks what the idea is. The narrator goes on:

> I had some idea that you and I might go to Regent's Park together. You shall sit in your little armchair and turn your wheel as you will, while I gracefully recline inside upon the larger seat and dispose my feet carelessly upon the smaller one. *En route* we will observe the life of the great metropolis, and mark the ambition, misery, and vice stamped upon the faces of its inhabitants. Perhaps we may even enter upon some interesting discussion with a motor-bus driver on the way.

Motoring in Britain dated from 1895, when the Honourable Evelyn Ellis brought the first petrol-driven car from France, a 4 hp Panhard & Lavassor machine. This make of car had done well in the first of the long-distance races in Europe and had completed a 732-mile course in 48 hours 48 minutes, proving the definitive victory of the petrol-driven car over the steam car. Ellis backed motoring in Britain to the extent of £20,000 of his own money, and although he was a pioneer in daring the authorities to prosecute him (the 4 mph speed limit plus a man with a red flag syndrome was still in operation) he was soon joined by J. A. Koosen in a Lutzmann and Sir David Salomons. An exhibition at Tunbridge Wells late in 1895 and another motor show at the Imperial Institute, London, in 1896, thrust the motor car into the public domain. In November 1895 *The Autocar* magazine was created, in confident confirmation of the future of motoring. The speed limit was pushed up from 4 mph to 12 mph in 1896, and the first London to Brighton run on 14 November that year commemorated the victory of the motor over the law.

Ellis's 4 hp Panhard & Lavassor motor created a stir wherever it appeared. On its maiden run 56 miles were covered in 5 hours 32 minutes, exclusive of stoppages, averaging 9.84 mph, and whole villages turned out to look at the vehicle, making rustic jokes. Occasionally it was stopped by the police, but they were satisfied by Ellis showing them his carriage licence.

J. A. Koosen had bought his car at the behest of his wife, who conveniently kept a diary:

1895

Nov 23—Took train to Lee and tried to make our motor work; wouldn't; came home at five.

Nov 24—Awfully cold; played with our motor—no result.

Nov 25—After luncheon saw to our motor, but didn't get it out of shed.

Nov 26—Drove to Lee and took Smith and Penning (engineers); Penning spent the day on his back without results.

Nov 30—Motor went with benzoline for first time; awfully pleased.

Dec 2—Waiting for new oil from Bowley & Son.

Dec 9—Drove to Lee at 10; motor sparked at once and went well. After lunch started for home in motor-car; came round by Fareham; had lovely drive; police spotted us; awful crowd followed us at Cosham; had to beat them off with umbrella.

Dec 10—Policeman called at 1.30, took our names re driving through Fareham without red flag ahead.

Dec 13—Went drive round common; tyre came off; sent her to Penning (engineer).

Dec 27—Frightened an unattended horse attached to a milk-cart, which bolted and sent the milk-cans flying in all directions.

That archetypal figure, the motor salesman, arrived on the scene. As the trade-in value of cars was only fifteen per cent he was forced to be exceptionally persuasive

Jan   4—Lost nut off air valve; pushed home.
Jan 14—Motor got stuck; made noises; sent her to Penning.
Jan 19—Moted [sic] to Eastney Lock; Jack got out to hold unattended
          horses, and I drove the car into the curb and smashed frame.
          Shoved into a stable close by.

Koosen goes into motoring history as the first man to be fined for a motor traffic offence: 1s plus 15s 7d costs; the second was a Scotsman in Berwick-on-Tweed, who was surrounded by all 13 of the local constabulary, and subsequently fined 6d with 19s 6d costs. Despite a country parson filling his petrol tank with water and asking if it mattered, and oiling the engine with a bicycle oil-can, the way was set for the Edwardian motoring boom.

The Edwardian car was expensive to buy, complicated and

costly to run. Turn-of-the-century cars were underpowered, and could not exceed 4 mph up hills. Any gradient more than 1 in 9 beat them, and a recommended test ground was Petersham Hill near Richmond, which averaged 1 in 15 with one steep bit 1 in 9½. The salesmen were already fly and glib, maintaining that the best of all test grounds was Savoy Hill, leading to the Embankment, which they claimed was 1 in 8½, though really it was 1 in 13.4.

No gentleman could be expected to mess around in the crude smoking interior of a motor car, and the new domestic was introduced, the motor servant—'He is a new type of man, and will require the wages of other engineers'.[1] Motoring in vehicles without hoods or windscreens called for special clothing. Tweed and cloth were out, for the air whipped them out into balloons; perforated leather was recommended, with the stipulation that the coats should button closely round the wrist. Trousers should be bound tightly around the ankles; and the

Motoring called for a new type of clothing, for men and for women. The artist here knew more about fashions than about cars

experts advised the adoption of a garment shaped like a bell tent from which the rain would run. Peaked caps, as used on the continent, were not recommended, as these were 'only seen on the heads of the drivers and conductors of electric tram-cars &c'. Goggles were a must.

One kept one's car not in a garage, which was French and therefore rather naughty, but in a motor stable. Green motorists who thought that machinery *per se* was strong and robust put their vehicles in damp motor stables, and were rapped sternly over the knuckles by their betters. Motor stables had to be on the large side, for no gentleman would think of having fewer than three cars. As for cheap cars, it was a disgusting notion, and the Automobile Club should be ashamed of itself for running an exhibition of cars priced at less than £200 at Hereford.

The new race of motorists were not particularly considerate or good drivers, though the 1896 act demanded that if anyone in control of horses lifted up a hand to stop a car, the car must stop (if possible). Side-slips (skids) were unfortunate, but there was not likely to be another car about, and horses and people were soft anyway. 'Lady cyclists were formerly a great danger, as they were apt, when a motor was heard approaching them from behind, to fall off their machines, apparently in terror; but this distressing spectacle is now [1906] comparatively rare'.[2] A driver was respectfully recommended, if he and not his motor servant was at the wheel, to practise reversing, for it was undignified to have to push a car out of a hotel yard because there was no room to turn. The early cars were fitted with something called a 'sprag', which if the gears failed when going up a hill, would come into operation, and hold the car.

In 1903 a 10 hp Panhard, a small car, cost 4d a mile to run. The price of petrol varied enormously from a copper or two to 1s 3d a gallon, depending on the cupidity of the garage proprietor. A doctor with a 10 hp car maintained that it cost as much to run as two horses, but that nevertheless the motor car was invaluable. The medical profession was the first to use the car for anything other than sport or gallivanting around. Sportsmen found the car a delightful toy, and used their twelve-bores from

moving cars; if they hit anything with their cars they were
advised to go back in case there was a stew or a soup to be made
from some broken creature.

Part of the expense of motoring revolved around the price of
spare parts. As tyres cost £24 15s a pair and were always
bursting, the more economically-minded motorist kept to
solid tyres. It was a brave man who went out without his motor
servant, for things could go wrong very easily, and the only way
the engine could be got at was from underneath. There were
few instruments, and the first sign of an engine over-heating was
the smell of burning paint. Pistons were easily ruined (and were
painted with aluminium paint by unscrupulous second-hand car
dealers), and some of the more powerful cars used as much oil
as petrol. A motorist who drove every day and did his own
maintenance would need to spend an hour a day cleaning, oiling
and adjusting.

To many people, the very uncertainties of motoring were part

*By 1911 the motor bus had displaced more than 2,000 horse-drawn buses, though there
were still a few horse-drawn 'pirates' on the London streets*

Victim: "WHAT HAS HAPPENED .   WH-WHERE
AM I ?"
   Doctor: "YOU HAVE BEEN KNOCKED OVER BY A
MOTOR-CAR ; BUT IT IS ALL RIGHT—YOU WILL
RECOVER."

*Motor cars were a source of humour. Although not particularly funny, this cartoon was
typical of the genre*

of the charm. Icy roads, rain, clouds of dust, these made the
adventure more exciting. There was a passion for fast cars,
shared by King Edward, who was proud of having exceeded
60 mph on the Brighton Road as early as 1906. The king favoured
the Daimler and the Mercedes, which were painted a rich claret
colour, and he enjoyed choosing new cars. Like many motorists
he hated being overtaken or, indeed, having any car in front of
him, and would urge his driver to pursue and pass as though the
honour of England were at stake.

In 1904 there were 24,201 cars in the United Kingdom, one
third of them in London. British makers had come late on the
scene, and the bulk of the cars were German or French;
American cars were not recommended. Motor cabs, known as
'Clarences', had just come in. There were few motor buses as
yet, but the possibilities of the internal combustion engine as a
transport aid was seen as early as 1906 when home county
farmers sent their produce to London by road.

The roads were terrible; the widespread use of the railway had
caused the neglect of the fine highways brought into being by the

stage coach. The decline of the turnpike system meant that no one was much interested in keeping the roads in good order. The poor quality of road surfaces, however, helped to keep car speeds down and reduce the number of accidents.

Many people hated the coming of the motor car. 'It made people independent of their near neighbours, and while it enlivened the lives of the well-to-do it spoiled county society for the less well circumstanced'.[3] *Punch*, as usual, was well-attuned to genteel discontent, and proposed the Anti-Motor Show, featuring the Spiky Turtleback, a huge steel dish-cover studded with twelve-inch spikes and attached to the wearer's back by springs and straps; the Vesuvian Jacket, made of gun-cotton with detonators as buttons and coloured red with yellow stripes, and the Pedestrian's Repair Outfit, containing a wooden leg. The fox-hunting fraternity refused to allow the new-fangled monster near them.

The march of progress was inexorable. In 1905 the chief constable of Guildford had a count taken of the cars that went up the High Street—they numbered 50,000. The most significant thing was that people became casual about cars, mentioning them in passing, and motoring terms took their place in the English language. The journalist W. Robertson Nicoll, though he never spoke of motors or motoring, referred to himself as being 'out of gear'. Between 1905 and 1907, motor prices went down by a third, and in 1908 the era of the cheap car arrived with the importation of the Ford. Nevertheless the small popular family car did not interfere with the prestige of the top names. In 1907 the De Dion Bouton had seven distinct models on the market varying between 8 and 30 hp. The works of the car were immensely improved, though there was less emphasis on the coach work; in the early 1900s it took forty days to paint the coach work on a Mercedes or a Rolls-Royce.

The motoring enthusiast bought a new car as soon as technological advances warranted it, throwing another second-hand car on to the market for another motorist to buy at a fraction of its cost. A three-year-old car was worth only 15 per cent of its original price. There was a good deal of swapping and changing,

as Arnold Bennett records in his diary on 17 December 1907:
'Pett Ridge said Arthur Morrison had sold his Japanese pictures
to the British Museum for £4,000, and bought a motor car.
Also that B. Pain (Barry Pain the humorous writer) had bought
a car off W. S. Gilbert and sold it again'.

The mania for speed and power so manifest in naval matters
produced a variety of monster cars. As early as 1902 on a private
road at Welbeck, Nottinghamshire, Charles Jarrott drove a
70 hp Panhard at 79.25 mph. The Nice Race Meeting of 1903
brought together the fastest models then built, but gloom was
cast over the meeting by the death of the celebrated Count
Zborowski in his racing Mercedes. The first significant entry of
America into the motor-racing stakes was in 1904 at Daytona
Beach in Florida, where W. K. Vanderbilt clocked up 92 mph
in his 90 hp Mercedes. In the same year a French car topped the
100 mph mark. These fast speeds were calculated on the basis of
the flying kilometre.

*The Victoria Embankment was one of the first stretches of road to be treated with tarred
macadam*

Various inventors, many of them of an unpractical turn of mind, began in 1904 to build cars that aroused excitement and acquired notoriety. The hitherto unknown Bellamy produced an 8 cylinder 165 hp car with a projected speed of 115 mph; this was topped by Dobelli of Rome who exhibited in London a 180 hp monster with four massive cylinders, an engineering curio rather than a serious rival to Mercedes or Darracq. In 1905, speeds were reckoned over the measured mile, and in Florida a Napier covered this distance at 105.8 mph and a 120 hp Mercedes at 109.5 mph. Average speeds were much higher than the previous year, and in a 100 mile race a 90 hp de Dietrich machine averaged 76.5 mph.

These great achievements boosted interest in motoring, and by May 1906 there were 44,098 cars registered in the UK. Something had to be done about the roads, and a stretch of the Victoria Embankment was experimentally treated with tarred macadam, which proved extremely effective. In 1909, 2,500 miles of main road were tarred in London alone.

1906 saw the inauguration of the French Grand Prix at Le Mans, and it was felt that motor-racing depended on the success of this meet. Britain was restricted by the 20 mph speed limit of 1903, and in the autumn of 1906 Mr and Mrs Locke King decided to lay out a track in their own ground near Weybridge—Brooklands—with accommodation for 100,000 people.

Commercial vehicles were hampered by limitations imposed on weight; until 1905 no commercial vehicle was legal in England if its unladen weight exceeded three tons. Motor buses were first licensed by the police authorities in 1904, and by 1910 had displaced 22,000 horses and 2,200 horse omnibuses. A few operators retained their horse-drawn buses, and because of their cut rates were known as pirates. These continued to run as late as 1912, as shown by a conundrum published in the magazine *Tittle-Tattle:*

What is the difference between the LGO Co's busses [sic] and the pirates? The former have acetylene lamps, the latter a set o'lean horses.

Although attempts had been made to introduce motor-cabs

The New Cab Tariff

" Oh, constable, the taximeter says we've come between two and a half and two and four-sixths miles. The driver says his taximeter is slow, and we've come between two and four-sixths and two and five-sixths miles. I'm sure we've only come about two and a sixth, so we're going to split the difference. What do you make the fare ? "

Cab fares were a cause of much confusion, as reflected in this cartoon of 1906

in London during 1904, 1905 and 1906, it was not until 1907 that the General Motor-cab Co put 100 vehicles on the road, and these proved so successful that by the end of the year there were 723 taxis in London, a figure that quadrupled in the next year. By April 1910 there were 4,941 taxis, though there remained on the streets 1,200 hansom cabs and 2,500 horse-drawn four-wheelers. The hiring rate for taxis was as high as 8d per mile. The word 'taxi' was received into the English language in 1907, and given a certificate of acceptance in 1912 with the stage play *The Girl in the Taxi*, immortalised by the phrase, 'If you can't be good—be careful'.

Parallel with the development of the motor-car was that of the motor-cycle, which was a triumph of logic over preconceptions. Motor car designers took a long time to throw over the idea that the car was an adapted horse-carriage, whereas the motor-cycle was functional from the start. The French were the dominant force in car manufacture until the end of the decade, while the leading motor-cycle manufacturers were British.

By the middle of 1905, 34,700 motor-cycles were registered in the United Kingdom, and became increasingly popular among the young and those who could not afford a car.

The motor-car revolution was seen as similar to the railway revolution. But there was one main difference. The railway had been an instrument of democracy, while the car represented private ostentation at its most arrogant, the final triumph of the haves over the have-nots. Perhaps the ultimate in Edwardian status symbols was the 1911 Rolls-Royce 'Silver Ghost', costing £1,154 (more than most people earned in ten years).

Many of the pioneer motorists were members of the Aero Club, and C. S. Rolls was not only a key figure in motoring circles but a balloonist. 'Balloonacy', as the sceptics called it, became fashionable, with meetings at Ranelagh and Hurlingham. The most spectacular publicity stunt was a race between a balloon and cars, starting from the Crystal Palace; it was won by the balloon, for the cars were forced to abandon their challenge at Farnham when darkness fell, while the balloon went on to Basingstoke.

One of the status symbols of the age, the Rolls-Royce

A cartoon strip dealing with 'Balloon-acy, the Coming Craze'

Like pioneer motoring, ballooning was a rich person's sport, and the magazine *The Car* attempted to convert its readers to the new craze. Ballooning was elegant, exclusive, health-inspiring and full of mild excitement, and although the decline set in about 1909 when aeroplanes became the rage it retained a following until World War I. In 1906 a rich newspaper proprietor, Gordon Bennett, instigated a series of long distance races, the first being won by an American who clocked up 402 miles—from Paris to Whitby in Yorkshire. Sport-loving ladies found ballooning much to their taste, considering it more feminine than motoring, but for the time being left aeroplanes to the men.

As early as 1894 Hiram Maxim had constructed an aeroplane that would probably have worked had he had a light aero-engine at his disposal. In 1900 he complained that he had spent £17,000 on the problem of a heavier-than-air machine. In the event he was beaten to it by the Wright brothers in 1902. In 1906 the *Daily Mail* offered £10,000 to the first person to fly from London to Manchester; this was won by a Frenchman, Paulhan. Blériot had already taken the *Daily Mail* prize of £1,000 for the first cross-channel flight. He and the other aeronauts were fêted by Lord Northcliffe, who in the columns of the *Daily Mail* emphasised the importance of flight; the Blériot plane was set up in Selfridge's in Oxford Street, and the music hall brought the good news to the masses:

> There's a wonderful time coming soon,
>   For they tell us we're all going to fly!
> And we'll take daily trips to the moon;
>   What a picnic for both you and I!

Many Englishmen refused to take the aeroplane seriously. The journalist R. D. Blumenfeld declared that 'these things represent a foolish waste of money. Besides, flying across the Channel means nothing after you have done it. You can't carry goods or passengers'.[4] The preference for the airship owed something to the supremacy of French aeronautics, and it was invested with great possibilities. Illustrations were published of the airship of the future crossing the English Channel, with passengers sitting in deck-chairs on the decks, open to the elements.

Nevertheless the *Daily Mail* prizes acted as an incentive. When a prize of £1,000 was offered for the first circular flight of a mile by a British-built aeroplane, industry roused itself, and on 30 October 1909 the money was won by J. C. T. Moore-Brabazon flying a machine built by Short Brothers. Two years earlier, the first short aeroplane flight in England was accomplished by an American, S. F. Cody, in a 'power-kite' of his own invention, somewhat obscurely named British Army Aeroplane No 1.

British Army Aeroplane No 1 did not indicate a startling anticipation of the role which aircraft were to play in the war, and although the Royal Flying Corps was instituted in 1912 it was pathetically ill-equipped, consisting in 1913 of four squadrons of aeroplanes and one of airships and kites, Despite the pre-1909 enthusiasm for ballooning, the British were well behind the Germans and the French in building airships, known as dirigible balloons. In 1908 Count von Zeppelin had built an airship 446 ft in length with a lifting capacity of well over ten tons. The Zeppelin was to be one of the great psychological weapons of the 1914 war.

Notes to this chapter are on page 294.

CHAPTER FIVE

THE SEXUAL REVOLUTION

Eugenics and Birth Control

THE WORD eugenics was first given currency in 1833, and made respectable by Francis Galton (1822–1911), the cousin of Charles Darwin. Galton had written that the active and ambitious classes deferred marriage until they could afford it, and there was thus a permanent obstacle to the fecundity of the 'more elevated classes'. The improvident and the weak-willed were on the other hand very prolific, and in time this would lead to the deterioration of the race, and civilisation would revert to barbarism.

To resolve this problem in a rational manner, the science of eugenics—the deliberate breeding of the superior person, the first superman—was introduced. The Edwardians pursued the study and propagation of this concept with enthusiasm. They took as their text Galton and his followers, some of whom had gone into eugenics because Galton had founded in 1904 a Research Fellowship at London University. The Eugenics Record Office was started in a room in Gower Street, and a few years later was renamed the Eugenics Laboratory. Galton was a man of many parts, explorer, meteorologist, and doctor. The police forces of the world owe him a great debt, for in 1892 his book *Finger*

SHALL
BABIES
BE ABOLISHED?

A question asked not entirely for fun

Prints laid the groundwork of that method of criminal detection. But his chief claim to fame were his admirable studies in heredity, *Hereditary Genius* (1869) and *Natural Inheritance* (1889).

One of Galton's strongest supporters, Dr James Crichton-Browne, wrote:

> A recognition of the obligations which man owes to his fellow-men, and the promptings of love's divine self-abnegation, impose restraints on some of the competitors, who, instead of forcing their way to the front, as they are well able to do, stand aside and allow themselves to be beaten by those less fitted to survive.[1]

It need not be asked who were the most fitted to survive. The rich. The eugenists conveniently overlooked the fact that the cream of the rich, the old aristocracy, were theoretically low on the list. In his *Physiology of the Mind*, the Victorian pathologist Henry Maudsley stated that the last members of an old family were nearly always consumptive or insane, the two qualities most deplored by eugenists and discovered with alacrity in the lowest echelons of society. There was only one difference: the upper classes were made insane by in-breeding, the lower classes by drink.

The tone of eugenics in the Edwardian period can be judged by the first shot fired by Galton in 1901, when he read a paper to the Anthropological Institute on the 'Possible Improvement of the Human Breed under existing conditions of Law and Sentiment'. The law took no cognisance of the desirability of only perpetuating an élite, and eugenists looked longingly at certain of the United States, where criminals and the insane were unceremoniously sterilized—especially if they were Negroes as well—the Negroes were breeding 4-per-cent quicker than the whites. The British eugenists also envied the no-nonsense attitude of their American colleagues—the American Breeders' Association was formed in 1903.

Respectability was given to the whole eugenics movement by referring back to the classics, in much the same way as homosexuality was made less reprehensible by keying it in with Plato's *Republic*, the book that also provided a starting-point for eugenics. Plato discussed the possibility of improving the human species by arranged marriages, by letting warriors have the first pick of the fair. In Plato's *Laws* there is a proposal to tax bachelors over thirty-five. Aristotle was also brought into the canon, for in his *Politics* he urges the desirability of arranged marriages for the benefit of the children.

The British eugenists had close ties with Germany, where eugenics was known ominously as 'race hygiene'. The effect of eugenics in Germany was considerable, for the theory of the superman had as a supporter not only the eugenists but Friedrich Nietzsche (1844–1900). His superman was to be developed by giving unbridled freedom to the struggle for existence, in which power and pleasure were the only criteria. Historically speaking, Nietzsche's philosophy was a development of that of Schopenhauer. Both of these men were sick, distraught creatures, seeking for a compensation in their ruthless dreams, but nevertheless Nietzsche was seized upon as a guiding spirit by those advocates of the superman who were contemptuous of the gentility of the eugenists.

It was logical to extend the concept of the superman to include the super race, and 'race hygiene' became not only anthropologically but politically exciting. It is of interest to recall that the two composers most influenced by Nietzsche and Schopenhauer—Richard Strauss and Richard Wagner—were key figures in the iconography of Adolf Hitler (though his own tastes were more for *The Merry Widow*). The Nordic blond hero stalks through Wagnerian opera as if aware that the eugenists were about to make him respectable.

Fascinating as the prospect of the superman was, how could racial improvement be effected? The answer was simple. 'Sexual selection, guided by the eugenic ideal rather than by sordid desires, would seem the surest way'.[2] How could the information be acquired to determine whether a match was likely to produce satisfactory progeny? Eugenists were quite willing to make an off-the-cuff decision. The poor, on moral grounds, were bad risks. If pressed, eugenists mentioned the name of Mendel (1822–84), whose paper on plant hybridisation was published in 1865 but largely disregarded until 1900. Most eugenists, however, did not feel at home among gametes and zygotes, preferring to leave to the geneticists the hard work involved in the study of Mendel.

Galton was more to their taste. He was a lively and interesting writer, but apt to see significances where there were none. He had to decide whether the mental and moral qualities of men are inherited according to the same laws that govern the production of eggs by fowl. He tackled this like a dilettante rather than a scientist. He obtained records of what he termed the good tempers and bad tempers of married couples, and tried to find out what proportion of their children were good or bad tempered. He went through old lists of the results of examinations at Cambridge to see what proportion of the sons of those who had gained distinction in these examinations had themselves done well. It need hardly be added that finding out whether a married couple was good or bad tempered depended as much as anything on whether they liked or disliked the observer. The Cambridge 'investigation' meant little, as a child could inherit brains from a mother as well as a father.

Eugenics thus got off to an unfortunate start, as its founding-father was statistically suspect. Eugenics was also centred on physical characteristics. Those unfitted to perpetuate the race were weedy, undernourished, in poor physical shape. Opponents of eugenics pointed out that the 'big blond beast' of Nietzsche, the unthinking ideal product, was not exactly the most desirable type of person to be turned out by the conveyor-belt. And surely, if physical well-being was a prime factor, what would be done about Caesar, an epileptic?

There were some sharp minds in the eugenic movement, but far too many of its members were sublimating their hatred of the lower classes. Many eugenists would, if attention had been directed towards them, have been weighed in the balance and found wanting.

One of the leading figures in British eugenics was Karl Pearson. Born in London in 1857, educated at King's College, Cambridge, he was called to the bar in 1882, a career that did not suit him. He preferred to enter the new field of eugenics, and was appointed Galton Professor of Eugenics at London University. He was awarded the Darwin Medal by the Royal Society for his numerous contributions to the mathematical theory of evolution and heredity. A statistician of rare ability, he was highly regarded as the expert on eugenics after Galton died in 1911, and in 1925 he wrote the definitive biography of Galton.

But behind the impressive façade Karl Pearson was not all that he seemed. Although he did not die until 1936 at the age of 79, he was under the illusion that he had tuberculosis and doomed to die young, an illusion that was not amenable to the statistical method. As an expert on eugenics it might be supposed that he would choose his love object rationally and according to the dictates of his science. There is an element of high comedy in his choice of the novelist Olive Schreiner, who had a frantic desire to wear men's clothes, who proved too much of a handful to Havelock Ellis, and, the final absurdity so far as Pearson was concerned, was a Lesbian.

One of the crispest of Pearson's colleagues was Major Leonard Darwin, president of the Eugenics Education Society from 1911. Darwin poured ridicule on the ostensible goal of eugenics, the

Nietzsche superman; this was better left to the Germans (who did, after all, carry through the charade). Darwin emphasised that the decisive factor in the struggle for existence was general ability, a difficult thing to measure. Not that the eugenists were particularly keen to measure general ability, as they were now hooked, after the random methods of Galton, on investigating children—and children have their own unpredictable ways of turning out differently to hypotheses framed by investigators. The Binet-Simon tests of 1915 were a kind of Bible to latter-day eugenists.

Major Darwin horrified social reformers in his view that the poor deserve to be poor and that their ranks are continuously swollen by the arbitrary descent of the unfit from the upper layers of society. This was comforting for eugenists; it confirmed their intuitive feelings that the poor had only themselves to blame, and that the pressures of society and the wicked capitalist system had nothing to do with the existence of a wretched sub-stratum of society. For, when the pros and cons of eugenics are finally sifted, the whole movement was a weapon of class, a sublimation of the view that the poor were multiplying so fast as to imperil the bastions of the middle classes.

With few exceptions, the Edwardian eugenists were afflicted with an immense arrogance. This was illustrated by a controversy between Pearson and Havelock Ellis carried on with a rancour that would be surprising if one were unaware that they were both rivals for the masculine hand of Olive Schreiner. Pearson claimed that Ellis 'had done much to perpetuate some of the pseudo-scientific superstitions'. Ellis replied ironically that Pearson:

> . . . is careful to tell us at frequent intervals, before he himself entered the field [of eugenics] all was 'dogma', 'superstition', 'nearly all partisan', at the best 'quite unproven'. I am inclined to think that these terms, which spring so easily to Mr. Pearson's pen, are automatic reminiscences of the ancient controversies he has waged with theologians and metaphysicians.[3]

Eugenists also had a penchant for dashing generalities. In his book *Eugenics*, Edgar Schuster summarises, after some inconsequential tests:

> Whatever are the innate differences between university professors, small tradesmen, and the denizens of the Liverpool slums, by the time they reach adult life there is little question that the order in which they would be placed with regard to their intellectual qualities is the same as that in which they are here written.

Some lunatic fringe eugenists believed in telegony. This means that if a woman had a child by one husband and subsequently another child by another husband, the peculiarities of the first husband would exert an influence not only on his own child but on the other man's. Maternal impressions, the action of external factors on an unborn child, were also treated with some respect.

The eugenists could not agree whether war was a good thing for mankind or not. The commonsense view was held by Havelock Ellis, who flirted with eugenics in his book *Man and Woman* (1894). He maintained that it was a remarkable tendency of the warlike spirit to exterminate itself. The fighting stocks were killed off, leaving the prudent, those who fought and ran away. This was disputed. Reckless fighters would be braver and win more quickly than those who fought and ran away, to be regrouped to fight again, and thus prolong a war. In the context of the time, with war just over the horizon, this was not an academic point.

In France and Germany, 30–50 per cent of conscripts were rejected as unfit for any kind of war service, though standards were speedily relaxed when war began. In 1911, 64,000 men offered themselves for enlistment in Great Britain; 45 per cent were turned down. One eugenist did comment that if war occurred the men who were killed would be on an average physically superior to those in their age group who had escaped the risk. But war, and the prospects of war, were far less important than the eugenic duty to restrict the birth-rate of the poor.

Why should the eugenic movement, which had been created well before the twentieth century arrived, have been so influential in Edwardian England? Briefly, the answer lies in the effect of birth control and the coming of the welfare state. In 1906, taxation was levied for the education and preservation of large families of the poor; no longer would their high birth rate be countered by a high death rate in infancy. This taxation was a double-edged weapon to eugenics, for those taxed would limit their own families to suit their pockets and would at the same time be subsidising the erotic behaviour of the lower classes, who lacked the knowledge, the will or the inclination to limit their own families.

It is not surprising that desperate measures were proposed by the eugenist high command. Major Darwin advocated sterilisation of the poor by means of the 'harmless and painless' X-rays, the new fad. This was called 'negative eugenics'; the encouragement of the superior classes to propagate was termed 'positive eugenics'. Such inducement could be monetary, and the eugenists proposed a rating reform. Big families needed big houses; parliament should subsidise rates on these. No one needed telling that the poor with big families did not own houses to pay rates on. Eugenics should be taught at school; the marriage laws should be looked at with a view to prospective spouses having to obtain a medical certificate, and the poor must be implanted with the ethics of love and marriage. Love was not blind, nor did it laugh at locksmiths. In every heart there should be an image of the ideal lover, to serve both as a guide and a goal. The fact was overlooked that it was unusual for a girl of the lower classes to have retained her virginity past the age of fourteen.

Between 1700 and 1800 the population of Great Britain increased by 30 per cent; between 1800 and 1900 it increased by 300 per cent. Some saw this as good; there was more labour to do more jobs and so create trade and prosperity. Others saw it as too many people chasing too few jobs, drawing an analogy with Ireland in 1846, when there was a peasant population of 8 million, living like pigs. Famine and emigration brought the population down to 4 million. The Irish, engage in internicine wars and quarrel with their English overlords as they may, then became prosperous. The Black Death in the fourteenth century reduced England's population by two-thirds; the fifteenth century was the happiest time for the agricultural workers, before or since.

Victorian Britain managed to cope with the population increase, though in the worst quarters of London unemployment was never less than 25 per cent. The colonies absorbed several millions. In the eighteenth century birth control propaganda had been directed at the man about town, but later the emphasis shifted to the respectable married man. During the nineteenth century more than a million tracts were sold on birth control, and many more were distributed free. Two pioneers were Francis Place (*The Principle of Population*, 1822) and Richard Carlile (*Practical Hints on How to Enjoy Life and Pleasure without Harm to Either Sex*, 1826). An English reprint of an American treatise on birth control, *The Fruits of Philosophy*, sold 42,000 copies between 1834 and 1876.

Notwithstanding the torrent of abuse heaped upon birth control, it became more widely adopted and by increasingly efficient methods: vulcanisation of rubber led to the rubber sheath, and in 1886 the soluble quinine pessary was perfected. In the 1870s, two freethinking reformers decided to republish the by then obsolete *Fruits of Philosophy*, and were involved in a tragi-comic court case, for the law saw birth control literature as obscene. The case drew public attention to the facts of contraception, and from 1878 the birth-rate of the United Kingdom dropped. The middle classes were the most significant converts, followed by the 'improved working class', who saw in the restriction of the size of their families a way to ascend the class ladder.

Birth control, despite frowns from some quarters, became respectable; society ladies distributed large quantities of birth control booklets to maternity hospitals. Though condemned by the bishops, the clergy gave their support. The Reverend Dennis Hurd was very pleased with his findings, as described in his book *A Christian with Two Wives*: 'The two girls are happy; they have three sons each, and they might have had ten, but I think three plenty for one woman; it just develops her nature and character, and makes her more lovely'.

At the Manchester Church Congress of 1888, a Professor
Symes said, 'I have the strongest reason to know that the subject
is engaging the attention of an immense number of people in all
classes in England and elsewhere'. As the old century gave way
to the new, more and more people planned their families,
though because of the prohibition on the sale of birth-control
literature many continued to use old-fashioned methods, such as
douching, withdrawal, and the utilisation of the so-called safe
period, which varied from authority to authority—one writer
specified this as just one week a month.

Official attitudes to birth control did not change very much
though the propaganda was more open, and there were advertisements on the 'gates of fields in the deep country' and on the walls
of railway station urinals. Advertisements in periodicals and
newspapers were bitterly attacked, and readers of *Myra's Journal*
in 1905 would soon acquire 'a second-hand knowledge which
would place them on an equal footing with an experienced
prostitute'. More reprehensible than advertisements for contraceptives were tracts on induced abortion, making use of
pills of lead plaster; a liquor in which copper coins had been
boiled; quinine crystals, and various salts.

The medical profession closed its eyes to the new wave. The
Lancet declared that birth control was a 'distasteful subject', but
notwithstanding the aversion of the general practitioner to
discuss the topic there was evidence of an increased use of
contraception by the middle classes. In 1905–6 the Fabian
Society found that, out of 316 marriages investigated, 242
couples practised birth control. The most powerful indication
that even the most respectable members of the middle class
were practising it came with the census of 1911, where it was
found that Church of England clergymen, those prolific breeders
of Victorian times, were 30 per cent less fertile than the population as a whole.

In 1906 Sidney Webb, the doyen of the left wing intellectuals,
declared that between a half and two-thirds of married people
practised some form of birth control. A new generation of
propagandists emerged, though most of their books were not

written until the war and after. The most famous of these was Marie Stopes, whose *Married Love* (1918) became perhaps the most widely read book on birth control, and only marginally less influential was Margaret Sanger, whose *Family Limitations* was published in 1914.

The morals and motivations of the new school could not be reasonably questioned. Generally speaking, the police preferred to leave the propagandists alone, though in 1911 James White was arrested for selling *True Morality* in the market place in Stanley, County Durham; he was fined £20, but chose instead to go to prison. In 1913 the Malthusian League (Malthusianism, drawing its name from Malthus, the eighteenth-century clergyman who foresaw the dangers of a teeming population, was the Victorian name for birth control) organised twice-weekly meetings in Southwark, and within a month had distributed 25,000 handbills to the working classes.

The books on birth control issued during the Edwardian period were considerably better than those produced during the nineteenth century, which were furtive in tone. There was a big mail order business, supplying such books under plain cover. *Hygienic Methods of Family Limitation* (1913) pronounced the safe period risky; withdrawal difficult on the nerves; and advocated sheaths at between 2s and 6s a dozen, which could be washed and used four or five times; and pessaries at 2s a dozen.

There was mutual distrust between the birth controllers, who wished to encourage the poor to practise birth control, and the eugenists, who preferred legislation and force, and were more interested in its benefits to the upper and middle classes than to the poor. Notwithstanding a certain prurience on the part of birth control enthusiasts, there is little doubt that they were considering the welfare of the poor when they took what they termed 'the good news' to the masses.

The rise in the number of respectable advocates of birth control did much to rob the movement of its Victorian reputation, and the support of the popular weekly magazine *John Bull* from 1910 nullified a good deal of reactionary opinion. Those who attacked birth control saw that it could no longer be put forward as an unqualified evil, but the wide sale of contraceptives and birth control literature would, they argued, destroy sexual morality. This was put uncompromisingly by Lieutenant-Colonel Everitt, who told a House of Commons committee on patent medicines in 1912 that 'young people of both sexes are led to believe that they can have illicit intercourse without any fear of detection, and this, of course, leads to what may be called free love, amateur prostitution, and other evils of that sort'.

The overwhelming success of the birth control movement is demonstrated by the 1911 Census, which also makes clear that the eugenists' fears that the poor were breeding faster than the other classes were justified:

England and Wales, 1911 Social Class	Legitimate birth rates in social classes per 1,000 married males
1 Upper and Middle	119
2 Intermediate Class	132
3 Skilled Workmen	153
4 Intermediate Class	158
5 Unskilled Workmen	213

The middle classes had to overcome their scruples before practising birth control; they veered between listening to the strictures of their mentors, doctors and clergymen, and self-interest. Nothing illustrates so well the hypocrisy of the middle classes as their fulmination against birth control propagandists and their consistent use of birth control methods. The upper classes had no such scruples. In an interesting investigation carried out using Burke's Peerage, it was found that marriages among the aristocracy during the ten years ending in 1840 gave an average of 7.1 births to each fertile couple; the ten years ending in 1850 and in 1860 each gave 6.1 births. But from 1871 to 1880 they dropped to 4.36, and from 1881 to 1890 to 3.13. This was reckoned by statisticians to be below the figure needed to sustain the class, and it was facts like this that led the eugenics movement into such contortions in the first ten years of this century.

Edwardian Love and Romance

To a large section of the population the passing of Queen
Victoria meant little in the day-to-day business of life. They
mourned her, were appropriately enthusiastic about her successor,
and then relapsed into their normal routine. Victorianism did
not end with the accession of King Edward, and in many middle-
class families the old taboos and proscriptions were maintained.
If anything, some of the more reactionary families tightened
their control on their impressionable young, especially their
daughters, when they sensed that the mood of the fin-de-siècle
showed no sign of dispersing.

The 'improved working classes' were also concerned about the
morals of their children. The Education Act of 1870 was
beginning to bite in respect of the child-bearing age groups, and
the improved working class was at pains to disown its former
drinking, blasphemous image. In the lace-curtained terrace
houses of Balham and Clapham there was no shortage of gentility.

Gentility can imply an aversion to looking at facts, the
preference of an easy-going ignorance to knowledge, and a
fondness for stale archetypes. One of these archetypes was the
relation between the sexes. At no time was there a greater
interest in love and romance than among the middle classes and
improved working classes of the first decade and a half of the
present century. Romance was supplied by a host of hack writers
and ethereal lady novelists, and figured strongly in such books as
Baroness Orczy's *The Scarlet Pimpernel* (1905) and *The Elusive
Pimpernel* (1908). Love and romance were therefore seen
through the filter supplied by writers, such as the novelist
de Vere Stacpoole, whose *The Blue Lagoon* was the best-seller of
1908.

A characteristic supplier of antidotes to apprehension and
a copious provider of formulas for the marriageable was Elinor
Glyn. She produced a novel almost every year containing
heroines who were nicely saucy or haughty, epitomised by
Ambroisine in *The Reflections of Ambroisine* (1902). In a passage

at arms with a wealthy young man who uses phrases like 'snug little crib' and 'beastly hard luck' (and was thus rather common), Ambroisine is kissed against her will; she repulses the man with 'You are to understand that I will not be mauled—and kissed like—Hephzibah at the back door.' 'Hoity-toity', the man replies, 'what airs you give yourself! but you look so deuced pretty when you are angry.'

Elinor Glyn occasionally turned away from fiction to summarise her philosophy of love. 'The lowest creatures, the worst characters', she wrote, 'are raised when they love—because for the time it holds them under its sway, they cease to be utterly selfish.' Also 'The first thing to learn—and to drum into your head—is that no one can love or unlove at will', and 'Love improves the character: it brings kindness and tolerance for others, and a generosity unknown at other times.' Elinor Glyn was also inclined to see love as an aesthetic process: 'To bring love to perfection is just as difficult as to rear a delicate plant, and every one of its changes must be watched and guided.'

In real life, romance was found to be inconclusive and arbitrary. Guided by pre-set ideas and misled by the fantasies of fiction writers, its followers got themselves into difficulties, turning for help to the advice columns of the women's magazines. Some of these journals were edited by the most inappropriate of men. Frank Harris, whose *My Life and Loves* has only recently been brought out from under the counter to be sold openly, edited *Vanity Fair* from 1907 to 1910 and *Hearth and Home* from 1911 to 1912. The health and beauty column of *Hearth and Home* had Dame Deborah Primrose assuring readers that a prominent bust was not in good *ton*, and although Harris was quite likely to roar out to worried correspondents who called at the office, 'There's only one use for a woman—get out of here before I show you', he knew that the success of a woman's paper depended on the charisma of its advice columns.

Annie S. Swan, a no-nonsense daughter of a Scots farmer, whose hobbies were walking, cycling and golf, edited *The Woman at Home*, and herself replied to correspondents. A surprising number of the letters were written by men. Miss Swan

The fantasies of writers of fiction led many people astray. Romance was not as clear cut as it was in magazine serials

(in real life Mrs Burnett Smith) advised 'Wanderer' to leave his wife alone as, now that she was comfortable and in a good position, he might be accused of ulterior motives were he to persecute her any more. 'Crushed Violets' was advised to dismiss her careless lover from her mind, and console herself with someone else; while 'Her Friend' wrote telling Miss Swan of the case of a friend who had been replaced in a husband's affection by a younger woman. This letter filled Miss Swan with 'a great, sad indignation'. Probably aware that 'Her Friend' was the woman herself, she delicately asked whether the deserted woman was letting herself go in the matter of looks.

She was not afraid to administer a sharp tap on the wrist. 'Looker On' was advised to mind her own business; 'Bobby' was

" Look into my eyes and tell me that you hate me !"

How far could flirting go without being immoral? There was little help from Crosspatch
Patty *by E. Maria Albanesi for which this illustration was drawn*

told to write in a different tone; and 'Daisy Darling', who complained that her lover had tired of her and who wanted him punished, was told not to be a bore. She was puzzled by a morbid hysterical letter from 'Budah', whom she told to do some honest hard work; and did not discern the psychological motives behind a letter from 'La Desirée' who 'is afflicted with a mysterious charm which causes every man who meets her to fall in love with her'.

A good percentage of the letters related to suspicions, and her advice was to bring everything out into the open. There were also anguished queries as to how far flirting could go without being immoral, or indeed where could a line be drawn between everyday civility and flirting, at a time when comradeship between the sexes was a great talking point. Miss Swan took a sensible line on platonic friendships; these, she considered, were not possible. She mentioned an instance of one that had lasted seventeen years and then ended in marriage; a waste, she commented, of seventeen years. 'French Marigold' was involved in a platonic friendship, and clearly wished it to be less platonic; she was advised to talk it over with her parents.

A correspondent signing herself 'Revolting Daughter' wanted some share of the emancipation cake, but was too habituated to parental control to do anything about it. She was having a mild affair with a youth who worked in her father's music warehouse and was teaching her the mandolin. Like 'French Marigold', she was advised to tell the whole story to her parents.

Unquestionably Miss Swan was on the side of the establishment, and if all correspondence columns had been conducted with her assurance parents would have had nothing to fear. The main problems of the letter writers derived from their having taken too seriously the facts of life as emasculated by novelists. Most writers, no matter how they conducted their own lives, would not commit themselves in print. George Bernard Shaw professed to be sexually liberated, but when he was expected by fellow socialists to publicly denounce marriage he was obdurate, warning his disciples that disregard of the conventions brought too much friction into private life and that it was troublesome enough being a socialist and agnostic without professing free love. His ethos was based on the motto: 'Do not throw out dirty water until you get in fresh'. In other words, keep marriage until you find something better.

Marriage was the rock on which romance foundered, but it was also the sacred state that preserved the respectability of advice columns in women's papers. Speculations in the daily newspapers about the possibility of introducing 'marriage leases' were treated as the outpourings of atheists or—worse—socialists. 'It would seem', declared Annie Swan, 'that the cancer of selfishness and flippancy is more widely spread through society than we dreamed.' However, the danger was more apparent than real. 'The great bulk of British people are still sound in the fundamentals.'

Nevertheless, even the women's pages recognized that marriage was no longer the religious state that it once had been, and was now tied up with the concept of home and duty. Going into marriage also had an element of the heroic, and proved that the British, eschewing selfish indulgence and happiness, were not so degenerate as many thought.

Bernard Shaw urged his women friends not to burn their boats without the protection and status of legal marriage—unless they were economically independent. D. H. Lawrence was not so circumspect. 'Only through a readjustment between men and women, and a making free and healthy of this sex, will she get out of her present atrophy',[1] he declared. But he did not live up to his convictions and as soon as he could, in 1914, he married a Nottingham lecturer's wife with whom he had eloped. H. G. Wells, another pioneer in the re-evaluation of the married state, defended his own marriage by saying, 'In our period, if we had not married, half our energy would have been frittered away in a conflict of garden-wall insults and slights and domestic exactions'.[2] Yet in a paper read to the Fabian Society in 1906 he stated that, 'I no more regard the institution of marriage as a permanent thing than I regard a state of competitive industrialism as a permanent thing'.[3]

The influence of such novelists as Wells played a part in

"Oh, by the way," you hear him say,
"I wish you'd marry me some day;
"How would next Friday fortnight suit you?
"And—may I (what they call) 'salute' you?"

Marriage was no longer the religious state of the Victorians, but it was not usual to treat it with flippancy

determining attitudes towards marriage, and *Ann Veronica* was treated as a primer by emancipated women and by women who desperately wanted to be emancipated. Today Ann Veronica herself would cause few eyebrows to rise, but to her real-life contemporaries she epitomised a type to be emulated. The book was banned, preached against, and attacked by the editor of *The Spectator*, John St Loe Strachey, as '. . . the muddy world of Mr Wells' imaginings, a community of scuffling stoats and ferrets, unenlightened by a ray of duty and abnegation'.

The old brigade regarded marriage as being under greater pressure than was the case, and literature that tended to degrade the institution was treated in a hostile manner. Duty and obeisance to the will of society kept marriages going even in the saddest conditions, and where partners were, as Carlyle put it, 'gey ill to live with' a pretence was kept up. Divorce was still a rarity. Between 1906 and 1910 an average of 638 decrees nisi were granted each year, and the rate of divorce had hardly altered since Victorian times. Divorce action was extremely expensive; an undefended suit would cost between £50–£60, and a defended case could cost upwards of £500. When it is borne in mind that only 70 per cent of petitions were successful, ill-matched partners were reluctant to go through the traumatic process even when they could afford to. The poorer classes were in no position to engage in divorce proceedings, and in 1909 a royal commission was appointed to look into the laws of divorce with particular reference to the poor.

Adultery was still the inexcusable sin, except among the rich and the emancipationists, and was discussed in hushed whispers unless it could be made to appear comical. On the other hand, a breach of promise action was 'socially a dead letter for all but the ladies of the dramatic profession and the lower classes'.[4]

No matter how hazardous marriage might be, there was no shortage of contestants. Those who could not find their own mates applied to the matrimonial agencies or advertised in the columns of the Sunday newspapers. A number of interesting letters appeared in *Reynold's News* in January 1908:

A superior person would like to marry an honourable man. Would make a capable farmer's wife. Aged 33.

Two friends (30, 32) highly respectable, domesticated, honourable women, would like to meet two friends or brothers, steady honourable men, retiring from navy or mechanics.

Eva, 4' 11", 25, fair, wished to meet a refined dark man, with the added stipulations that he must be an abstainer and a non-conformist (in religion not habits). A Christian gentleman of means, of a loving disposition, sought a wife; an affliction was not objected to. The customs and taboos of society always create outsiders, and although such plaintive and pathetic letters were not by any means uncommon in Victorian popular papers, it is somehow surprising to find them in the Edwardian Sunday press. The call for marriage candidates of an 'honourable nature' demonstrates that the advertisers were well aware that male readers might con the correspondence columns with a view to adventure, though there is some doubt whether the more vulnerable were protected by this stipulation.

The problems of love and marriage can be read between the lines of the agony columns of *Reynold's News*:

PAT—tremendous row. Consequences awkward. Forbidden to play bridge. Happily no blame attaches to you. Say nothing. Be careful. E.

DEARIE—Enjoyed Saturday evening, especially cab ride between Waterloo and Vauxhall. Caught 1.20 am train to Clapham. All right at home. Meet me same time tomorrow. EVENING DRESS.

FAIR ONE—Do be patient, dear. It is all for your good. K. would make life intolerable if he knew. CHIP.

Though there was also promise:

Delighted to see you. Sooner the better. How would Tuesday 3.30 Charing-cross bookshop suit you? Girl in Gray.

Will charming young lady wearing green feather hat with white boa who caught eye of gentleman in Putney bus on Friday last communicate with Admirer? There was then no opportunity of speaking. Address this paper. P.S.T.

Women were able to escape into business. No longer was marriage the only career open to them

The young were often handicapped in their pursuit of love by the resentment and petulance of the old and middle aged. The old would not let Victorianism die. They were envious of the freedom of the young Edwardian woman who was going out to work in one of the professions, such as medicine, opened up to them by the stout pioneering work of progressive Victorian women. An army of young women were recruited to operate the telephone exchanges; in 1901 only 18 per cent of telephone operators were female, but in 1911 this had risen to 32 per cent and rose higher still by 1914, when there were 775,000 telephones in Great Britain. Even more significant was the revolution in business activity caused by the wholesale acceptance of the typewriter. Being a typist was considered a respectable occupation for a middle-class girl, and being twice as well paid as a shop assistant the typist became a person worth the courting by the mass media. The typist also created a new type of life-style, and was wholly responsible for the genesis of the tea-room and the cafeteria.

These well-bred young ladies, set uncertainly in the social structure between the shop-girl and the teacher, were torn between the influences of the home and those of the emanci-pationists—reluctant either to adhere to the moral standards of their parents or throw in their lot with the New Woman. They were therefore very much inclined to seek an answer to their uncertainties in fiction or the popular press.

The high-class newspapers and periodicals took a very priggish tone about the romance that was served up to an eager readership. Of Elinor Glyn's *Three Weeks*, the *Daily Telegraph* wrote that 'the record of these erotic passions . . . only avoids by a hair-breadth the accusation of growing positively squalid', a critique that did the book no harm as two million copies were sold in nine years.

In the end, the Edwardians had to adjust as best they could to their human needs. Only in retrospect can their age be seen as extravagant or ostentatious, greedy or immoral. The people themselves were still in thrall to their Victorian upbringing, and were confused by the diverse promptings of what they recognised as a different age, though in what ways it was different they could only guess. At one time, the bemused had found help and consolation in the Bible; thwarted and hopeless love would find final consummation in the hereafter. The Edwardians did not have this straw to cling to, but sought succour in women's magazines and in the tabloid newspapers pandering to bewilder-ment. Genuine information about love and romance, the counter-feits for sex, was hard to come by, and the glib answers of journalists were not good enough. Although it was the age of Havelock Ellis and earnest studies into the psychology of sex, such works were not for the masses, and middle class and working class investigators had to find consolation in such insipidities as Edward Carpenter's *Love's Coming of Age.*

In many cases it was reassurance rather than information that was wanted. The Edwardian young were vouchsafed glimpses of the ideal love, and built fantasies upon this which toppled before the inroads of reality. It is the theme of thousands of Victorian novels, and the Edwardians had no monopoly on unrequited love, on misunderstandings, or on fickle fate. But unlike the previous age they had nothing to fall back on.

The Feminists

The lethargy and the apathy of Edwardian men in politics, the arts, and everything except the pursuit of pleasure was countered by ferocious energy on the part of their women folk, which reached its apotheosis in the suffragette movement, but which was apparent in a variety of diverse activities. The women of the middle classes and the upper classes played whist and bridge with a concentration and a devotion that their husbands could rarely match, hordes of women cyclists tried to demonstrate that women were no longer the weaker sex, and in hockey, golf, ping-pong, diabolo and Swedish drill women were as active as men. Lady beaglers in masculine garb tore through hedges and fell into ditches, ju-jitsu and fencing were practised by belligerent young women with unyielding verve, and when the British leisured classes made ski-ing in Switzerland an in-sport the women were as much in evidence as the men. In 1912 a Miss Maitland had the temerity to win an all-comers ski competition.

The game of bridge was introduced into London clubs in 1894 as Russian Whist, but the vogue did not really get under way until 1907 when auction bridge was evolved ('Strange game of esoteric charm, Bridge of a myriad sighs and curses'). The power of bridge was such that it all but killed fashionable 'At Homes' and nearly finished musical evenings, though that, declared the *Morning Post*, would be 'a crowning mercy'. Bridge was coincident with the rise of women's clubs. In 1913 there were twenty-two clubs for women in London, including the Ladies' Army & Navy.

IT TAKES TIME.

Miss Weston: "AND HAVE YOU PLAYED
MUCH GOLF, MR. JONES?"

Mr. Jones: "WELL—ER, NO, CAN'T SAY
I'VE *PLAYED* MUCH, BUT I'VE WALKED ROUND
THE LINKS SEVERAL TIMES IN THESE CLOTHES,
AND I'M BEGINNING TO UNDERSTAND THE
LANGUAGE."

*In sport, the arts, and business, women were no longer content to be the weaker sex, and
could be formidable adversaries, as this 1901 cartoon makes clear*

Women were no longer restricted to their homes and a dull
round of social visiting; increasingly, restaurants and tea-shops
catered for feminine restlessness. Harrods opened a Gentlemen's
Club and a Ladies' Club; in the latter tea was served to the
accompaniment of Harrods Royal Red Orchestra. In 1903 the
Daily Mail referred to the number of 'quick lunch' establishments
opening, at which the customers helped themselves, and there
was a splurge of vegetarian restaurants, the clients of which
were predominantly women entranced by the new fad, nut
diets.

The stage was set for women to exert their influence. They were venturing into politics. The Hon Mrs Alfred Lyttelton, author of *Warp and Woof*, a play dealing with the oppression of the dressmakers, was an active member of the Women's Liberal-Unionist Association and the Victoria League; Mrs Brodrick, wife of the war minister, was on the executive committee of the Ladies' Grand Council of the Primrose League, of which the vice-president was the formidable Lady Ancaster, a society hostess in the grand manner.

Some of the women had thrown off not only their stay-at-home ways but their stays as well. They wanted it conceded that not only were they men's equals, but they were their superiors, infinitely brighter, better and finer. Their rallying cry was 'Votes for Women!'

In 1903 the Women's Social and Political Union was formed. This was not another Women's Liberal-Unionist Association or Victoria League; the WSPU was militant and aggressive. Its leading figure was Mrs Pankhurst, widow of Dr Pankhurst who had been prominent in women's suffrage since 1868, when, as a barrister, he had defended women ratepayers in a test case. The Liberals had disillusioned him, and after Gladstone 'had thrown the women overboard' in 1884 the Pankhursts deserted the party and flirted with the Independent Labour Party. Dr Pankhurst died in 1898, and Mrs Pankhurst felt free to leave Labour; the Manchester Suffrage Society was dreary and old-fashioned, and, worst of all, democratic. Mrs Pankhurst deemed herself the king-pin in the 'votes for women' movement, and gathered round her a select group of new women, malcontents and despairing spinsters.

One of these was Annie Kenney, a cotton operative who had lived all her life at Lees, near Oldham, and had started work at ten years old. Thin, haggard, hysterical, Annie Kenney was the stuff of which disciples are made. She tried to join the local committee of the card and blowing-room operatives, but the men were aghast at the prospect of women trade unionists. They told her she would not like it, as textile unionists were a drunken lot, more interested in whippet-racing than anything else, and held their meetings in public houses. Other members of the movement included Miss Kerr, the office manager, whose main motivation for being a suffragette was her hatred of her architect father; Beatrice Sanders, the wife of a Fabian; Aela Lamb, a frail orphan anxious for revenge on society; Mary Home, who kept the newspaper cuttings and the research material, a pale young woman with a hare lip, the daughter of an Indian Army officer; Vera Holmes, a singer in Gilbert and Sullivan opera; and Jessie Spink, a shop assistant who carried a portrait of Mrs Pankhurst on her breast, and who, aflame with aspiration, changed her name to Vera Wentworth to become a novelist.

However, Mrs Pankhurst's two greatest allies were her daughters Sylvia and Christabel, whom she overpowered with her rancour and bitterness. The eagerness of these three women to get the vote became an obsession. The movement was helped because many politicians thought that women should get the vote; these politicians were on the left wing, and did not realise that when women did get the vote they would be the most powerful force against them (if there were no women voters today the Labour Party would always be in office).

The suffragettes' most loyal supporter was the veteran Labour politician Keir Hardie, who lived a frugal life at 14 Nevill's Court, just off Fetter Lane in London. His walls were covered with engravings of socialist heroes of yesteryear, and he had a collection of fossils gathered when he was a coal miner. The prim anti-sexual demeanour of the Pankhursts appealed to him, brought up in a Calvinistic environment. He gave them tea and scones, and saw them and their movement through a veil of sentiment.

The Fabian Society was wholeheartedly behind women's franchise—theoretically. But many of its members were disappointed by the women who were out to achieve it. If women wanted to be free, wrote H. G. Wells, good luck to them; free love and birth control would necessarily replace domestic chains. He was disillusioned. 'It became increasingly evident that a large part of the woman's suffrage movement was animated less by the desire for freedom and fullness of life than by a

The gallery of the House of Commons became a gathering point for ardent suffragettes

passionate jealousy and hatred of the relative liberties of men'. For one woman who wanted to live generously and nobly there were a score who merely wanted to make things uncomfortable for the 'insolent, embarrassing, oblivious male. They did not want more life; their main impulse was vindictive'.[1]

In 1905 the Women's Enfranchisement Bill was talked out ·in the Commons by Henry Labouchere, who objected to women getting the vote on the somewhat obscure grounds that they could not be soldiers; when another member pointed out that he was not a military man, Labouchere exploded in patriotic rage. Mrs Pankhurst had watched the scene from the public gallery, and went down to break the news to her colleagues. There was in indignation meeting, joined by Keir Hardie, at which one of the old timers, Mrs Wolstenholme Elmy, decided to tell everyone about the early days of the movement back in 1865.

Despite events in London the movement was still centred in Manchester. It was clear that the Conservative government was doomed, and when Sir Edward Grey arrived to speak in the Manchester Free Trade Hall in October 1905 it was as a future cabinet minister that he was treated. The suffragettes were present in force, and when Grey refused to answer questions about votes for women, Christabel Pankhurst and Annie Kenney created a scene, spitting and scratching at police officers called to remove them. Manchester made the mistake of making martyrs of them; summoned to court, Miss Pankhurst decided to go to prison for seven days, Miss Kenney for three, rather than pay nominal fines.

The matter received wide publicity in the London press. The *Evening Standard* was for the girls going to prison, the *Daily Mail* declared that this only proved that women did not deserve the vote. Keir Hardie telegraphed that it was a dastardly outrage to send the girls to prison, but it would do immense good for the cause. The implications were seen by Winston Churchill, who was at the Free Trade Hall, and he went to Strangeways Gaol to pay the fine, an offer that was refused by the governor. It is possible that by turning down the fifteen shillings the governor of the gaol cost his country hundreds of thousands of pounds.

The suffragettes realised that by being sent to prison they would win public sympathy. Now that the Liberals were set for power, the future cabinet appeared at the Albert Hall to answer questions. The chance was too good to miss, and the suffragettes created a scene and unrolled a 9 ft banner from the balcony. At an Asquith meeting in Sheffield, Annie Kenney began to wail, and her companion, Sylvia Pankhurst, was uncomfortably aware that the audience would think that Miss Kenney was mad. Men in the audience struck her with fists and umbrellas, and she was ejected, but still not imprisoned. It might be different in London. It was. The *Daily Mail* gave the movement the label 'the Suffragettes', though *Punch* preferred 'the Insuffrabelles'.

Society eccentrics, such as Lady Carlisle and her son the Honourable Geoffrey Howard, backed the suffragettes, and the maverick journalist and half-mad W. T. Stead offered enthusiastic support, having to be forcibly prevented from kissing Annie Kenney.

At this stage the movement began to get substantial financial help, and the Pethick Lawrences allied themselves to the suffragettes. The Pethick Lawrences had founded a co-operative dressmaking venture, a holiday hotel for working girls, and had built a children's holiday home. Lawrence's monthly paper, the *Labour Record*, was a platform for suffragette thought.

The new government was more openly sympathetic than the Conservatives had been towards enfranchisement. Two hundred MPs formed themselves into a Women's Suffrage Committee; these included members of the opposition who had been steadfastly against the movement but now realised this was a wonderful chance to embarrass the government. Mrs Pankhurst thought that now was the time to jump in and create a major disturbance in the House of Commons, but her daughters dissuaded her. Some idea of Mrs Pankhurst's egotism can be gauged by her tearful reproof: 'You have balked me—both of you! I thought there would have been one little nitch [sic] in the temple of fame for me!'[2]

Keir Hardie remained the spearhead of the 'votes for women' lobby, and in April 1906 the matter was brought up again. The suffragettes in the gallery were over-anxious; when they saw policemen ranged around the wall, they erupted, were ejected, and thus alienated their supporters in parliament. In May a deputation representing 260,000 women was advised to be patient. But the suppressed hysteria was bubbling over, and there was increasing violence on both sides when meetings were interrupted. One suffragette lashed out with a dog-whip at a steward attempting to eject her, while Annie Kenney was again sent to prison, though other suffragettes avoided martyrdom by having their fines paid by well-wishers.

To many people the whole business seemed to be getting beyond a joke. Women, who saw no purpose in getting the

A cartoon strip dealing with the increasingly militant suffragettes

vote and were quite happy with the power they already wielded, banded together to show that the suffragettes were atypical. A petition was presented signed by 243,852 women resolutely anti-suffragette. The male viewpoint was that ladies, whatever their grievances, should behave in a ladylike respectable manner. There was an ironical news item: 'Two suffragettes the other evening made their way into a private house where a reception was given in honour of Mr Asquith, and created an unpleasant scene. They were disguised as ladies'.

The novelist Elizabeth Robins, who was also an actress known for her interpretation of Ibsen, caught the spirit of the time and smartly turned out the play *Votes for Women* and the novel *The Convert*. The Court theatre, never averse to topical themes, put on the play in April 1907. Christabel Pankhurst was becoming the heroine of the movement, outshining her mother and sister, who complained of her 'incipient Toryism' and ruthlessness. Those who spoke quaveringly of the good old days of the 1860s were being ousted in favour of professionals who could raise money. The movement's income was £3,000 in 1906–7; £7,000 in 1907–8; reaching £20,000 in 1908–9, and £32,000 in 1909–10. More than 5,000 meetings were held in 1907–8; the paper *Votes for Women*, founded the same year, had a circulation of nearly 40,000 by 1909–10.

The full militancy of the suffragettes became evident on 23 October 1906 when they held a meeting in the lobby of the House of Commons. Their all-embracing wish was realised; they were all sent to prison. The national press welcomed the strong line of the Cannon Row Police Court magistrate, and amusedly quoted Christabel Pankhurst's statement, 'Four working women from the north went to prison, and their husbands are enthusiastic'.

Women's prison life in 1906 was squalid and degrading. Keir Hardie demanded for the suffragettes the status of political prisoners, which would have meant better treatment, but this was refused. Several women were released by undertaking to keep the peace; Mrs Montefiore considered no cause was worth having vermin in the hair. Sylvia Pankhurst stuck it out and received some of the glare of publicity that had fallen too strongly on her more exotic sister. She made a little money by writing about her terrible experiences in Holloway Gaol. Rival suffrage movements, such as the National Union of Women's Suffrage, headed by Mrs Fawcett, praised the courage of the imprisoned suffragettes— except the Pankhursts. The non-militants did not want anything to do with that family.

The spirit of martyrdom was abroad; every progressive woman wanted to go to prison. The police obliged. Fourteen days in Holloway was as good as a testimonial, as can be seen from an advertisement in the journal *Votes for Women*: 'SUFFRAGETTE leaving Holloway Prison on the 28th inst. desires post as SECRETARY, or would undertake typewriting at home'. The small Labour Party representation in parliament watched developments with disquiet and started their own movement, the Women's Labour League. Keir Hardie was caught in the middle and disowned by the suffragette high command.

Christabel Pankhurst thought her sister Sylvia was getting too much attention, and threw herself into another Houses of Parliament battle so as to get arrested. When suffragettes were released there was joy all round; in addition Sylvia was troubled by the attentions of W. T. Stead who gave every indication of trying to ravish her. In 1907 seventy-five women and one man were arrested in an assault on the Houses of Parliament, the object of which was to seize the mace. Included in the round-up were two lady painters from Norway and Italy who had nothing to do with the show. The Pankhursts went about the country spreading the suffragette message, and Mrs Pankhurst narrowly escaped being rolled in a barrel in Newton Abbot. Cabinet ministers were cautious about open meetings, and audiences were admitted only by tickets. The suffragettes resorted to forged tickets. Accosting ministers at meetings and receptions became a new tactic.

A further attack on parliament was carried out by twenty-one suffragettes hiding in two furniture vans; funds were raised by a week of self-denial; sympathisers rattled collecting boxes at

THE HAUNTED HOUSE

By permission of the "Daily Chronicle."
The Haunted House—a vision of the House of Commons during the Suffragettes' Reign of Terror.

A newspaper cartoon indicating the prevalent attitude towards 'Votes for Women'

street corners; and John Galsworthy donated autographed copies of his books to help the cause. Winston Churchill was an especial target for suffragette hatred; he described the suffragettes as hornets, 'allying themselves with the forces of drink and reaction'. In the summer of 1908 a great demonstration was held in Hyde Park. Thirty special trains were run from the provinces. The organisers counted on an audience of 250,000. *The Times* declared that the numbers that actually came could be treble this; the *Daily Express* commented: 'It is probable that so many people never before stood in one square mass anywhere in England'. The government was challenged to do something, faced by this support. It would not. After a demonstration in Parliament Square, where the women were manhandled by the police and by roughs, two suffragettes took a cab to Downing Street and threw two stones through the window of No 10. It was the beginning of a new campaign.

A schism between militants and non-militants was splitting

the movement, but the former were winning. For the opening of parliament on 13 October 1908 it was decided to rush the House of Commons. Handbills were printed; a 'votes for women' kite was flown over the parliament building; and a steam launch, with posters announcing the forthcoming attraction, patrolled the river. For what was called the Battle of Parliament Square, the police were massed in cordons, 5 ft deep, and instructed to make as few arrests as possible. A show trial with Christabel Pankhurst fizzled out, though she was sent to prison. *Punch* thought of a way to stop demonstrations: pass an act making it a penal offence for any newspaper to publish the names or photographs of any females offending against public order.

Christabel Pankhurst and her mother were now in prison together. Mrs Pankhurst broke the rule of silence and was put in solitary confinement; she obtained the intervention of the powerful C. P. Scott of the *Manchester Guardian*. The government were at a loss what to do; Asquith's motto of 'Wait and see' hardly applied to the mounting energy of the militants. Worse was to come. When an attempt was made to eject another demonstrator from the ladies' gallery of the House of Commons, it was found that she had chained herself to the metal grille and could only be silenced by being gagged. At meetings, violence accelerated. In the streets women would spring out of vans to write slogans in chalk on the pavement before chaining themselves to railings.

The latest weapon in the suffragette armoury was the hunger strike, suggested by Mrs Pankhurst after her release. The first woman to carry out this threat whilst in prison was a sculptor, who was set free after ninety-one hours of fasting. The police combined their forces to keep the suffragettes out of Parliament Square; the women counter-attacked by breaking windows in government offices. In Liverpool, a suffragette armed with a hatchet climbed on to a roof, tore up slates, and hurled them on to the roof of a hall where the war minister, Haldane, was speaking. An iron bar was thrown through the windows of a railway carriage, and there was an epidemic of window-breaking. The offenders were forthwith sent to prison where they went on hunger strike; but now they were not released, but forcibly fed. This created a furore. Public sympathy, which had been waning, was now reviving. Lady Constance Lytton, who had once rejected militancy, was now burning with fervour and anxious to be incarcerated with other stone-throwers; she seized the opportunity to throw a stone at the radiator of Sir Walter Runciman's car, knowing that as she had a weak heart, prison and forcible feeding would probably kill her, making her the first authentic martyr of the cause and eclipsing all the achievements of the Pankhursts in one fell swoop. To her disappointment, she was released as unfit soon after being given a six-week prison sentence.

Disguised as charwomen, two women broke a stained-glass window during the Lord Mayor's Banquet; two others, disguised as street hawkers, threw an empty ginger-beer bottle into Asquith's car, and Lady Constance Lytton made her second bid for glory by dressing up in poor clothes and assuming the name of Jane Warton, seamstress, before getting arrested. Forcible feeding made her very ill, and in 1910 she had a paralytic seizure, but this did not stop her from window-breaking in 1911. In 1912 she had a stroke, and remained bedridden until her death in 1923. She wrote of herself as:

> One of that numerous gang of upper-class, leisured-class spinsters, un-
> employed, unpropertied, unendowed, uneducated . . . economically
> dependent entirely upon others . . . A maiming subserviency is so conditional
> to their very existence that it becomes an aim in itself, an ideal.[3]

Insight of this quality was rare. Lady Constance Lytton was, far more than the Pankhursts, a tragic figure in the comic opera convulsions of the movement. She was thirty-nine when she joined; when she came out of prison she was fobbed off with a £2 a week job as a junior organiser. Unlike many of her colleagues, Lady Constance believed deeply in what she was doing. The sociologist Masterman saw agitation for the vote as an 'outlet for suppressed energy and proffered devotion'; H. G. Wells dismissed the suffragettes as 'a fluttering swarm of disillusioned and wildly exasperated human beings, all a little frightened at what they were doing'.

Militant leaders of 1910. Left to right: Lady Constance Lytton, Annie Kenney, Mrs Pethick Lawrence, Christabel and Sylvia Pankhurst

In 1910 Asquith called a general election to strengthen his hand—a miscalculation as he lost a hundred seats to the Conservatives, though he retained office through the co-operation of the Irish members. The suffragettes called a truce, hoping for a more acceptable posture on the part of the government. It gave time for everyone to review the matter, and meditate upon the impact of the feminists.

Nothing shook the fabric of society so much as the activities of the militant suffragettes. It seemed as though the sex roles were being reversed, that the viragos were gaining control. The government was seen as effete and powerless, incapable of any sensible action, unable to adjust itself to changing conditions,. and more intent on retaining its dignity than making any strenuous efforts to seek for a formula. It was the case of a weak administration refusing to face the fact that it was weak, and unable to go for a compromise as this would be seen as the victory of a group of hysterical women over gentlemanly statesmanship. The extremists on both sides lost sight of the topic. Votes for women was an excuse for anarchy and repression.

The death of Edward VII threw the suffragette movement into confusion, and Christabel Pankhurst, to the distaste of sister Sylvia, proclaimed her devotion to the throne and all it stood for. With this proof that the suffragettes were human, and the prospect of another bill, significantly named the Conciliation Bill, coming before parliament, it seemed as though there was a chance for peace. The bill did not go through. The militants redoubled their efforts and on 'Black Friday' scenes of unparalleled ferocity occurred in Parliament Square, when 115 women were arrested; the police behaved with zealous brutality, striking the women with their fists, kicking them when they were down, twisting and wrenching arms, rubbing faces against the railings, and pinching breasts. The more refractory women were marched down side streets and beaten up.

Police behaviour was as much a cause for concern as the activities of the suffragettes. It confirmed the belief of the

A new phase of suffragette activity began with attacks on property, especially West End shops

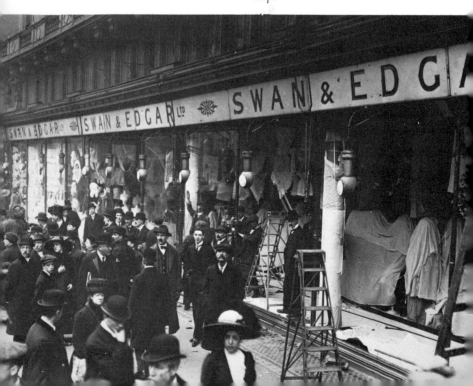

working classes that the police were instruments of government tyranny, even though their attitude towards the suffragettes was one of indifference. In previous years it seemed that the police had instructions to take things coolly, to make as few arrests as possible consistent with preserving order. A government inquiry was requested into the actions of the police, but this was refused by Churchill, for whom a confrontation with the suffragettes was becoming an obsession almost as reprehensible as suffragette violence.

Attempts on the House of Commons were self-defeating. In pitched battles the police always had the ascendancy. Attacks on property were less easily dealt with, and the West End shops were a target for women armed with hammers. Among the stores desecrated were Swan & Edgar, Marshall & Snelgrove, Jay's, Liberty's and Burberry's. It is said that in Bond Street hardly a shop window remained intact. The suffragettes turned their attentions to Knightsbridge and Kensington High Street. The frenzy of destruction was the most alarming thing that had happened yet. A desperate attempt was made to tighten the net round the ring-leaders, and Christabel Pankhurst fled to Paris and directed operations from there.

Harsh treatment had resulted in several deaths, but conditions in Holloway Gaol had eased; Sylvia Pankhurst described it as a veritable Liberty Hall. A wing had been given over to the suffragettes, and cell doors were left unlocked. The composer Ethel Smyth had joined the movement and was writing music for it, including 'March of the Women' and '1910, a Medley'.

The new phase of activities involved arson, destruction of the contents of pillar boxes and the giving of false fire alarms. Street lamps were broken, slogans were painted on the seats on Hampstead Heath, keyholes were stopped up with lead pellets, house numbers were painted out, chairs were flung into the Serpentine, cushions in railway carriages were slashed, flower-beds were damaged, bowling greens and golf courses were cut up, telegraph and telephone wires were severed, and envelopes containing snuff and red pepper were sent to every cabinet minister. The glass of a jewel-case in the Tower of London was

An attack on Buckingham Palace resulted in the arrest of Mrs Pankhurst

smashed; thirteen paintings were mutilated in Manchester Art Gallery; refreshment pavilions were burned down in Regent's Park and Kew Gardens; empty houses were destroyed, and an old cannon near Dudley Castle was fired, terrifying everyone within earshot. The bombing of Lloyd George's new house may have had some connection with votes for women, but little else in this roll call of vandalism had. It was destruction for destruction's sake, a vendetta of hatred.

The government's only satisfaction was that it had found the means to counter the hunger strikes in prisons. The Cat and Mouse Act was passed; a suffragette on hunger-strike was released on ticket-of-leave, and picked up again and put back into prison when she was strong enough.

The war between government and suffragette could have gone on continuously, but both sides experienced a sharp shock on Derby Day 1913, when Emily Wilding Davison threw herself in front of the king's horse and was killed. She had made three attempts to kill herself in prison by flinging herself over corridor railings. The movement had found its first authentic martyr. The self-aggrandisement of the Pankhursts, the repressed naughtinesses of the rank and file, the orgy of destruction were brought into perspective. And so was the reason for it all. For it became apparent that female suffrage was not very important after all. Many continental countries had it, and no disaster had resulted. A movement that arose in China demanding the vote for women had had an immediate success; the Chinese government happily passed a bill, and the women went back to their domestic duties.

The suffragette movement was a symptom of a deep sickness in the state of the country. Publicity made it seem more important than it was; indignation was artificially engendered by newspapers realising that they had a series of scoops on their hands, and when the tempers were easing off the militants did something else to incite the government, the police, and the small traders who were more interested in the fate of their plate glass windows than the whys and wherefores of votes for women.

Whether or not the suffragette campaign was, in the words of H. G. Wells, nagging and ignoble, it did prove how vulnerable England was to internal strife. Fortunately the militant workers did not grasp the lessons, nor was there a liaison between the working classes and the suffragettes, who opened an office in Bow to explain the sex war to the poor. Although the government behaved in a thoroughly block-headed way, it was psychologically checkmated by the perverse attitude of the suffragette high command. The Pankhursts simply could not be reasoned with. Their crusade became an obsession, and they were masochistic in the way they gloried over their imprisonment and the hardships they endured. The forcible feeding that so shocked the nation was the answer to hunger strikes, but the suffragettes never seemed to realise that this was, by and large, a response by a civilised regime. It did not occur to them that they could have been left to starve. Incarceration in Holloway gave meaning to the lives of scores of insipid, bored members of the traditional leisured classes. It was pathetic that old and sickly enthusiasts should have been conned into bravado, and have paid for it with their lives.

What did the suffragettes hope to achieve by getting the vote? It is interesting that few of them bothered to think about this; if they did, they thought that paradise would be opened to them. Mrs Pankhurst was sufficiently unhinged to believe that when women got the vote they would cease to menstruate. Envy of men and men's liberties had turned in upon itself.

The male supporters of women's suffrage—Shaw, Galsworthy, the poet Zangwill (licensed buffoon of the set)—shirked martyrdom; they stood on the sidelines and cheered. The Pankhursts were woolly suburbanites with an urge to destroy; responsible followers, such as the Pethick Lawrences, who backed the early endeavours and were later cast off, suffered most. Pethick Lawrence himself was held responsible for the attacks of suffragettes on private property and made bankrupt. Conveniently for the Pankhursts, they had no property that could be sequestered.

In later years, confinement in Holloway, mass demonstrations, and the glorious excitement of window-breaking in the West End became nostalgic topics. There was reticence about the fag-end of the great crusade against sex inequality. H. G. Wells dismissed it in a sentence: 'as Europe collapsed into war, the Vote was flung to women to keep them quiet',[4] an unchivalrous statement that was not correct. By mutual consent, hostilities between the militant suffragettes and the government ceased when the real war started. Most of the suffragettes then diverted their astonishing energy into helping the nation, by taking over the jobs of men who had joined up; they became window-cleaners, plumbers and tram-conductors, joined the nursing services or the new munitions industries. Other women succeeded in coping with the flood of refugees from Europe, especially Belgium, and with a measure of government assistance managed to harbour a quarter of million of them.

The suffragettes were too busy to continue campaigning for the vote, and those who had been most vociferous accepted its coming with a disarming casualness; they were amused rather than angry by Lord Curzon's apoplectic speech declaring that women voters would be the downfall of the Empire.

In February 1918 it was all over. Women had the vote. No longer would MPs automatically throw letters from lady constituents into the wastepaper basket, but it is doubtful whether female suffrage was significant for a good many years.

Notes to this chapter are on page 294.

CHAPTER SIX

ALARMS AND EXCURSIONS

The War Lords

BALFOUR, CAMPBELL-BANNERMAN, and Asquith were termed in a previous chapter as the men at the top. But were they? Perhaps it might be more correct to describe these prime ministers as men who were trying to stay at the top in the face of difficulties caused by their own supporters, who were trying to cope with national and international matters whilst striving to avoid the knife in the back. Their worries were dispersed over a range of topics, and the time at their disposal was insufficient to deal with international matters that they may well have been able to solve better than their foreign secretaries. It is not surprising that, with such pressing burdens as the upsurge of the working classes, the menace of trade unionism, the maniacal belligerence of the suffragettes, the Irish problem, and the administrative difficulties caused by the stirrings of the welfare state, prime ministers relegated the anxieties arising from foreign affairs to the lower levels of the consciousness. Why keep a foreign secretary and bark oneself?

Britain's foreign secretaries, though capable and dutiful, were not fitted for the duties that they should have carried out. They lacked percipience and ruthlessness, and strove endlessly to perpetuate the status quo, pacifying and appeasing if need be.

When they did venture into taking a firm posture, there was an even chance that they would be wrong. A prime example was the support of Sir Edward Grey for the Turkish uprising in 1908, which led to the unseating of the old order that had strong links with Britain and the setting up of a Turko-German understanding.

Actions were taken in the realm of foreign affairs before World War I that were unthinking, meaningless and arbitrary, and those who were concerned with the possible results of muddled diplomacy were often contemptuous, brash and explosive. The most ardent and colourful of the war lords was Sir John Fisher, First Sea Lord between 1904 and 1910. Born in 1841, a midshipman in 1854, Fisher had seen action on the China station. He became the protegé of Admiral James Hope, whose motto was 'favouritism is the secret of efficiency'. It was a motto Fisher never forgot.

At the first opportunity Hope promoted Fisher to lieutenant; in 1869 Fisher became a commander and went back to China, and in 1872 he returned to Britain and specialised in torpedo warfare. In 1881 he was appointed to command *Inflexible*, the largest ship in the Royal Navy, built in 1876 with 18in-thick armour-plating. In 1882 he took part in the bombardment of Alexandria, organised the first armoured train and commanded it in various skirmishes with the Egyptians. After being invalided home, he collaborated with journalist W. T. Stead in *The Truth about the Navy*. In 1886 Fisher was appointed Director of Naval Ordnance; five years later he became Admiral-Superintendent of Portsmouth Dockyard, and gradually rose from Third Sea Lord to become First Sea Lord in 1904.

Fisher's background shows that here was a man, experienced in both administration and command, who knew what he was talking about. Arrogant and overbearing, with a delight in making enemies in politics and within the service, he perhaps could have saved Britain from involvement in the war, by the simple expedient of knocking Germany out before she had re-armed, by 'copenhagening' the German fleet in harbour without warning of war. Fisher was an early disciple of the principle of the first strike. His attitude was exemplified by a sequence of

Britain felt safe in the care of the Royal Navy. It was axiomatic that it was the best in the world

apophthegms published in 1919—'Think in Oceans—shoot at sight', 'Surprise—the pith and marrow of war', 'Rashness in war is Prudence, Prudence in war is Imbecility', 'Hit first! Hit hard! Keep on hitting!' 'The three requisites for success—Ruthless, Relentless, Remorseless'.[1]

To his contemporaries, having Fisher about was akin to harbouring Attila the Hun. In the delicate mincing world of international diplomacy he was seen as a savage incomprehensible intruder. The army hated him; he saw the army as an appendix to the navy, and a minor appendix at that.

When he took over the navy in 1904 he decided that he had to be cruel to be kind. Since 1815 the navy had been resting on its laurels; only in 1860 was hanging from the yard-arm abolished, only in 1880 had flogging with the cat-o'-nine-tails been suspended. The fleet was antiquated and obsolete, and the first thing to do was to get rid of the relics of a vanished age, which amounted to 154 ships including seventeen battleships. These were to be replaced with just four types of vessel, battleships with a speed of 21 knots, armoured cruisers, destroyers with a speed of 36 knots, and submarines. The emphasis on future ships was on big guns and speed, rather than on armour plating.

The navy would be disposed differently, with ships being withdrawn from the Mediterranean and placed in the North Sea, directly facing the ultimate enemy, Germany. At a time when many statesmen wondered which nation Britain would fight, Fisher had no doubt at all. He demanded absolute readiness for war; he was disgusted that for a third of the year the navy was in Portsmouth Harbour, disorganised and languishing.

Fisher's most startling coup was to introduce *Dreadnought*, his first super-ship. Built in eleven months, *Dreadnought* rendered obsolete every other warship in the world, including those in the Royal Navy. Fisher's design team did not stop there; it was responsible for the birth of Fisher's second category, the armoured cruiser, which was large and very fast. These vessels, renamed battle-cruisers in 1912, did not live up to expectation as they were used in situations that Fisher deplored, where their speed proved of little avail. The dreadnoughts and the armoured

Lord Fisher declared that the submarine would accomplish a vast revolution in naval warfare, but the Admiralty dragged its feet, and the Germans proved that Fisher was right

cruisers only made complete sense in the context of Fisher's aggressive policies, and historically their evolution was less important than his anticipation of the role of the submarine.

Having studied the naval war between Japan and Russia in 1904, Fisher realised that the Japanese won because their ships were marginally faster than those of the Russians. In one of his cogent angry letters, dated 20 April 1904, he declared that the war would have swung the other way if the Russians had had submarines: 'It's astounding to me, *perfectly astounding*, how the very best amongst us absolutely fail to realise the vast impending revolution in naval warfare and naval strategy that the submarine will accomplish!'[2]

Fisher had been an advocate of the torpedo since 1872, and realised its suitability as a weapon for the submarine. In 1903 he had watched a demonstration in Portsmouth Harbour, in which the old ironclad *Belleisle* had been sent to the bottom in seven minutes by a torpedo, even though the ship had been specially strengthened. By the time Fisher left the Admiralty in 1910, he had achieved the construction of sixty-one submarines. Without him, the navy reverted to its apathy, and when he returned in 1914 the number of submarines had decreased to fifty-three, and of twenty-one being built only five were any good.

The dreadnoughts were a mixed blessing, for they encouraged Germany to build an equivalent fleet. The British naval estimates had risen from £23,778,400 in 1898–9 to £36,889,000 in 1904–5, and although the scrapping of obsolete ships had effected some economies in upkeep, there was a clamour to keep the expense down—a clamour that rose to a roar when the Liberals took over. The Liberals needed the money for their social services scheme. The cutback on the building of dreadnoughts was countered by the Admiralty, and a compromise was reached.

To some extent, the dreadnoughts were status symbols, designed to overawe the Germans. They were seen as the One Simple Answer. Fisher did not see the dichotomy between his own 1904 views on the supremacy of the submarine and the

Deck A

„ B

„ C

„ D

„ E

„ F

Transverse Section of the Cunarder "CARMANIA."

Deck A—Promenades and Lounge.
  „   B—Promenades, Drawing Room and State Rooms *en Suite.*
  „   C—Promenades, State Rooms, and Dome of Saloon.

Deck D—Dining Saloon.
  „   E—Second Class State Rooms.
  „   F—Third Class Accommodation.

In 1903 German passenger liners crossed the Atlantic in record time; the Cunard Steamship Co Ltd countered this with a massive shipbuilding programme backed by government money. This is a cut-out section of one of their ships

construction of dreadnoughts that were the born victims of offensive submarine warfare. The enthusiasm of the government for the dreadnought is only fully understandable when one considers what was happening in the world of passenger liners. In 1903 the Germans had won two blue ribands for crossing the Atlantic in record time. The instinctive response to this had been a loan by the government of £2,600,000 at a very low rate of interest for the building of two turbine vessels with an anticipated speed of 25 knots, the *Mauretania* and the *Lusitania*. In 1907 a British passenger liner crossed the Atlantic in a time that was not bettered until 1929. To the Edwardians it was inconceivable that anyone but the British could be supreme at anything to do with the sea.

The modernisation of the navy was accompanied by far-reaching reforms in structure and administration, and here Fisher came up against the full forces of reaction, headed by Admiral Lord Charles Beresford, who denounced Fisher's North Sea policy as a fraud upon the public and a danger to the Empire, and demanded an official inquiry into Admiralty policy. This acrimonious situation was much enjoyed by the Germans who realised that Fisher was a very real threat to them, and that while he was in control of naval fortunes the possibility of a first strike was always possible. It was well-known that he had the ear of Edward VII, who relished the rough-talking, rumbustious First Sea Lord. Those with a long memory backed the king against Beresford.

From 1905 to 1907, during the time of the feud with Fisher, Admiral Beresford had been in command of the Mediterranean Fleet. Fisher had little interest in the Mediterranean, as it was too far away from the enemy, Germany, whose only interest in the Mediterranean was on behalf of its ally, Austria, who had a base at Fiume on the Adriatic. Beresford was slightly younger than Fisher, but although he was sixty he preserved some of the qualities of his youth, when he was a bosom friend of Edward VII, then the Prince of Wales. His father was the celebrated rake, the Marquis of Waterford, and Beresford had inherited the family high spirits and penchant for the gay life.

He shared with Prince Edward the affections of the Countess of Warwick. Beresford's wife had got hold of a letter from Lady Warwick to Beresford, and was indulging in a little discreet blackmail. The Prince of Wales became involved in the intrigue, and in 1890 Beresford called at Marlborough House and accused him of being a blackguard and a coward, shaking his fist in the prince's face. Edward was not a man to let such affronts be forgotten. It was perhaps not surprising that Beresford lost the duel with Fisher, and was ordered to haul down his flag.

To Fisher this defeat of his rival was as important as a judicious 'copenhagening' of a foreign fleet, but his boastful demeanour alienated many who had regarded him highly. His dreadnought policy was also showing the kind of dividends no one welcomed. The year was 1909; reports were coming in that the Germans would have dreadnought parity by 1912. Four battleships a year had been planned; the Admiralty now wanted six and, when even more alarming intelligence came, put this demand up to eight, a demand that was refused by Lloyd George and Winston Churchill. To the Conservative opposition, the opportunity was too good to miss, and they instigated a motto, 'We want eight, and we won't wait'. A compromise was reached, but the country looked round for a scapegoat and found one in Fisher. It was claimed that he had been caught on the hop by the German acceleration in ship building. The inquiry that Beresford had called for was granted, and although Beresford was rapped over the knuckles for his ungentlemanly behaviour, and although the Admiralty was exonerated, Fisher was chided for his secrecy, for his policy of keeping his own plans to himself. This chill reprimand encouraged Fisher to resign, and for four vital years he was obliged to sit on the sidelines and fume. When he was recalled, it was too late for his particular strategy: the capture of Heligoland—which had aimlessly been exchanged not so many years previously for Zanzibar and was now an important cog in the German war machine—and the landing of an amphibious force on the Baltic coast for a direct assault upon Berlin.

His concept of the army was as a bullet fired by the navy. But by 1914 France, who had little trust in naval power, had her way—the British Army was to be an auxiliary of the French, to fight uncomplainingly on their left flank.

Fisher had made a prestige navy into a fighting navy. Could anything be done with the army after the Boer War had shown it to be a creaking anachronism? It was an army in which Guards officers based in London lived at home or in clubs, played cricket or tennis, and were regular visitors to fashionable Sandown Park, Hurlingham or Ranelagh. It was considered rather odd if a subaltern could not get four months leave a year, odder still for a captain to spend more than six months in the year anywhere near his regiment. The hunting-shooting seasons saw the flight not only of foxes and various small birds but of Guards officers into the great outdoors. No officer could live on his pay: a Guards officer needed £300 over and above that, and an officer in the prestigious 10th Hussars £500 extra on top of his pay.

It was an army in which the soldiers spent their lives drilling and scrubbing out their quarters, conditioned to blind obedience to an officer élite. 'We make the private soldier in many cases a fool', admitted one officer, 'because we start with the assumption that he is a fool'.[3] The Boer War, said Sir Alfred Milner, had been 'an avalanche of military incompetence'. Staff work had been haphazard, manoeuvres and marches were carried out in a stilted clumsy manner, and the weapons and equipment provided were inferior to those of the enemy. It had taken a long time for the idea to sink in among commanders in the field that the British Army was not fighting half-naked savages with spears but wily white men from a good European stock.

The government at the outset of the South African war did not take the Boers seriously. The commander-in-chief, Lord Wolseley, complained, 'I always come away from these meetings of Ministers in saddened frame of mind when I have listened for some time to the military folly talked by most of those who comprise that Committee . . . The whole time was taken up in worrying over the number of field guns we should order, and the machinery we should erect to make guns, ammunition etc'.[4]

Lord Lansdowne, secretary for war 1895–1900, proved as useless in that role as he was as foreign secretary (1900–5). He had gone to the War Office 'with the comfortable knowledge that nothing was required of him beyond *vis inertiae*. Then unfortunately the South African hostilities supervened. Long before their conclusion Lord Lansdowne had sagaciously removed himself to another sphere'.[5]

Into the post left vacant jumped another time-server, William Brodrick, a man desperately anxious for office. Observers recorded that Brodrick seemed to take a gloomy pleasure in informing the House of Commons that the war was going very badly. Brodrick was diligent in reorganisation; Winston Churchill described how Brodrick made army corps 'by a mental process and a scratch of the pen'. His management was denounced as 'mess, muddle and make-believe'. Six army corps dreamed up on paper, a concession to panic, did not prevent his reluctant departure to the India Office in 1903. The kiss of death had been given by King Edward's confidant, Lord Esher: 'A very capable man, rendered incapable by circumstances—by military officials, all with ill-defined duties, all pulling different ways instead of all pulling together'.[6]

Lord Esher himself wisely avoided being made secretary for war, the graveyard of reputations, and the job fell to H. O. Arnold-Forster, whom the king cordially disliked. He complained to the prime minister that Arnold-Forster lacked polish and was socially uncouth, and Balfour agreed, saying that Mr Forster's manner was not his strong point, 'but though he wants manner, he does not want *tact*'. The prime minister, however, happy that somebody had taken on the post, was too sanguine, for Arnold-Forster went into the job 'with the enthusiasm of the apostle and the spirit of the martyr; he suffers from a superexcitation of the nerves such as six hundred years ago produced the *stigmata* and other evidences of an overheated imagination'.[7]

Arnold-Forster was no more fit to reform the army than the unfortunate Brodrick, and alienated not only the king but the officer class when he abolished inter-regimental polo tournaments. He spent much of his time probing into his predecessors'

files, and undoing what they had done. There was the affair of
the jam. There had been 1,350,816 tins of it, holding a pound
each. Arnold-Forster discovered with triumph that the pound
had been an apothecary's pound of twelve ounces, and created
something of a stir by his diligence in uncovering the inconceivably
uninteresting. His army reform plans were inconsequential and
muddled. The sceptics looked at his background: nephew of the
poet Arnold, and adopted son of W. E. Forster, pioneer of
elementary education. Arnold-Forster did not wear his hyphenated
name with the aplomb of a Campbell-Bannerman. He had also
been unfortunate enough to write schoolbooks, a book called
the *Citizen's Reader*, and the weirdly entitled *In a Conning Tower*,
mistakenly thought by more than one indignant buyer to be
written by a naval officer.

Alternatively arrogant and subservient, Arnold-Forster was
relentlessly doomed as soon as he crossed the threshold of the
War Office. Brodrick had been the butt of Winston Churchill,
who had sardonically demolished the myth of the six army
corps: 'The first three army corps are incomplete, the fourth
consists of Sir Archibald Hunter, the fifth is in the War Office
file, and the sixth Mr. Brodrick has taken with him in his
pocket on his trip to the Mediterranean'.[8] But Arnold-Forster
was more vulnerable. For, unlike Brodrick, he was slightly
common, and his quietus was dealt by the king's secretary,
Knollys, in a letter to Esher, on 1 December 1904, though it
took some time to bundle out the body:

> You will probably agree with me that it would not be judicious for the King
> to press Arnold-Forster too hard, as if circumstances, owing to the way in
> which he is behaving, obliged him to resign, it would be unfortunate if his
> friends (I suppose he has *some!*) went about saying he was got rid of by the
> King, or to please H.M.[9]

These then were the war lords of the first half of the Edwardian
age—Lansdowne, Brodrick and Arnold-Forster, presided over
by the bland Balfour. They were collectively too little regarded
to involve Britain in any dangerous adventure. They were minor
figures by any standard, basking in the glories of state.

Their low calibre was reflected by the attitude of the prime minister, Balfour, who wished to rule with the minimum of fuss and to ignore the threat of Germany. There was no army officer of the quality of Fisher to shake the war ministers into animation. Wolseley and Roberts were old and unenthusiastic. Such re-armament as had taken place after the Boer War, when artillery was re-examined and ground troops equipped with the short Lee-Enfield, had been carried out not by the ministers but by their subordinates, with a vague nod of approval from above.

The man who replaced the unfortunate Arnold-Forster was Richard Haldane. He had met Asquith when he was a barrister, and while recovering from illness Haldane paid frequent visits to Asquith's house in Hampstead, where he met the Liberal intellectuals. Haldane was orientated to German thought—Campbell-Bannerman's nickname for him was Schopenhauer—and he also took an interest in the lower levels of society and flirted dispassionately with socialism. He was on amiable terms with the Fabian Society, whom he expected to find a group of Utopian faddists bent on bloody revolution and instead discovered a bunch of wordy theorists with whom he could swap banter.

Haldane gradually moved into the power centres of liberalism; he and Asquith gave annual dinners at the Blue Posts, Cork Street, at which the coming generation of statesmen were present—Balfour, Rosebery, Curzon and Grey. His private life was less satisfactory, and he was jilted by Miss Munro Ferguson.

A visit to Germany in 1890 confirmed Haldane in his belief in Teutonic organisation, and during the Boer War he was distinctly a hawk. Asquith looked on him as the think tank for the Liberal party, and there was no question that Haldane was destined for high office. Despite their aversion to Campbell-Bannerman as Liberal prime minister, Asquith, Haldane and Grey each served under him, though Haldane did not get the post he wanted. Haldane asked, 'What about the War Office?' Campbell-Bannerman retorted, 'Nobody will touch it with a pole'. Haldane took up the challenge.

His aim was a compact fighting army, and, with the Liberal preoccupation with economy and money for the poor, Haldane

" A Little British Army, etc. "

HALDANE, R.A. (or rather R.B.): "There—now I call that a
very neat job"

*The press welcomed Haldane's Territorial Army, and this cartoon was typical of
many of the time*

had to consider two factors—saving and efficiency. Out were the
expensively-maintained coastal defence batteries that would
accomplish nothing, no matter how a war went, and out too
were garrisons in such places as St Helena and China. The
militia were to be abolished and replaced by a territorial army,
and there would be a reduction in the strength of the Guards.
This created a furore, but the former prime minister, Balfour,
backed Haldane's reforms, having recognised that the War
Office had done little when he was in office.

Despite his affection for Germany, Haldane was aware that
it was from that quarter that danger would arise. On 8 January
1906 Grey wrote to him, 'Persistent reports and little indications
keep reaching me that Germany means to attack France in the
spring'. Grey's intelligence service was no more efficient than
that of his undistinguished predecessors, but dimly he was
discerning the mood. If any of his colleagues sensed the same
thing they took care to conceal it, preferably from themselves.
The more reactionary Liberals regretted that such an acute,

intelligent man had been put in at the War Office, though they
were partly mollified by the 1907–8 army estimates, which were
down on the previous year.

Grey was happy to see Haldane go off on a visit to Germany
instead of him, a trip encouraged by King Edward, who got on
well with Haldane. Unlike his predecessors, Haldane was
neither awkward nor prickly, and this stood him in good stead
in Germany, where he was allowed to examine at close quarters
the organisation of the Berlin War Office. He met von Moltke,
the nephew of the great German military tactician, who praised
Kitchener. The kaiser was impressed by Haldane, and they
discussed the new British Army in which the German ruler
appeared to take a brotherly interest. By the time Haldane came
back, he had reached a *modus vivendi* with the Germans, though
this was not to be built upon.

Each in his own way, Haldane and Fisher were creating a
modern military machine, but there was no co-operation between
the two services. Fisher declared that Haldane had fallen into
the 'vulgar error' of imagining that the army and navy were run
in more or less the same way, and talked 'twaddle'. Haldane
deplored Fisher's method of keeping his plans to himself.
Haldane also had his own economy-mad colleagues in the
cabinet to contend with, as well as the aged Lord Roberts, who
was stomping the country seeking to denigrate the territorial
army. The only thing Britain could do to save herself, he
maintained, was to start conscription. As things were, the
country could not resist invasion. The word invasion triggered
off a number of predictable responses, and there was a spate of
spy stories. It was said that the Germans had thousands of
rifles in a cellar of a bank near Charing Cross, ready to be
taken up by German sympathisers when the grey hordes landed
on the coast; and the appearance of an airship in the skies over
London created terror, though it was only advertising some
commodity.

These stories were widely reported in the sensational newspapers. The kaiser got to hear of them and added his own iota of
confusion, saying that it would be a good idea to drop mines in

the Thames and the Solent when the fleet was congregating, a comment that made its way back to London to create more heartache.

Lord Roberts had been in the army since 1851, starting off in the Indian Army where he had won the VC. He did well in wars in Abyssinia and Afghanistan, and after the set-backs in the Boer War he was sent out to South Africa, being one of the few men to emerge from that mêlée with any credit. 'Bobs' was the darling of the troops, immeasurably better known to the rank and file than Haldane, though Haldane had created an excellent impression among the higher ranks. No one doubted Roberts' worth or his personal courage; he was the 'hero of innumerable adventures that might have been specially enacted to please the boys of a preparatory school'.[10]

There was little question that now Roberts was a liability rather than an asset. He got the ear of the king, warning him that Haldane's model army was the laughing stock of Europe and that the territorial army would be useless in a war because of its defective training.

A more formidable rival was Lord Kitchener, who was mercifully commander in chief in India and thus a long way away. Taciturn and severe, it was said of Kitchener that he had never spoken to a private soldier, that his family treated him with awe rather than affection, and that he was a war machine on two legs. Furthermore, Kitchener did not want to come home as he was hoping to become viceroy. However, it was clear that he did not hold Haldane in very high regard, dismissing him as an unpractical theorist and the territorial army as a bunch of play-boys who would come to nothing. Basically Kitchener did not like civilians; he would have preferred the administration of the army to be out of the hands of politicians. Nor did he like the navy; the navy was an instrument to transport a vast army across the English Channel, and whether or not Haldane wanted a vast army there would have to be one, for the war with Germany would be long and arduous, calling for a degree of endurance only anticipated by the American Civil War. Kitchener had little confidence in the French: the Germans would 'walk through the

French Officer: "THE GREAT THING IS, AFTER ALL,
MY COMRADE, DIGNITY AND ELEGANCE."
(A Drawing by Jean Victor Bates.)

Lord Kitchener did not like civilians, the Royal Navy, or the Territorial Army. In the event of war he thought the Germans would walk through the French lines 'like partridges'. Cartoonists found the French army funny rather than fearsome

French line like partridges'. But all this was academic; it was more important to be viceroy of India, a country whose role was an agreeable subjugation.

Nevertheless, the territorial army arrived. In June 1909 the king presented colours to 108 territorial battalions at Windsor. It was the outcome, wrote Haldane, of three years of missionary enterprise.

The war, when it came, ran according to the grim forecast of Kitchener. The territorial army provided a cadre after the British Expeditionary Force—the best trained army in Europe, thanks to Haldane—had been decimated. Haldane did the best he could under the conditions imposed upon him: limited expenditure and no conscription. Clever as he was, he was no military tactician; he could not have foreseen that the supremacy of small-arms fire and the machine-gun would inaugurate the phenomenon of trench warfare, and that defence and offence would be evenly matched. Bedevilled by opposition from a section of the army and some of his own party, not to mention the Conservatives, Haldane provided a sharply-honed weapon that was too subtle for the situation. Fisher had envisaged a navy that would operate with such a force as Haldane had created. They were both prophets of the next war but one.

The American Threat

Britain acquired her Empire in a prolonged fit of absentmindedness, and it was a surprise to many that there were profits to reap as well as thousands of square miles to police. The finding of gold in Australia and South Africa enriched the home country, and India was plundered with endless zest. Britain's dominant trade position and her unique geographical location made the policy of splendid isolation possible, but as the nineteenth century drew to a close there were indications that other nations wished to have a bite of the cherry. In a speech at Leeds in 1888 Lord Rosebery said: 'The other powers are beginning a career of colonial aggrandizement. We formerly did not have to trouble ourselves with colonial questions, because we had a monopoly of colonies. That monopoly has ceased'.[1]

By that time the French were out of the race, following their definitive defeat in the Franco-Prussian War, and their falling behind in industrial reorganisation—partly due to the absence of a home supply of coal. France was still the hereditary foe, but she was treated like the grand old warrior who had gone to seed, and if there was enmity it was tepid. She had her empire, a good deal less profitable even on a pro rata basis than Britain's, and although she was hanging on to it, there was a certain despair, as though the Republic was not certain that she could. Germany was another matter. She was a late starter; the assortment of states that had formed Germany before the unification had made a colonial policy impossible.

The Germans were irked by Britain's refusal even to consider that they should have an empire, and in 1885 Bismarck was incensed by the British foreign secretary's insistence that British friendliness towards Germany was incompatible with a German pursuit of a colonial policy. 'We should be curious to learn', wrote Bismarck sardonically to his minister in London, 'why the right to colonize, which England uses to the fullest extent, should be denied to us'. As Germany was becoming industrialised at a faster rate than England, the conditions for a confrontation were already being built up.

But these conditions were already being built up elsewhere—in the United States. The Americans had shrugged off in an amazing way the after-effects of the Civil War, which had killed 600,000 of their young men, and although there was a great slump in 1873 and another one in 1893 (when there were 15,000 business failures and 574 banks went broke) the march of America towards commercial parity with Britain was unnervingly steady.

The first signs of the US colonial mentality were seen in 1878, when the country of Colombia granted a concession to a French company to drive a canal through the isthmus of Panama. President Hayes saw this as a threat to the United States, and that such a canal must be under the control of America and 'virtually a part of the coast-line of the United States'. Shortly afterwards the United States interfered in a conflict between Chile and Peru; this almost caused a war between Chile and the United States when crew from an American ship were killed in Valparaiso.

The key to an overseas empire was a supply of coaling stations. For a fleet that depended on steam, these were vital. America saw the Pacific as its area of influence, and a convenient coaling station, the Samoan Islands, was divided between the United States, Britain and Germany, though this arrangement proved so difficult that in 1900 Britain withdrew from the islands, receiving concessions from Germany in other parts of the world.

But the most dangerous events of the time so far as Britain was concerned occurred not in the Samoan Islands, nor Alaska (bought from Russia in 1867), but in Cuba. Cuba was under Spanish rule, and in 1895 a revolt broke out against the Madrid government, which was not quelled even though 200,000 Spanish soldiers were sent to the island. The Cubans adopted guerilla tactics, and the wire entanglements and blockhouses built by the Spaniards failed dismally to cope with the insurgents. The Spaniards then took to organising concentration camps, in which the death rate arising from brutality and disease was very high.

The Americans watched the situation with unease, for the rebels were burning the sugar plantations, and American business had a $50 million stake in sugar, tobacco and iron. By 1897 Cuba was in a condition of anarchy, and militant Americans were in favour of going in and cleaning up the mess. They were actively abetted by the sensationalist press, which drummed up a war, though for a time it was thought that reason would prevail. An American warship paid a 'goodwill' visit to Havana, to reassure American residents and businessmen that they had not been forgotten, and in return a Spanish cruiser visited New York. These amiable gestures were forgotten when the Hearst press published an indiscreet letter from the Spanish minister in Washington condemning the president of the United States as weak and a bidder for the admiration of the rabble. Yet even this, despite the bellicosity of Theodore Roosevelt, a devotee of war and slaughter and all manly sports, would not have led to war. In February 1898 the battleship *Maine* was destroyed probably by a mine in an explosion in the harbour of Havana, and 260 men died. Although President McKinley and the Spanish government were desperately trying to avoid war, war remorselessly came.

It was welcomed by the Hearst press and by American business. Senator Thurston of Nebraska was unapologetic: 'War with Spain would increase the business and earnings of every American railroad, it would increase the output of every American factory, it would stimulate every branch of industry and domestic commerce'.[2] There were other reasons; the Americans were suffering from a sense of inferiority, a sense of deprivation. They had not fought, except amongst themselves, since they had thrown the British out in the War of Independence. Why should they not enjoy themselves at the expense of the Spaniards, a nation long in decline? Spain had an empire. They would take it away from her and go into the colonial business themselves. Probably the Europeans, who saw all this going on, were distressed because the Americans had got in first.

Not surprisingly the Spanish Government backed down in every conceivable way, willing to let the Americans walk over them in any manner they pleased, but President McKinley, realising that a satisfactory and convenient war would guarantee him office for a second term, did not lay the vital documents before Congress. The Spanish-American War was brief and almost bloodless. It was declared on 19 April 1898 and on 1 May the Spanish fleet was destroyed in the Philippines; an army was sent to Cuba, landing at Santiago instead of Havana, 700 miles nearer the United States, and in August it was all over. The Americans lost in battle 379 soldiers and fewer than twenty sailors, despite military maladministration that vied with that of the British in the Boer War.

It was an easy, if not a particularly efficient way to win colonies. H. W. Nevinson, the journalist, was in Spain covering that end of the operation. There was little for him to do, for the Spanish heart was not in the war; the best Spanish battleships were still in harbour. They had not sailed and they had no intention of sailing.

The Philippines, Puerto Rico and Guam were ceded outright to the Americans. Cuba was temporarily occupied until an independent government, more amenable to the Americans than the Spanish administration, was installed. This coup, allied with an incident that occurred in 1895 in Venezuela—the United States accused Britain of attempting to control Venezuela when a difference of opinion arose relating to the border between Venezuela and British Guiana—brought America to the attention of Britain in no uncertain manner.

As a result of the Spanish-American War the Americans found they were treated with a good deal more respect. The militarists decided that they liked empire-building, even though there were inconveniences attached to the acquisition of foreign lands—the Philippinos did not like the Americans any more than the Spaniards, and rose up against them. Unfortunately for the United States, the world had already been carved up between the European powers, and the only way to increase territory was to tackle the empire of some power that had once been great, but was now in decline. It is possible that the French empire was considered, but even the most enthusiastic of imperialist powers blenched at the prospect of acquiring the thousands of square miles of sparsely inhabited African desert, with a doubtful supply of minerals beneath the ground.

But what about Holland, with its rich empire in the East Indies? America had bases in the Philippines for any attack on Sumatra or Java. But there were now political inhibitions about taking the territories of other countries and it would be difficult to find a pretext for annexing the Dutch East Indies.

Suspicion of American motives had been felt in Britain from about 1895. In March 1898 Arnold Bennett was present at a discussion between the owner of the magazine *Woman* and the editor of the *Morning Post*. They 'suddenly began to talk about the chances of war. I was astonished at the eagerness for it, and the certainty with which they predicted where and between whom it would occur . . . We ought to have fought the U.S.A. a year or two ago, when they wanted a war. We should have thrashed them easily, and that would have cleared the air of the war cloud'.[3]

Did the United States want a war with Britain? In December 1895, Theodore Roosevelt wrote to Cabot Lodge: 'Let the fight come if it must. I don't care whether our sea-board cities are bombarded or not; we would take Canada'.[4]

Perhaps the most important factor that prevented a conflict at this time was that although America had most of the hallmarks of an imperialist power she lacked economic incentive. She did not seek fresh markets for her goods. In 1900 the United States exported four per cent of her manufactures, while the figure for Germany was twelve per cent and Britain twenty-five per cent. Had the United States wanted to export more manufactured goods she would have had no difficulty in finding markets, for she was well ahead in the products of the industrial age, such as typewriters, and sewing-machines (in both of which America had the virtual monopoly), telephones and other advanced equipment.

The factor that could have swung the balance in favour of open conflict between America and Britain would have been an alliance between Germany and Britain. It is significant that Joseph Chamberlain, the colonial secretary, gradually dropped his dream of such an alliance; he knew the temper of America well, as he was married to an American. It is interesting to speculate on what would have happened had America gone to war with the combined forces of Germany and Britain, for unlike both those countries the United States only kept a small standing army, numbering fewer than 100,000 men in 1900. It is even more interesting to see that such a war was a contingency, recognised by men who afterwards would have been aghast at such a possibility.

The Edwardian age opened with America emerging as a classic imperialist power, the features of which were laid down by Lenin:

1 The concentration of production and capital, developed to such a high stage that it has created monopolies, which play a decisive role in economic life.
2 The merging of bank capital with industrial capital and the creation, on the basis of this 'finance capital' of a financial oligarchy.
3 The export of capital as distinguished from the export of commodities, becomes of particularly great importance.
4 International monopoly combines of capitalists are formed which divide up the world. [5]

Despite the warlike utterances of a number of American statesmen, there was a greater fund of goodwill in America towards Britain than Britain believed. The US government did not attempt to make capital out of the Boer War, despite the attempts of Irish-Americans to raise an Irish brigade to fight the British in South Africa. Congress petitions for intervention or mediation came to nothing.

There was still sufficient apprehension in Britain, however, to merit comment. In July 1902 the Dutch press feared that a pretext might be sought by Britain for seizing the Dutch East Indies, to prevent them being taken over by America or Germany, both of which had colonies near by. By this time, however, anxiety had shifted from American politics to American business, represented by the gigantic figure of J. P. Morgan.

After the great crash of 1893, Morgan had supplied the United States government with $62 million to avert utter catastrophe, and in 1901 Morgan and his associates formed the United States Steel Corporation, capitalized at $1,321 million, which controlled sixty per cent of the nation's steel-making capacity. In 1902 Morgan bought a number of British shipping lines. British industry was long-established and old-fashioned. It bobbed about on the pond of free trade and was not helped, as industry was in the United States and Germany, by an elaborate screen of protective tariffs. Even such dominating firms in the world of heavy industry as Armstrong Whitworth and Vickers were dwarfed by the American combines.

The uneasiness of Britain was reflected in the popular press. In May 1901 *The King* magazine published a mock proclamation:

> Whereas we, Pierpont Morgan I., have now acquired, obtained, and taken possession of the United Kingdom, with all its dependencies, plantations and appurtenances in full suzerainty for US, our Heirs and Successors, till further orders, and Whereas WE are apprised, guess, calculate and suspect that unregistered English persons are still at large in this our Kingdom . . .

And in the gossip column of the same paper: 'Mr. J. Pierpont Morgan is staying in Paris, and will shortly visit Aix-les-Bains, where he is very popular. He has not yet decided which town he will buy'.

It was fortunate that the 'American invasion', as it was known, encompassed not only businessmen:

On the whole, I think the influx of the American element into English society has done good rather than harm, whilst there are many old families which, both in mind and pocket, have been completely revivified by prudent marriages with American brides . . . Bright and vivacious, it may with justice be said that it is by the American girl that we have been conquered . . .[6]

The businessmen, as it turned out, were less alarming than had been anticipated and, even to the old school, presented a refreshing contrast to their English equivalents. The rich Americans had a peculiar penchant for philanthropy, incomprehensible to English businessmen who diligently kept their money to themselves. Andrew Carnegie, a big figure in steel, poured thousands of pounds into higher education in Scotland. In this altruistic field, the Americans were following the example of George Peabody (1795–1869) who gave half a million dollars towards building tenements for the London poor.

As the Edwardian age proceeded, the American threat diminished, until the mere idea of an armed conflict between Britain and America became laughable, though the Germans tried to stir up trouble in the United States when it was clear to them that an alliance with Britain was out of the question. Troublesome matters that arose during the decade was amicably settled; a certain rapport was awkwardly founded between King Edward and President Theodore Roosevelt, who had settled down after his earlier rumbustious days as a fighter for Cuban freedom and an advocate of war. Grey, the foreign secretary, handled the Americans with considerably more ease than he dealt with the European powers. Although a certain bitterness was felt when the American slump of 1907 reacted sharply on the British economy, it was seen more and more that British and American interests coincided. In March 1908, Theodore Roosevelt wrote to Arthur Balfour that he had 'ugly doubts as to what may befall our modern civilization'.[7] Ten years earlier he would not have cared.

In Search of an Ally

England at the start of the Edwardian period was in the position of a neurotic old lady who suddenly feels lonely. She had shrugged off friends for twenty years, and now that she wanted some, whom could she trust? The nicest kind of friends were those who spoke the same language (the Americans) or who belonged to the same family (the Germans), but these were always putting provisos in the way, and in the end she had to settle for someone else, someone who had been a bit of a bother in the past, but who was probably not too bad after all. The French too were lonely and disconsolate.

Genuine friendships were hard to come by in 1901, and British friendship was not especially welcome. Britain was suspect militarily, her economy was static, and her people, as seen from the other side of the channel, were decadent. According to the British newspapers, people would not fight except with their mouths; industrialists, less concerned with patriotism than the main chance, sold arms to the enemy and provided brown paper boots to the army; and there was a commercial policy of absolute indifference and indolence. The only factor that was incalculable was the Royal Navy, seemingly invincible.

When it was clear that the entente cordiale between France and Britain was on, misunderstandings were cleared up. In 1904 a bargain was struck with France that she could have a free hand in Morocco if Britain were allowed a free hand in Egypt. This understanding had been forecast by *The Times* in March 1903:

> Here popular feeling has been altered very decidedly in favour of France, perhaps not without regard to the contrasted attitude taken up by another nation . . . the controverted questions which agitate the relations of France and England are not of the first order of importance . . . quite trifling in comparison with the great interests which both have in common.

The Russo-Japanese War provided a test of the friendship. Britain had previously signed a treaty with Japan, but France had a long-standing treaty with Russia. *The Economist* put the dilemma well: those who were lauding the Japanese victories were advised to 'moderate their exultation over Russian defeats. After all they are the defeats sustained by the friend of a friend'. Nor did the British acclaim too loudly their pleasure that the Russians did not get the terminus of the Trans-Siberian Railway they wanted (ostensibly the reason for the conflict, though Japan was more interested in the acquisition of Korea). The Japanese victory lessened the Russian threat to India. Other nations were not too sorry about the Russian humiliation; although America faced Russia across the Bering sea. As the war went on there was some American rethinking: in August 1905, Cabot Lodge wrote to Roosevelt that it was not in the American interest 'to have Russia too completely crippled'.

It was now felt that Britain could approach Russia, and the way was paved by offering a loan. A convention was held in 1907 in which Tibet, Afghanistan and Persia was recognized by both parties as buffer states. Persia, the tricky one of these three, was divided into a large Russian zone, a small British zone, and a neutral zone in the middle. In 1909 the Persians got rid of a particularly obnoxious shah, and the Russian troops went in and put him back. As a bonus, they shelled Persia's most sacred shrine. But Russia was now a friend, and furthermore a friend who was building up her already vast army, and reinforcing her strategic railway systems with cash supplied by France.

Many cynical politicians thought that with such a friend as Tsarist Russia Britain could well do without any enemies. Russia had watched what was happening in the Balkans with disquiet. The British had not much interest in the Balkans, where there were always wars, and were bored with Turkey, on whose behalf Britain had nearly gone to war with Russia thirty years before, and there was anger towards Grey, who had been on the side of the Young Turk revolution in 1908. The days had long since gone when Turkey was seen as the poor innocent in danger of being crushed by the Russian bear. She was now nothing but a nuisance. The Russians on the other hand were neurotically interested in whatever was going on in the Balkans. When Austria, without warning, parley or apparent purpose, walked in and annexed Bosnia and Herzegovina, Russia was aggrieved, and the bitter animosity excited throughout Russia against Austria was a considerable factor in the chemistry of the start of World War I.

The issues in the Balkans were totally alien to British thought;

each Balkan nation was a virtual land-mine. Since Turkey went into decline, Russia and Austria were the powers most interested in this conglomeration of arrogant and self-opinionated states. The key to them all was Serbia, which was under Russian protection.

Since 1905 there had been a trade war between Austria and Serbia, and even then it appeared that Serbia was an ill-fitting piece in a rather tedious jigsaw puzzle. Germany was also interested in Serbia, for vital to her development as an imperialist power was the railway to Constantinople, part of the projected Berlin to Baghdad railway route which would ensure that Turkey remained under the German thumb, and would alarm Russia and Britain, with their interests in Persia and India. Such a railway had to go through Serbia and, with the Russians alienated, there seemed no prospect of them welcoming the German engineers into the country.

If Belgium was traditionally the cockpit of Europe, Turkey the sick man of Europe, Germany the eagle and Russia the bear, then assuredly Italy was the hyena. In the neurotic quest for allies, Britain had not paid much attention to Italy, to which she had, in the nineteenth century, administered sharp slaps when it seemed as though Italy was going too energetically into the empire-building business. Italy had hoped to get Tunisia with the British nod of approval, but the French had stepped in first. True, Italy did manage to acquire a slice of empire in Eritrea, though her adventure in Abyssinia had turned rather sour. An offer by Britain to let Italy have a modest slice of colonial cake led the Italians to pontificate on a grand Anglo-Italian carve-up of north Africa. This was considered impertinent by the British politicians, and Italy was coolly snubbed. She was forced to stand on the side-lines and watch while Britain and France acquired their African empires.

In the old days Turkey had ruled the Balkans ruthlessly and harshly, and the troubles there related directly to her growing decrepitude. Not surprisingly the Italians, deprived of an empire in north Africa, looked across the Mediterranean at Libya, which since 1835 had been directly ruled from Constantinople.

In 1911 the Italians seized Libya. To their delight this move was approved by France, who had had a good deal of trouble with the Turks, especially in the hinterland where south Libya merged imperceptibly into French territory.

To the surprise of other colonial powers, Italy ruled Libya in a civilised and enlightened manner, building roads, railways, schools and hospitals, and respecting the religious feelings of her new subjects. Detached observers could not help comparing the Italian attitude with that of the British in north Africa, and a scandal that had occurred in 1906 was dredged up to illustrate their differences in colonial rule. In that year, a group of British officers stationed at Denshawi in the Nile Delta amused themselves by shooting pigeons belonging to the villagers. The villagers tried to stop this slaughter, and a woman was shot. The officers were ill-used and one died of sunstroke. The villagers were brought to trial; four were hanged, two sent to prison for life, and eight flogged. 'The arrangements were admirable', wrote the British official on the spot, 'and reflect great credit to all concerned . . . the Egyptian, being a fatalist, does not greatly fear death, and there is therefore much to be said for flogging as judicial punishment in Egypt'.

Technically, the Italians had an alliance with Germany, but this was recognized as not worth more than the paper it was written on, for it was clear that, in any alignment of power, Austria would side with Germany, and Austria was the country most antipathetic to the Italians. In any event, Italy was not worth courting.

In the search for friends, Britain was not only counting the heads but counting the armies. What was there in the way of cannon fodder? Russia had plenty, and could call on a million combatants in the event of war, but she was dreadfully deficient in arms, especially artillery. She was also short of ammunition; there were only a thousand rounds in reserve for each light gun and rifle. After the débâcle of the Russo-Japanese War, the Russians had spent great sums on their navy—expending £24,477,487 in 1913, more than any other country except Britain and the United States. Four Russian battle-cruisers laid down in 1912 had the requirements demanded by Sir John Fisher in his reorganisation of the Royal Navy—speed and fire-power.

Italy, whichever way she turned, did not seem militarily important. Her army, which on paper numbered 289,000 men, lacked heavy field artillery, and what guns there were were old 'rigid' guns. The standard rifle, though excellent, had been in service since 1891. The machine-gun, which was to be the dominant weapon of the war to come, was conspicuous by its total absence. Italy's naval programme was languid, and in 1913 she had only one dreadnought. Though she had a strong torpedo-boat force, the navy by and large was top-heavy with ancient vessels. Of all the maritime powers, Italy had the smallest number of battleships.

In the coming confrontation with Germany, the role of Japan was uncertain, but in the event of a German naval presence in the East the Japanese navy was well qualified to take care of itself and perhaps nullify a German attempt on India or Australia. Japan's was the fifth navy in the world, after those of Britain, Germany, the United States and France.

The understanding that when war came the British would serve on the French left flank necessitated an appraisal of the French army. On a peace-time footing in 1914, it numbered 823,251 men, but the French boast that this could be more than trebled in a short time was warranted by events. French equipment and artillery were immeasurably better than the Russian or Italian. On 1 September 1914 France had 1,135,000 rifles, 25,000 carbines, 106,200 sabres, 2,158 machine-guns, 4,098 field guns, 389 heavy guns, 192 mountain guns, and 200 aeroplanes.

It was assumed that Belgium would become involved in the war, being invaded either by Germany or by France and Britain. In the year preceding the war, Belgium's army estimates were on a par with those of Sweden or Australia, and few believed in her 350,000-strong army (in the event it numbered 117,000). The Belgian army was ill-equipped with obsolete weapons; the standard rifle was an 1889 model. The war caught the Belgians in the midst of reorganisation, when they were thinking about building a fleet.

Britain's appraisal of possible allies was governed by the belief in a short sharp war, with Germany caught between the nutcrackers of the French and Russian armies, her navy destroyed or bottled up, and her industry rendered mute by a relentless blockade. In the event, counting the heads did not do much good; they had to be in the right place at the right time. No one in Britain, except Kitchener and his circle, foresaw the ineptitude of the French war-machine and its pursuit of an *idée fixe*—a strike through Lorraine—although the French knew that the Germans intended an offensive through Belgium and the unprotected north of France.

The Battle of the Marne proved conclusively that something had gone wrong, and the musical-chairs diplomacy of the preceding decade had failed. Somebody had not only shot the pianist and changed the rules of the game, but had dismantled the piano as well.

Notes to this chapter are on page 295.

CHAPTER SEVEN

SPORT AND ENTERTAINMENT

The Sporting Life

SPORT FLOWERED without let or hindrance between 1901 and 1914, and historians never tire of pointing out that it was the golden age of sport, with amateurs rubbing shoulders with professionals, good humour in the grandstands and hardly a trace of bottle-throwing or hooliganism; Britain was triumphant in all fields, walking away with fifty-six gold medals at the 1908 Olympic Games.

Many of the rich gave over their lives to sport. The poor were less fortunate; the only sport they took to their heart was football, with cricket decidedly a second best. In association football there were still amateurs, such as the Corinthians, among the leading clubs. They were not seen by the working classes as giant-killers—as are today's amateur clubs coming face to face with the big battalions—but as gents who had condescended to perform before their inferiors. Class distinctions were as clearly defined on the running track, the cricket pitch and the football field as in the outside world.

Except perhaps in cricket, techniques were unsophisticated. The emphasis in football was not on tactics but on attack, and there was a good deal of what would now be considered over-

Mr. Jerry Builder, who desires to purchase building plots, is directed to Snowheath Estate.

The crowd, imagining him to be going to the great football match, follow.

Fearing that he has mistaken his way, the builder again inquires.

This time the "footer" crowd overhear his inquiry, and mildly explain to him that he has taken them miles out of their way, causing them to miss the football match.

Hoping to arrive by half-time, they quickly retrace their steps, having briefly explained their opinion of himself to Mr. Jerry Builder.

The poor were devoted to football; it was their sport, and they would go to a great deal of trouble to watch a match

Emphasis in association football was on attack, and there was much over-zealous tackling and hard play

zealous tackling and hard play, though scheming fouls involving play-acting had not yet been codified. The customary practice was to play five forwards, with the backs up in attack somewhere in mid-field. Play therefore fluctuated from one end of the field to the other, there was little plan or purpose behind the attacks and none of the delicate by-play or strategy that marks the best football today. Association football employed professionals, who ran till they dropped for a maximum of £4 a week. It was lively, unquestionably, but lacking in subtlety; speed and dash were what the man on the terrace wanted.

The dominant force in the game was the Football League, a breakaway movement formed in 1888. This was orientated to the Midlands and the North; the teams in the Football League played for workers in industry, whose Saturday afternoons were consecrated to football, and occasionally other sports: cock-fighting was still practised in the North, and the working classes were also fond of whippet-racing and pigeon-racing. By the end of the nineteenth century, the South was getting the flavour of football, and typical of the immense interest being

The 1901 cup final at the Crystal Palace between Tottenham Hotspurs and Sheffield United drew 110,820 spectators, the largest crowd ever to watch a football match

shown was the 110,820 attendance at the 1901 cup final at the Crystal Palace. The game was between Tottenham Hotspurs and Sheffield United and ended in a draw, two all, including one disputed goal. During half-time the spectators flocked on to the pitch and milled about, and the police were powerless to stop them; it was the largest crowd ever assembled to watch a football match.

The Football League was free from the affectation and gentility that had marked public school football, previously the bastion of the game. The commercial game was hard and rough, and although the amateurs had competed for the F.A. Cup in the past they soon dropped out of the running—all except the Corinthians—and started their own cup with its own rules, refusing to recognise the penalty kick which they considered the prerogative of the common professionals with their propensity for foul play.

Although there was plenty of money in professional football, if only on account of the large gates at the Saturday afternoon games, little of it rubbed off on the players. In 1901 it was ruled that no player should receive more than £10 for a signing-on fee, and when, in 1905, a player was transferred from one club to another at a cost to the buyer of £1,000, the Football Association stepped in with a ruling that £350 was to be the top transfer fee—a petty move that fell into disuse within a few months. There was a certain amount of bribery and corruption, and football clubs and officials were wealthy.

In international matches there was virtually no competition from abroad, and all comers were soundly trounced, whether it was Germany in 1901 (beaten 12–0 and 10–0), or Austria in 1908. There was no doubt at all who would win the Olympic football tournament in 1912.

In Rugby football, too, there had been a breakaway movement in the late nineteenth century to differentiate between amateurs and professionals. Rugby Union and Rugby League pursued their separate paths according to different rules. Rugby League was played mostly in the industrial north. Wales, weak in soccer, was strong in Rugby, and in 1905 was the only side to beat the New Zealand All-Blacks. In England there was sufficient interest in Rugby Union to merit the building of the stadium at Twickenham, which thereafter became its headquarters. Those who played Rugby Union were gents, those who played Rugby League were common; there were also class differences between Rugby and soccer, and middle-class grammar schools with aspirations made a point of saying in their prospectus that Rugby, not soccer, was played.

Amateurs and professionals in football, gentlemen and players in cricket. Cricket pervaded the whole fabric of Edwardian life, and although it was never followed with the intensity of football by the industrial working classes, they found pleasure in watching the giants of the age. One of the few areas in which Edwardian democracy operated was village cricket, where for the space of a few hours class distinctions were brushed aside and there was no dishonour in the squire being eclipsed by the blacksmith. In the great country houses cricket was a feature of the leisured life, with full-time groundsmen committed to maintaining pitches equal to that of the Oval and pavilions that vied with those on county grounds.

Village cricket was a great leveller, and squire vied with blacksmith without loss of dignity

The Grand Old Man of English cricket, W. G. Grace, had just left first-class cricket when the reign opened—he could afford to; in 1895 a testimonial of over £5,000 was raised for him by the *Daily Telegraph*. Although he played in a few minor matches and lived until 1915, the Edwardian public had to be content with his legend and his successors.

They were days of good wickets and fast scoring. In 1901 in six consecutive innings, C. B. Fry scored 106, 209, 149, 105, 140 and 105. In that same year sixty batsmen scored more than 1,000 runs each, and three topped the 3,000 mark. In 1902 Sussex scored 705 for nine declared against Surrey at Hastings; in 1903 Jessop scored 286 in 180 minutes for Gloucestershire, and in 1904 in the match between Derbyshire and Essex both sides topped 500 runs in the first innings. The match between Worcestershire and Oxford University produced 1,492 runs. In the Test Matches against Australia in 1905 the Hon F. S. Jackson captained England, won the toss five times out of five and headed both the batting and the bowling averages. In 1906 T. Hayward scored a record 3,518 runs, and in the same year

G. H. Hirst scored 2,385 runs and took 208 wickets—the only double 'double' ever completed. In 1909 Hobbs and Hayes scored 371 runs in 165 minutes for Surrey against Hampshire. The decade was, indeed, notable for the brightest of cricket. One of the feats of 1911 was the scoring by E. Alletson of Nottingham of 189 runs in 90 minutes, his last 89 being made in 15 minutes.

Nor was there any shortage of bowling triumphs. In both 1906 and 1908 T. Wass of Nottinghamshire took 16 wickets in a day; in 1901 Yorkshire dismissed Nottinghamshire for 13 runs, and in 1902 Australia was dismissed for 36 runs with Wilfred Rhodes taking 7 wickets for 17 runs. The English team on that occasion is generally regarded as the best-balanced side ever put into the field by this country. In 1905 Rhodes demonstrated his supremacy by taking six wickets for nine runs for Yorkshire against Essex.

The captain of the 1902 side against Australia was C. B. Fry, who epitomised the quality of Edwardian sportsmen. Born in 1872, Fry was the gentleman autocrat at his most unselfconscious. In 1892 at the inter-university sports taking place at Oxford he put down his cigar in the dressing-room, went out and set a world record for the long jump that held for 21 years, then went back to his cigar. He played football of the highest standard, taking part in a cup final, and was a boxer, a fine swimmer, a golfer, played competitive tennis, was adept at the javelin, and was a good shot, fisherman and horseman. He was also a talented writer, promoted naval training for boys, and was a keen motorist. All in all, a *Boy's Own Paper* hero. Typical of the aristocratic players was the Hon F. S. Jackson, who split his time between soldiering (serving in the Boer War), hunting, shooting and cricket. In the Gentleman v Players match at Lord's in 1894 he and his fellow opening bowler bowled unchanged throughout the match, Jackson taking 12 wickets for 77 runs. Born in 1870, the son of Lord Allerton, he was educated at Harrow and Trinity College, Cambridge, and personified the well-born cricket amateur.

Cricket was the sport everyone could participate in without

loss of dignity. Urchins played it in the squalid streets of the East End with dustbins as wickets; the lower middle classes set up their stumps on the beaches of the south coast; the rich spent their week-ends at the game, and attendance at the Eton-Harrow match was a must on the social calendar. Of course, there were those who complained that it was a slow game, out of key with the frenzied tempo of the new age. In 1901 *Punch* put forward a number of suggestions for shortening the game: let the batsmen go in fetters; extend the distance between the wickets to a quarter of a mile; have two bowlers at each end, both bowling simultaneously; increase the fielding side to twenty-two but allow only six to bat (chosen by ballot); have six stumps at each end; let the bat be abolished in favour of the broom-stick; instruct umpires to treat every application in the most favourable sense to the 'outs'; let the innings of a batsman be closed at twenty runs and a match come to an end when declared by a tenth of the spectators as 'tedious'—all of which were scorned by the MCC.

To the man in the street, rowing was the University Boat Race, a free spectacle with opportunities for celebration in the riverside pubs. The purists rather resented the interest of the masses in this contest, were disgusted by the betting that 'contaminated' the event, and deplored the ungentlemanlike behaviour of members of the crews in writing about rowing for the press. Athletics was also of limited appeal, and the 1908 Olympic Games passed without extravagant press coverage, despite British supremacy in most events. The fastest time for the 100 yards sprint was 9.8 seconds in July 1901, and for the mile 4 minutes 16.8 seconds in July 1902; these remained unbroken by the 1908 games. The record for the high jump was less than 6 ft 6 in, the long jump record was just under 25 ft. In the tug-of-war at the Olympic Games the United Kingdom had a walk-over for third place, as only the Americans decided to compete against the three United Kingdom teams (all made up of policemen).

Hockey, widely played in the universities and public schools, was now considered a suitable sport for young ladies, who were

Croquet was still widely played, and at one time it seemed as though it would eclipse lawn tennis in popularity

also entering the male purlieus of cricket and football. 'Have you not observed', asked a *Punch* humorist:

> That all the girls you meet
> Have either hockey elbows or
> Ungainly cycling feet?
> Their backs are bent, their faces red,
> From cricket stoop or football head.

Hockey represented an early instance of what might be called the St Trinians syndrome ('I caught her a crunch on the knuckle. A clip on the knee and the cheek'), and mixed hockey, energetically called for by the women, was invariably declined by the men. England dominated the hockey scene, and were never beaten in an international (though the only country outside the British Isles that participated in hockey internationals was France).

Tennis vied with croquet for attention, and at one time it seemed that it would go under. The magazine *The World* reported that 'the lawns that were erstwhile cumbered with tennis nets now bristle with croquet hoops, and the sedate mallet has driven out the frisky racquet'. Competition tennis had yet to make an impact, and it was mainly a sociable game or a source of humour.

> 'I wonder why Mr Poppstein serves with three balls?'
> 'Old associations, I suppose.'

There were few links between lawn tennis and real tennis, which was played in an indoor court. The latter form was dominated throughout the period by one player, E. H. Miles. Lawn-tennis was a late starter, deriving from a game called sphairistike patented in 1874. In 1877 the All England Croquet Club became the All England Croquet and Lawn Tennis Club, and Wimbledon became the centre of the lawn tennis world. Edwardian lawn tennis, compared with present-day standards, was a slower game, with less emphasis on the serve and more on placing the ball. Real, or royal tennis, called court tennis in America, was a rich man's sport, for it cost £2,000 to build an indoor court, whereas almost anyone could play lawn tennis. It was ironically suggested that tennis matches could be played with one's neighbours over the hedge; one would not necessarily have to meet them. It was ferociously played by middle-aged men under the illusion that they were young, and was a useful adjunct to courtship, though the long skirts of the women players handicapped them, and rushing the net was decidedly out. Croquet was a much more amiable game, and part of the social background rather than a competitive event. It gave women the opportunity to cheat, as they could shuffle the ball forward under their long dresses without fear of detection. Played on vicarage lawns, it was the ideal way of spinning out the long Edwardian summers. Both games were given prestige by Edward VII, who took up lawn tennis shortly after it was invented and indulged in croquet at Marienbad when he was on one of his cures.

Modern boxing, as distinct from pugilism, dates from 1866 when the laws against prize-fighting became more rigidly enforced; though the fairground bruisers were still in operation and the bouts organised in the East End were as vicious as anything in the roll-call of bare-knuckle bouts. The Amateur Boxing Association, founded in 1884, made boxing respectable. Its major innovation was to restrict the number of rounds.

The upper flight of professional boxers aspired to appear under the aegis of the National Sporting Club. In 1901 a case was brought against the club for manslaughter when Billy Smith, fighting under the name of Murray Livingstone, died in the ring. The aim of the Crown was to put a stop to future competitions and, had the jury brought in a verdict of guilty, the history of boxing in Britain might have been cut dramatically short. Fairground boxing-booths provided a cadre for the professional ring; and for young working-class men who happened to be strong and quick on their feet, the ring seemed an escape from unemployment or menial jobs, the emoluments offered for one fight being usually more than a man would earn in a week of toil.

Heavyweight boxing in Britain was dominated by Bombardier Billy Wells, who held the title for nine years, and in the lesser weights Jimmy Wilde—still a name to be conjured with in public bars—had by 1914 fought 200 contests without being beaten. Britain's triumph in the boxing events in the 1908 Olympic Games was due to the non-participation of America. The aristocrat amateur was significantly absent from the boxing ring. Boxing was rough and tough, and little prestige was to be gained from being battered about the head and body, even over the three rounds that the Amateur Boxing Association specified. For every Jimmy Wilde and Bombardier Billy Wells, there were a score of punch-drunk has-beens shuffling round the streets.

Wrestling never made much of an impact on the industrial masses, but various regional forms were practised, each part of the country having its own speciality. There was the Cumberland and Westmorland, the Lancashire (known as 'catch as catch can'), the Cornish, the Devon, the Scottish, and the Irish. There were also a bewildering variety of foreign systems, including 'Glima', the national style of Iceland, which had a curiosity value during the 1908 Olympic Games. The English forms did not match with the Graeco-Roman style popular in Europe,

A Golf Story

(*A golfer recently, in attempting to loft over a house, landed his ball down the chimney. That is the story as reported. We have ventured to supply the remainder*)

" My good woman, don't make such a fuss. Can't you see I'm badly bunkered in your confounded fireplace? "

Golf was a very popular sport, and golfing stories made their rounds, a source of inspiration to cartoonists

and the British felt that they were at an unfair disadvantage, as the Graeco-Roman style had little resemblance to classic wrestling and derived from the French wrestling schools of the 1860s. Competitive wrestling had little appeal as a spectator sport; it was too slow-moving and the rules were too obscure to excite spectators nurtured on the slap-bang-wallop of professional boxing or the frenzied running about of association football.

The prime minister, Balfour, made golf an in-sport, but even so it would have made headway as a sport eminently suitable for overweight middle-aged men, with someone to carry the clubs, and respectable for women and the lower middle classes. It was a sport that did not need any great mental or physical preparation, and businessmen found that a round of golf did not take too much out of them. Where there is demand backed by money there is supply, and new courses sprang up with startling rapidity in the outer suburbs of the cities and towns. The new golfers soon got to grips with drivers, spoons, brassies, mashies, irons, niblicks and putters, and were discreetly pleased when the solid gutta-percha ball, which had been in use since 1848, was replaced in 1902 by the more easily played, rubber-cored and wound so-called Haskell ball, a mass-produced American invention.

The handicapping system made it possible for apprentice golfers to match themselves against experienced players without a round becoming too one-sided. Golf, unlike cricket, was never a social leveller; if anything it acerbated the class divisions, encouraging businessmen to gather together in exclusive cliques. A good deal of informal business could be done over eighteen holes. Golf also initiated a modest revolution in domestic matters; for it provided a man with a viable excuse to go off for an afternoon without his wife sensing another woman in the offing.

The age was dominated by three players, J. H. Taylor, James Braid and Harry Vardon, but in anticipation of the future an American won a major tournament in 1913 against the best that Britain could offer. In many sports the Americans were becoming a threat to British supremacy. An interesting, as yet unbeaten record was set up in the same year; on a course at Herne Bay a golf ball was driven more than a quarter of a mile.

Cricket of a fairly high standard was played by such luminaries as cartoonist Bernard Partridge, playwright J. M. Barrie, actor C. Aubrey Smith, and novelist A. E. W. Mason, while golf had the prime minister as its most valuable PRO. More prestigious than either of these sports was horse-racing, a sport in which Edward VII had an almost psychotic interest, possibly justified by the immense sums of money he made at it. Between 1886 and 1910 his stallions earned £269,495 in stud fees, and his horses won £146,345. Wealth was always a criterion of what was worth while to the king. He maintained that the happiest day of his life was in 1896 when he led in his Derby winner, Persimmon. To cap his delight the horse had been quoted at 5–1 against. The Jockey Club took action against anyone who infringed the rules, bloodstock breeding improved, and the 'monkey crouch' style of riding changed horse-racing tactics.

On Derby Day the British from all ranks of life gathered together. Ascot was a fashionable event in the social calendar;

every year King Edward moved to Windsor for Ascot Week in the middle of June, and towards the end of July he made a regular visit to the Duke of Richmond for the races at Goodwood. The French nobility were always in evidence at Ascot; 'they appreciated the *haute école* and that observance of the things *stylé* that is dear to their hearts'.[1]

It was well known that the ladies who went to Ascot to show off their finery did not know much about horse-racing. One joke of the period made this clear:

> Uncle: 'Ah, Milly, I'm afraid you've lost your money over that one. He's gone the wrong way!'
> Milly: 'Oh, no, uncle, I'm all right. George told me to back it 'both ways'.'

After the death of Edward VII there was a surrealist touch in the so-called 'Black Ascot', when everyone appeared dressed from head to foot in black.

> The men wore black silk top hats with morning or frock coats, black trousers, black waistcoats, black ties, while in their black-gloved hands they carried tightly rolled black umbrellas. Their funereal ladies must have seemed like strange giant crows or morbid birds of paradise strutting at some Gothic entertainment.[2]

Perhaps the gesture would have appealed to the king; the last thing he was told before he died was that one of his horses had won a race at Kempton Park, and the Ascot extravaganza might have pleased him. Anyway, pretty women always looked well in black.

Showbiz

To many of the rich showbiz was life, and life was showbiz. They pursued their pleasures with a diligence that was lacking in any other aspect of their lives, and prominent amongst these pleasures was the theatre. The cinema had arrived on the scene, but it was in its early stages, and there was no kudos in being seen in picture palaces in the suburbs—the cinema had yet to make the West End.

Edwardian theatre encompassed a wide variety of genres. The frivolous did not flock to the theatre of Galsworthy or Bernard Shaw, kept going by the patronage of the intellectuals and the improved working classes, but they did to the new respectable music halls of the syndicates, the theatres showing inane farces and spectacular melodrama, and, especially, musical shows.

Music hall had passed its best; the drive and the verve that characterised it in mid-Victorian times had been replaced by the cult of the comedian. Twenty years before Edward came to the throne, an Act of Suitability, demanding safety curtains and the exclusion of food and drink from the auditorium, had forced most of the smaller halls to close down and the local stars into other professions. The emphasis shifted to large music halls with a wide appeal, for 'family' entertainment with a minimum of smut, and this led gradually to the control of halls passing to one group, who despatched their stars from one place to another, feeding the demand for hero and heroine worship.

The Coliseum in St Martin's Lane was the dream music hall come true. Opened in December 1904 and costing £80,000 more than anticipated, it had a triple revolving stage that could be rotated at 20 mph, a stage of 10,000 square feet weighing 160 tons, and a special tramline leading directly into the Royal Box, on which ran a tram made entirely of glass. The Coliseum contained an information bureau, a multitude of confectionery stalls, a telephone box (at a time when telephones were few and far between) and a letter box. With four shows a day, presented with a panache that few music hall owners had ever been able to afford, the theatre was lavish, expensive and gorgeously vulgar. It was not surprising that King Edward soon availed himself of the opportunity to use the glass tram so kindly placed at his disposal by the progenitor of the Coliseum, Oswald Stoll.

Stoll was born in Australia in 1866, and when his father died his mother brought Oswald to England, and married into the provincial music hall business. Her new husband owned the Parthenon music hall in Liverpool, and after his death she and her 14-year-old son managed it, then moved to Cardiff to open a music hall there. It might be supposed that Stoll knew all there was to know about the music hall by 1904. Though not yet forty, he was old-fashioned in his ideas, and although clean, the shows at his Coliseum were dull, and it was known as the Morgueseum. A simulated Derby was put on (at one performance a jockey was thrown off his horse and killed), chariot races were run, there were massive choirs clothed in surplices, and although the Coliseum's motto, blazoned across the programmes, was 'Pro Bono Publico', the public were not interested in their own good but only in being entertained. Spectacle and music did not necessarily guarantee amusement.

Stoll introduced the novelty of making all seats bookable, including the sixpenny balcony (not gallery, for gallery had low connotations), but this back-fired for the sixpenny public was not used to this procedure. The box office became ankle-deep in postal orders, without accompanying names or addresses, the resulting chaos necessitating the employment of a chartered accountant to sort out the mess, which he did by giving tickets to everyone who declared that he had sent in his money.

The Coliseum, the mirror of the new improved Edwardian music hall, did not get off to the start that Stoll had hoped for, but he was sanguine, for he was chairman and managing director of a chain of music halls that included Empires at Hackney, Holloway, New Cross, Stratford and Shepherds Bush in London, and Hippodromes, Coliseums, and Empires scattered throughout the United Kingdom, in Leeds, Bradford, Birmingham, Liverpool, Newcastle, Manchester and Nottingham, and other towns where family fun was in demand. Occasionally the managers were not so strict with their artists as Stoll, and when a comedian at the Shepherds Bush Empire overstepped the mark and cracked a blue joke, this lapse cost Stoll ten guineas. No doubt it proved even more expensive to the unfortunate comedian, for the circuit system was in operation, and a black mark registered against a performer would affect his career not only in the Stoll empire but in that of Edward Moss, whose major property was the London Hippodrome. The circuit system of sending stars from hall to hall meant that select performers could earn more than

£1,000 a week, and the glamour attracted the small fry, who clamoured for work in the life-enhancing environment of the music hall. Seven hundred chorus girls once attended an audition for a show, only twenty of whom were acceptable.

To counter the effect of the Moss and Stoll chains, previously unallied theatres and music halls joined together in self-protection. One of these syndicates comprised the Tivoli, the Oxford, the London Pavilion, the Canterbury and the South London. It was an indication that the independent music hall, catering for a local audience, was dying, though one or two of them, including the Britannia in Hoxton, kept going against all the odds. Shows were becoming stereotyped for the mass audience. Although Sarah Bernhardt and Ellen Terry appeared at the Coliseum, and good one-act plays were staged as part of the programme, the basic elements of the spectaculars were blandness and unction, pseudo-Cockney song and sweet melody, an eagerness not to offend. Stoll received a knighthood in 1919, as the man who cleaned up music hall and made it respectable.

Many of the qualities of respectable music hall entertainment promoted by Stoll were present in musical theatre, the dominant form of which was the musical comedy. This had been gaining popularity over burlesque and comic opera since 1892 when *In Town* brought the new genre to the public. *The Belle of New York* (1898), with Edna May as the leading lady, established the American musical in Britain.

In 1903 the new Gaiety was opened in the presence of the king and queen, neither of them averse to entertainment that did not demand too much of their mental powers. The musical comedy presented then was the now forgotten *The Orchid*, which made a star of Gabrielle Ray, so that she became a 'postcard queen'; a favourite Edwardian way of conferring immortality was to portray stage heroines on picture postcards. The Gaiety became a cult, with the Gaiety Girls the epitome of desirability. Show girls had always been fair game for stage door johnnies, whether Victorian swells or Edwardian knuts, but the charisma had never been exploited with so much energy. Whether or not the Gaiety stage door was, as historians put it,

London's West End was rich in theatres and music halls. In this superb Edwardian night photograph of Leicester Square the Alhambra can be seen through the trees

the gateway to romance, the girls became transformed into the Baroness Churston, the Countess Poulett and the Countess of Drogheda. The inane vacuous stories being unfolded on stage were transferred to real life.

The keynote of Edwardian musical comedy was escape. Musical comedy had started as being refreshingly modern, but now audiences wanted to be wafted into a never-never world. The promoters tended these delicate blossoms, and saw that it paid handsomely. Frank Curzon was a typical entrepreneur of the period. Having made money in tailoring, he built the Piccadilly Hotel and resurrected the Strand theatre, opening it in 1901 with *A Chinese Honeymoon* that had been tried out in the theatrical outback of Hanley in 1899. With songs such as 'Martha Spanks the Grand Piano' and 'Twiddly Bits' the show was a runaway success, notching up 1,076 performances. By 1903 Curzon controlled the following theatres: Avenue, Camden, Coronet, Prince of Wales, Comedy, Criterion, Wyndham's and the Strand. For prestige reasons he occasionally dabbled in straight theatre, putting on Gerald du Maurier at Wyndham's.

Producing a musical comedy was not exactly a licence to print money. Some shows were too banal even for an Edwardian audience and the more discriminating favoured the meatier light operas of Edward German—*Merrie England* (1902) and *Tom Jones* (1906). But whereas *Merrie England* ran for only 120 performances the later musical comedies enjoyed a more popular success; *Our Miss Gibbs* (1909) ran for 636 performances, *The Arcadians* (1909) for 809, and *The Quaker Girl* (1910) for 536.

The most dramatic triumph of fantasy over reality, of long drawn-out sweetness, was Lehar's *The Merry Widow*, put in production as a stop gap when the supply of English musical comedies was running out. It ran from June 1907 until July 1909, and King Edward VII saw it four times. An Eton schoolboy, Osbert Sitwell, saw it, and later pondered over its significance:

> It held a suitably designed mirror to the age, to the preference for restaurant to palace, for comfort to beauty, and to the idealization of Mammon. Mammon underlay the smudgy softness and superficial prettiness of the whole performance, as the skull supports the lineaments of even the youngest and freshest face.[1]

For the farewell performance the theatre was besieged all day long, the earliest arrival taking his place at 5.30 in the morning.

Franz Lehar, born in 1870, a young Austrian bandmaster, followed this up in 1911 with *The Count of Luxembourg*, which he composed in two months. It was the kind of plot the audiences loved. A comic grand duke wanted to marry a music hall girl, but before he could do so the girl needed a title, so a marriage was arranged between the girl and a spendthrift count, on condition that he did not see her and divorced her after three months. There was £20,000 on the deal. Naturally the count (hero) did see the music hall girl (heroine) and what was £20,000 to a man in love? What indeed? echoed the audience, entranced. But Lehar's second offering to the English stage did not have the success of *The Merry Widow*, and *Gipsy Love* of 1912 faded even faster.

The mood had changed. In 1907 when *The Merry Widow* opened war was far away, but five years later there were rumblings of a change. The old-fashioned burlesque was being remodelled into the modern revue, and in 1913 *Hullo, Ragtime* broke vulgarly on to the scene, thin in plot and music, but fast paced and abounding in vigour. It brought new thinking into the theatre and new dances into the ballroom—the bunny hug, the chicken scramble, and many of the devotees of the older school breathed a sigh of relief when, during the war, *The Maid of the Mountains* proved that romance was not dead. Also in the pre-war format was the record-breaking *Chu Chin Chow*, of which, because of a certain degree of nakedness in the production, Sir Herbert Tree quipped: 'More navel than millinery'.

Nudity, in fact, was becoming a draw in the theatre, and paralleled the emphasis in fashion on the sensuous and the alluring. Gaby Deslys had appeared in London in 1903 as a soubrette, singing naughty French songs and wearing naughty French clothes. As early as 1900 Annette Kellerman did a physically revealing swimming and diving act, and was a dominant influence in persuading women to adopt the close-fitting bathing costume, hiding little. Maud Allan was one of the first women to appear on the stage with bare arms and legs. But no matter what went on after the show, when it was tacitly recognised that the goal of the show girl was a liaison with a toff, the accent was on teasing and titillation, as far from Victorian strip tease (*poses plastiques* and *tableaux vivants*) as they were from present frontal nudity. The titillation was given a veneer of spurious artistry; Maud Allan received most applause for her dance of Salome, when she was a good deal more naked than when expressing Mendelssohn's 'Spring Song'.

Male impersonators were enjoying a vogue. Vesta Tilley in frock-coat, spats, silk hat, and lavender gloves was perhaps of more consequence as a singer than a woman in drag, but she bought her clothes from men's outfitters and for a time set men's fashions.

In *Our Miss Gibbs* the hats worn by the chorus girls cost sixty guineas each. Salaries for the principals were reaching astronomical heights, the choruses were getting larger, and were being subdivided into front row chorus, who would participate in the singing, dialogue and action, and the also-rans. The members of the front row chorus, experienced and wooed for rival shows,

Maud Allan in her celebrated Salome dance

were becoming as much in demand as the stars, and marriage was always breaking into their ranks. Musical theatre was big business. In 1913 one management spent £18,000 in producing the now little-known show, *Come Over Here*; in the course of an evening the chorus girls wore 650 frocks. The producer of *The Arcadians* spent £12,000 on improvements to the Shaftesbury Theatre in preparation for the musical comedy that only he had any faith in. £13,000 could go into a loser such as *The Dashing Little Duke*, while *The Duchess of Dantzig* lost £15,000. These were both attempts to capitalise on the vogue for Ruritanian high jinks. Even long-running shows such *A Country Girl* failed to show profits in London, and although *The Girl from Kays* ran for 432 performances in 1902, the loss of £20,000 was only recouped from the provinces and America. Nevertheless there were vast profits to be made for everyone—200,000 copies of the sheet music of the waltz from *The Merry Widow* were sold within a few years, an encouragement to music publishers to back promising outsiders. In an age in which the stage was never short of backers, it is not surprising that promoters occasionally ventured their arm on projects that everyone on the outside could see were doomed.

The disarming quality of the best of the musical comedies was that they were musically unpretentious, and composers such as Franz Lehar provided large numbers of excellent tunes. There were those, of course, who saw musical significance in *The Merry Widow* and its contemporaries, who persuaded themselves that they were in contact with great art rather than being self-indulgent. G. K. Chesterton in his column in the *Illustrated London News* lashed out at the pretentiousness of these people: 'The fact is that we have reached so high and rarefied a condition of humbug that the most serious things we have left are the comic songs'. *The Merry Widow* was a historical phenomenon, and it is interesting to note that it was Adolf Hitler's favourite entertainment.

In straight theatre, only one production in three was a success despite the low cost in putting on a play. A play running at half capacity could show a modest profit. There was not the backing for drama that there was for the musical, but pioneers such as Harley Granville Barker forced playgoers to face the facts of life with his own plays; *The Voysey Inheritance* and *Waste* have survived the froth and frivolity that constituted much of the West End theatre. Barker's management of the Court Theatre between 1904 and 1907 has been described as 'without question the most noteworthy episode in English theatrical history since Shakespeare and Burbage ran the Globe on Bankside'.[2] Granville Barker encouraged the resurgence of provincial repertory theatre, and at the Court he put on Euripides, Maeterlinck, Yeats and Galsworthy, but it was Shaw who made this theatre financially viable. One of his lesser works, *John Bull's Other Island*, was a runaway hit, seen by Balfour four times; on two of these occasions Balfour took with him Asquith and Campbell-

A scene from a domestic melodrama of the period, Alfred Sutro's John Glayde's Honour, *performed in 1907*

Bannerman, the leaders of the opposition. King Edward, who had earlier dismissed Shaw as a 'damned crank', went to see this play, and laughed uproariously, breaking a chair in the process. Shaw described the playgoers who went to the Court as 'not an audience but a congregation'. *Man and Superman* made Shaw the key figure of the period to the intelligentsia, and *Major Barbara* and *The Doctor's Dilemma* played to full houses. The Court Theatre had neither the capacity nor the location to attract large audiences, and the Shaw plays were transfered to the Savoy and the Haymarket theatres. Fashionable playgoers did not relish having to work at enjoyment, however, and this fact, combined with crippling rents, forced the plays to close. The Shaw/Barker regime was not typical of Edwardian theatre; away from the Court theatre it had to face the opposition of farcical drivel and spectacular melodrama using real railway trains at Drury Lane, and, as often was the case in Edwardian London, the second-rate triumphed. Later plays by Shaw, *Getting Married* (1908) and *Misalliance* (1910), ran in the West End, but not for long. His *The Shewing-Up of Blanco Posnet* was refused a licence by the Lord Chamberlain for blasphemy, and only a pot-boiler, *Fanny's First Play* (1911), could be rated a success in terms of number of performances.

The new school of playwrights did not obey the cardinal rule of giving the public what it wanted, and only when Shaw wrote *Pygmalion* for Mrs Patrick Campbell did the highbrow and the middlebrow theatre meet. The paying audience on the whole did not wish to be reminded of industrial unrest, as in Galsworthy's *Strife*, much preferring the saccharine of Barrie or the calculated daring of Somerset Maugham. The test of a successful Edwardian play was to be burlesqued, and this dubious dignity was conferred on Barrie's *What Every Woman Knows* (1908). Several of his other plays, such as *Quality Street* (1902), were almost parodies in themselves.

A scene from a Drury Lane spectacular, The Whip, *performed in* 1909

Nevertheless there was frequently an integrity in the intelligent Edwardian theatre that one is at a loss to find elsewhere, and one can have nothing but praise for Granville Barker and others for not only putting on meaty and demanding English fare but for encouraging foreign drama. Granville Barker also put on superb productions of Shakespeare when, from a box office point of view, they spelled death.

To a certain degree, drama had a clear field in visual story-telling. Maugham's dramas were in no way better than the average television play of today, but they were patronised by the public who wanted to see what ordinary people would do in set circumstances; the interest was in dialogue and narrative. The middlebrow theatre was doing what the cinema could do far better. However, in Britain the cinema had got off on the wrong foot, and was treated as a gimmick, with cinematography an auxiliary to music hall turns. Film clips of the funeral of Queen Victoria and the coronation of Edward VII were treated as fit entertainment for the groundlings, and it is characteristic of the lack of imagination shown that when Edward VII saw himself on film he was concerned mainly because his medals were on the wrong way round (the film was in negative).

The cinematograph was born towards the end of the nineteenth century; in 1893, Edison had done a one-minute film of the execution of Mary, Queen of Scots; in 1894, kinetoscopes had been set up in force on Broadway; in 1895, the Lumière Brothers had begun operations; but perhaps the most significant event was a fifteen-minute film in twelve scenes on the subject of the Dreyfus affair made by the pioneer Méliès in 1899. The British lagged behind, and one of the few manifestations of interest was the Brighton school of film-making from 1900 to 1905, in which the innovation of close-up was used. Whereas Méliès made his adventurous *A Trip to the Moon* in 1902 and the Americans produced the first 'classic' film, *The Great Train Robbery*, in 1903, the main contribution of the British was the trivial snippet of film to enliven a music hall programme. All the elements were there to exploit, but no one bothered. As with the typewriter and the telephone, development was left to the Americans, though it was the Italians who foresaw the possibilities of the cinema for spectacle when they made *Quo Vadis* in 1912, a year before the development of Hollywood and three years before Griffiths' *Birth of a Nation*.

The British also ignored the cinema's comic possibilities and let Charlie Chaplin, who had been a wolf in the first performance of *Peter Pan* in London and who had demonstrated his capabilities in the Karno Comedy Co, get out of their grasp. Chaplin made thirty-five films for Mack Sennett in 1914, while the British, leaders in visual humour, twiddled their thumbs. In the sphere of cinematography, as in many others, the British were too idle to capitalise on an entertainment winner and only the demand of the masses for this new medium caused it to be taken up. The home-grown product was cheap and vulgar with the aura of a second-rate music hall turn, and although by 1914 all the large towns in Britain had picture palaces, their offerings gave no indication that the cinema was to be one of the most important art forms of the century.

The middle classes and the intellectuals scorned cinema, the former because it reeked of innovation, the latter because it was common; the left-wing intelligentsia were even more contemptuous, for the cinema made a point of giving the lower orders exactly what they wanted (sex and violence) without attempting to improve them.

Innovation had a habit of nonplussing the English paying public, and when Debussy's *Pélleas et Mélisande* was produced at Covent Garden in 1909 they were caught between incomprehension and the desire to appear knowledgeable, states of mind shared by the critics. Opera came dimly within the orbit of showbiz. Provided that English opera was not put on, there was always a public for Covent Garden productions of the standards, under-rehearsed and shabby as they might be; the only stipulation the opera public made was that there should be a name singer (preferably not British). The operas of Richard Strauss were always good for a shudder, on account of his plots, and a laugh, on account of his music. Ballet was an integral part of the music hall scene, and it was via the Coliseum in 1909 that Russian dancers made themselves known to the British public. They heralded the invasion of the Diaghilev ballet in 1911, and the mellifluent absurdities of Isadora Duncan and Maud Allan were submerged in a riot of exotic dancing, exciting music and colourful costumes.

Strange new trends had already been forced on the public mind by the Post-Impressionist exhibition of 1910, called into being by the fact that the Grafton Gallery had a gap between exhibitions. Cèzanne, Gauguin and Matisse provoked lectures from psychiatrists and a chorus of disapproval from the established artists. Thesauruses were looted for the right words to describe this barbaric invasion—jejune, barbarous, imbecility (*The Queen*), weird, uncouth, tortuous (*Daily Telegraph*). Painters of the English establishment saw the show as a bad joke that would devalue art; art was concerned with conspicuous display. The new rich had their portraits painted by Sargent, and city councils commissioned artists like Brangwyn to decorate their walls with appropriate scenes. The status symbol of the genteel was the set of Francis Wheatley's street cries of London, reprinted in a limited edition.

Philip Burne-Jones, who had made for himself something of a corner in languorous hermaphrodites and was thought by most people to be dead, wrote to *The Times* a letter incoherent with rage, in which he suspected that the exhibition of Post-Impressionist paintings 'is a huge practical joke, organised in Paris at the expense of our countrymen'. The *Morning Post* complained that art students would find these 'hysterical daubs' . . . 'a justification of their own worst endeavours'.

The chorus of disapproval that greeted this quite small exhibition was out of all proportion to its impact on the general public, which rarely visited any of the minor galleries, and whose artistic horizons were governed by the Royal Academy exhibitions. It was symptomatic of a feeling of helplessness. It is understandable that the French artists on show were regarded as the vanguard of chaos, paving the way to the naked barbarism of the Russian ballet of the following year. To the establishment it seemed that a crack was appearing in the whole framework of civilisation, and anxieties about the cultural basis of the western world were mixed with general apprehension at the way more mundane things were going. Similarities were drawn between the anarchy of art and the anarchy of industry, the *malheurs* of Richard Strauss and the perversity of Debussy were matched with the incomprehensible behaviour of the suffragette movements.

No wonder that the disciples of the old order were outraged that not only did these sinister manifestations occur, but that the only response seemed to be tepid jibes in *Punch* and a rustle of order papers in parliament. The warmth and *schmalz* of *The Merry Widow*, the flattery of Sargent's brush, the harmless knockabout and cheeky Cockney of the music hall, all these were fading, rendered insignificant by the new brutal spirit of the times, a counterpoint to dark doings in Europe.

Notes to this chapter are on page 295.

CHAPTER EIGHT

CRIME AND PUNISHMENT

The Policeman's Lot

IN SPITE of the unrest and unease that pervaded the years 1901–14, crime remained at a modest level. This table showing the numbers of criminals convicted at superior courts in England and Wales makes illuminating reading:

	population	convictions
1850	17,773,324	20,537
1860	19,902,713	12,068
1870	22,090,163	12,953
1880	25,714,288	11,214
1890	28,763,673	9,242
1900	32,249,187	8,157
1910	35,796,289	11,987

In 1906, a typical year, there had been a total of 59,079 indictable offences committed, compared with 50,469 in 1899. This, incredibly, was less than two crimes per policeman and despite the strong feelings of hostility by the poor, who had constantly suffered at the hands of the police throughout the Victorian period. The police were then looked upon as instruments of class war, and were harried and mocked whenever the chance arose. A clear indication of this can be found in a host of music hall songs, where the police are shown as corrupt, vicious, unintelligent and comic. 'If You Want to Know the Time, Ask a P'liceman' indicates that this was all he was good for.

There was no equivocation about right and wrong. There was a criminal class, just as there was a working class and a middle class. Criminals were easily recognised, and when caught fair and square they would own up and make a clean breast of it; they abided by the rules of the game. According to the criminologist Dr Lombroso in 1876 'the born criminal has projecting ears, thick hair and thin beard, projecting frontal eminences, enormous jaws, a square and protruding chin, large cheek bones, and frequent gesticulation'. Moral insensibility, a dull conscience and a freedom from remorse were attributed to the criminal, and as he was generally lacking in intelligence he never took proper precautions before or after committing a crime.

By the start of the Edwardian period, the Metropolitan Police had settled in at new headquarters in Scotland Yard, and were acquiring new techniques. Although the principle of fingerprinting had been laid down in 1892, the police were still involved in anthropometry—the classification of criminals by physical characteristics, such as the shape of the head. A system of fingerprinting, introduced in 1902, caused alarm throughout the underworld, especially when fifty-four men were arrested on Derby Day for various offences, notably pickpocketing, and it was discovered, by comparing their fingerprints with those on record, that twenty-nine of them were old lags.

The possibilities of the use of this technique in crime detection were brought to the attention of a sensation-seeking public when a finger was found on a Clerkenwell warehouse-gate after a break-in. At Scotland Yard, the finger was identified as belonging to a pickpocket who operated in the Elephant and Castle area. Eventually he was picked up, and the absence of a finger provided excellent evidence. Fingerprints by themselves were not fully accepted by the courts, though a precedent was formed on 14 September 1902 when the perpetrator of a burglary in

Denmark Hill was brought to justice on the evidence of fingerprints alone and sentenced to seven years' imprisonment.

It was hoped that with new methods, such as fingerprinting, there would be a rise in the numbers of cases solved. In 1878 the CID had investigated 21,792 felonies, and arrests had been made in 10,849 of these cases. Yet of £157,283 stolen, only £19,785 were recovered. The public was not slow to accuse the police of incompetence, and something worse, and throughout the Edwardian period very few months went by without the police being charged with accepting bribes from prostitutes and brothel-keepers.

As for incompetence, the Metropolitan Police in the early 1900s was 2,000 under strength, the new techniques had yet to be tested, and the recording systems were in a mess—not until 1914 was the Criminal Record Office formed from the various individual departments dealing with records. The *Police Gazette* continued to use woodcuts for illustrations long after photography became a viable proposition for this purpose. Although the introduction of the telephone had revolutionised business life, the Metropolitan Police still preferred the telegraph, where messages had to be tapped out one letter after another, maintaining that this was safer than the telephone, where operators could listen in. This idea that telephones were not 'secret' persisted until about 1910, though as late as 1917 there were two police stations which were not on the telephone.

In 1903 Sir Melville Macnaghten took over as Chief of the Criminal Investigation Department. Born in 1853, he had been educated at Eton before taking over the management of the family estates in Bengal. He joined the CID in 1889.

He determined to make the Metropolitan Police a force above reproach. In 1904 a constable charged with perjury—accused of planting a knife and a hammer in the pockets of a suspected man—was sentenced to five years' imprisonment. The case was given wide publicity by the tabloid press, and the general public was well pleased that its intuitive suspicions about the police were justified. In 1906 a constable arrested Eva d'Angely as a common prostitute; she had, he maintained, been behaving in a riotous and indecent manner in Regent Street, and she duly appeared at Marlborough Street police court. To the reporters of the London weekly press, that depended for its success on juicy court cases, it seemed an open and shut case, but Eva d'Angely protested that she was a respectable married woman who had been waiting for her husband, and this plea was accepted by the magistrate. The police, the popular press reported, were celebrated for their persecution of innocent women, and it was high time something was done about it. The public image of the police would seem to have been irrevocably tarnished, but when the newspapers tried to get hold of Mrs d'Angely to keep the story boiling they found that she had disappeared to Paris. Discreetly it was decided not to pursue the matter for Eva d'Angely was, indeed, a common prostitute.

Another case stirred the fires. Two men were arrested on Boat Race night for being drunk and disorderly, and were incarcerated in Vine Street police station. Again it all seemed a cut and dried case, and only when the magistrates decided that the two men had suffered from 'brutal methods of treatment and procedure, denoting culpable negligence' did it become newsworthy.

It was not surprising that when the suffragettes appeared on the scene the police were in two minds how to tackle the problem. The statement by Mrs Pankhurst that 'the argument of the broken pane is the most valuable argument in modern politics' did not endear her to them. The police authorities could hardly pull punches when letters were being set on fire in pillar-boxes, and other targets for arson included empty houses, sports pavilions, boat houses, grandstands, railway stations, plus a school or two. Nor could the police ignore the fact that the British Museum and the Tower of London were attacked, pictures slashed, golf greens dug up, the glass of orchid houses at Kew Gardens smashed and telephone wires cut. The policeman's lot was decidedly not a happy one.

That the Metropolitan Police were not reduced to a chronic state of anxiety says much for the calibre of the average constable. There were cases that could not backfire. When a house in

Richmond Road, Kensington, was raided in 1904 in the belief that it was a brothel there was relief all round when twenty-five couples were found (including three coloured women) distributed amidst the five bedrooms, plus indecent photographs in the upstairs rooms. In the same year the police were involved with the Rev Mr Kendall, rector of Holsworthy, Devon, who was accused of having saucy photographs of Plymouth actresses and suspected of having unlawful relations with a Miss Andrews. The rector was awarded £1,000 damages for slander, and there were more red faces.

Constable Pullen was luckier. William Morris and Cecil Proutt one night in 1908 missed the last train from Liverpool Street station, and walked through Bishopsgate Street, meeting

"CAN YOU TELL ME?"

THE POLICE SAY THEY HAVE FOUND A CLUE AND DO EVERYTHING IN THEIR POWER TO MAKE SURE OF THEIR MAN. IS IT ANY FAULT OF THEIRS IF HE GETS AWAY?

(*Drawn by* G. L. STAMPA.)

The police were always good for a laugh, as reflected in this humorous drawing of 1907

The girl looked down at the sinister patch of red on her skirt.
"It l·oks like—like blood," she stammered.

It was the age of the suave amateur sleuth, such as Freeman's John Thorndyke, here about to solve another baffling crime

Constable Pullen en route and deciding to bait him. They asked the constable 'What's the time?' and Pullen pointed to the clock over the road. This procedure was repeated several times, and eventually the two men broke into the song 'If you want to know the time ask a p'liceman' whereupon Pullen, his patience exhausted, took them into custody. Next morning the men were fined 10s. Such cases were the small change of police business.

Britain's police forces were guaranteed a bad press if they slipped up, and journalists were certain of getting their names in print if they exposed a scandal involving the police. And not only journalists. In 1903 Sir Arthur Conan Doyle came across the case of George Edalji, the son of a Parsee country vicar, sent to prison for horse-maiming. Thinking the sentence of seven years was somewhat harsh, Conan Doyle decided to emulate his own Sherlock Holmes and investigate. He found that Edalji had been convicted because he was coloured, and that he was a studious, shortsighted man who had worked in a solicitor's office and written, at the age of twenty-seven, an authoritative book on railway law. Conan Doyle's series of articles in the *Daily Telegraph* in 1907 once more cast doubt on the quality of the police.

It was the age of the fictitious amateur detective; apart from Sherlock Holmes, there were, among others, Chesterton's Father Brown, Freeman's John Thorndyke, and Baroness Orczy's Old Man in the Corner. The 'old man in the corner' figured in two Edwardian collections published in 1905 and 1909; he sat in an ABC teashop drinking milk and tying and untying knots in strings, solving crimes that had baffled the police, for the benefit of a girl reporter. 'There is no such thing as a mystery in connection with any crime, provided intelligence is brought to bear upon its investigation', he stated. And intelligence, it was implicit, was notably lacking in the baffled police, who were invariably portrayed in fiction as incompetent inferiors to the brilliant sleuths.

Baroness Orczy was at one with the suffragettes in her belief that everything a man could do, a woman could do—better, and this included, for the baroness, police work. In 1910 *Lady Molly of Scotland Yard* appeared, featuring Lady Molly Robertson-Kirk 'head of the Female Department'—in fact as late as 1926 the CID had only one woman detective, and women police were not introduced until 1919.

It sometimes seemed that criminals were taking their tone from A. J. Raffles and other gentleman crooks. Violent crime was rare. Besides keeping the crime rate down, Macnaghten stopped major crime escalating as it had done in the United States. Murder was sufficiently uncommon for there to be no homicide squad at Scotland Yard, and firearms were generally eschewed. There were two instances during the period where the smooth fabric of the crime pattern was shattered and the police engaged in armed conflict with law-breakers.

The first occurred in 1909, when Paul Hefeld and Jacob

Violent crime was rare, but when it occurred it was relentlessly exploited by the press, who found it good copy. A payroll robbery in Tottenham in 1909 inspired several magazine serials

Meyer, described as 'Russians of doubtful character', snatched a payroll of £80 from outside a Tottenham factory. They were on foot, and were pursued by two policemen in the car that had brought the money from the bank. Hefeld fired three shots at the car; one missed, one smashed the windscreen, and the last pierced the radiator, stopping the engine. The policemen continued the chase on foot, with the two men firing at them.

A small boy who came along to see the fun was shot dead, and as the action moved towards Tottenham Marshes a bullet killed one of the policemen. Nothing like this had ever happened before. The telegraph began tapping out its slow message to the various police stations, and—knowing that this was a case where they could not be rendered speechless by acid-tongued magistrates— the London constabulary flung themselves into the pursuit on horseback, on bicycles, in carriages and motor cars, and even a bus. They were hindered by a vast crowd of well-wishers, and two men with shotguns who were bird-shooting on the marshes watched the whole cavalcade go by, not knowing the reason for it. By the time the two fugitives had reached the Chingford Road they had killed two persons and wounded twenty others.

An electric tramcar on the Chingford Road was held up at the point of a pistol to allow the two men to get aboard. An elderly passenger who objected was shot, and from the back of the car Meyer fired at the pursuers who had requisitioned a horse-trap. The horse was hit and the occupants thrown out; a tram-car travelling in the opposite direction was stopped, and reversed with the police on board. A car drew ahead of the leading tram and Meyer and Hefeld were forced to get out. They took over a milkcart, which was wrecked, and then a greengrocer's cart, which they abandoned before taking to the fields, heading for Epping Forest. Sportsmen with shotguns had now joined in. Hefeld fell wounded, but before he could be captured he turned his gun on himself and blew his brains out. Meyer carried on alone. He made for an unfinished building, where a plasterer threw bricks at him and was shot. Meyer took refuge in a cottage and tried unsuccessfully to hide in the chimney. He fled upstairs, locking himself in a bedroom. There was some doubt as to whether he killed himself or was shot by two armed policemen who followed him into the cottage. The whole affair was quite outside the experience of the police. The public felt that at last real life was taking on the colours of adventure fiction. This view was confirmed less than two years later when other foreign criminals demonstrated that gun battles were not, by act of God, restricted to the eruptive continent of Europe.

In December 1910 a small gang of aliens resolved to rob a jeweller's shop in Houndsditch; they took the premises next door, intending to break through the intervening wall. While they were busy with the crowbar, the proprietor of a fancy goods shop heard suspicious sounds, and summoned the police. The four investigating policemen were inquisitive rather than bent upon arrest, but a foot was put in the door when one of the gang tried to slam it in the leading officer's face. The gang panicked, shooting the four policemen and their own leader. Another policeman was killed when he tried to tackle one of the gang who left the house.

In the confusion the criminals escaped, and took refuge in Grove Street, Whitechapel. They had with them the shot member of the gang. A doctor, who was summoned, accepted the story that the dying man had been accidentally shot in the back, and did not report the matter to the police. When he returned to the house to see how the man was getting on, he found him dead and the others gone; only then did he tell the police, who searched the place and found a loaded pistol. There was a round-up of revolutionaries, and a small arsenal and a collection of anarchist literature were found in a house in Gold Street, off the Whitechapel Road.

The police came to a dead end in their investigations, and it seemed as though the whole affair would turn out to be inconclusive. A year went by before information reached the police that two of the wanted men had taken refuge in 100 Sidney Street, a squalid thoroughfare running between the Mile End Road and the Commercial Road. The police were told that the men were armed with Mauser pistols and a large stock of ammunition. It was perhaps typical of the lack of preparedness for any such contingencies that the ninety policemen recruited for the assault of Sidney Street were armed with inferior revolvers and rifles from a miniature rifle range.

It was difficult to clear the surrounding houses and to winkle out the occupants of the building; an elderly couple on the ground floor, no doubt thinking that their worst fears of the police were justified, screamed and had to be removed by force.

Bovril

"I have saved a cup for you"

Notwithstanding such events as the Sidney Street siege, the public's image of the policeman was stable enough for it to appear in advertisement form

Gradually the police cordon reached two hundred, and at dawn the door was knocked and gravel thrown at the windows. This drew the fire of the inmates, and one policeman was hit.

It was soon realised that the police weapons were nothing but toys, and a detachment of Scots Guards was summoned from the Tower of London. Everybody was keen to have a go. Sportsmen with shotguns saw this as their hour of glory (after all, only two men were up there, and they were foreigners and therefore of little account) and were disappointed that they were not called upon; so were the police, who offered to carry the house by frontal assault. Historic significance was given to what was afterwards called the Siege of Sidney Street by the arrival of Winston Churchill, the home secretary, who suggested that artillery should be brought to the scene and Royal Engineers should drive tunnels beneath the house. In the event, though the artillery arrived, it was not used, but the owners of nearby property had a few uneasy moments.

The police fired at the house, the gang fired back, and the crowd of spectators became bored. Their unspoken thoughts were answered by a wisp of smoke at an upstairs window; the house was on fire. The flames forced the two men down to the ground floor, and after a time the firing from the house ceased. The police and fire-brigade entered the burning building, but for a time they could not find the bodies of the two men—raising the suspicion that the police had in some curious manner let the men get away through the back of the house. Eventually the two charred corpses were found. Two hundred policemen, nineteen Scots Guards marksmen, and two pieces of artillery had been set against two armed men locked in a house from which there was no escape. A mystery grew up around the name of Peter the Painter, though there was a good deal of doubt concerning who he was, where he was, and what he had to do with the Sidney Street charade.

Such deeds of 'derring do' proved a welcome relief from the humdrum business of everyday life for both police and public, and helped to avert attention from the activities of the suffragettes, who had done nothing so spectacular as to engage in a pitched gun battle with the constabulary. It might be too cynical to say that the only thing learned at the Siege of Sidney Street was how to carry unwilling civilians from their homes; this proved useful in dealing with militant suffragettes.

Forgery and Fraud

Where there are large sums of money about and the motivating spirit of the period is greed then there will be fraud. Money was the god of the Edwardian age, and was pursued with a passion that the Victorians would have considered ill-bred. There was nothing disgraceful in the making of fortunes, and the shopocracy, the tradesmen who had lifted themselves out of the middle classes by the making of millions, were endlessly courted by the aristocracy. They could do no wrong, and their social gaffes were politely ignored. It was a shock to all, aristocracy and shopocracy alike, when William Whiteley, the 'universal provider' of Bayswater, was killed by his illegitimate son.

A gullible public eager for easy money were a ready prey for anyone with get-rich-quick schemes, such as the South and South-West Coast Steam Trawling and Fishing Syndicate, which was run by Charles de Ville Wells, a picturesque scoundrel immortalised as the man who broke the bank at Monte Carlo, not once but half a dozen times in the space of a fortnight. By 1906 Wells had come down in the world, having made and lost millions, and done a spell in prison. His colleague in the syndicate was an unfrocked clergyman named Moyle.

Wells and Moyle followed the standard pattern by inserting advertisements in the leading daily newspapers, offering a monthly income of £20 on every £100 invested. Hundreds applied and, although for the first month or so they received their 'interest', payments soon ceased. The syndicate also claimed to own a patent life-saving apparatus, the 'Enforced Breathing Apparatus', and had so much confidence in it that they displayed it at a fisheries exhibition in London. Wells had lost his touch and was soon convicted, being sentenced to three years. Other financiers and entrepreneurs were more astute.

A. W. Carpenter worked along the same lines as Wells and Moyle only on a larger scale. There were still a considerable number of private banks in existence and, notwithstanding the collapse of several of them in the nineteenth century, many people preferred to put their money into these small banks, encouraged by the large rates of interest offered. Carpenter owned the Charing Cross Bank, which he had started in 1886 as a corollary to his money-lending business. He offered six per cent interest for six-month deposits, seven per cent for twelve months, and ten per cent for five years. Carpenter had a gigantic ego, and was confident that his investments, using the money deposited in his bank, would pay off handsomely; his main interests were in Canada and in South African gold. In 1907 the magazine *Truth* began to have doubts about the Charing Cross Bank, but little was done and the public's attention would not have been drawn to Carpenter's machinations if he had not employed an accountant to put the bank's internal affairs in order. The accountant found evidence of incompetence and dishonesty on the part of Carpenter's underlings, and also became aware that the bank was based on very shaky foundations. The accountant asked advice of his solicitors, and in due course the affairs of the Charing Cross Bank were examined with a view to prosecution; it closed down in October 1910 with a deficit of nearly £2 million.

A good deal of fraud was possible because of the lenient attitude of a number of the large banks towards forgery, partly due to the lapse of the Bankers' Association which once prosecuted in all cases. Any moves that reflected on the unreliability of the banking machine were avoided, and bank employees involved in embezzlement were rarely punished; one offender was given £100 and a passage to Canada to get him out of the way. When the banks did prosecute they often used inexperienced barristers who were friends of bank officials. This rebounded, for the offenders gave their cases to better advocates, and frequently got off.

When prosecutions were undertaken, gangs of forgers were often uncovered, whose principals remained in the background to avoid risk. The usual method employed by forgers was to use a messenger boy, who would take a forged cheque to a bank and cash it. Outside the bank he would be followed unobtrusively by one of the gang. The messenger had previously been told to go to a certain shop and buy something. If the transaction went through, the forger would know that the coup had been successful; if the messenger boy had been stopped in the bank, or did not emerge from the shop with the goods, the watcher would slip away.

Specialists in forged cheques usually put in a good deal of homework on their subjects, and took pains to obtain genuine signatures to copy. One master forger went into business partnership with Mrs Hughes, known as the queen of begging-letter writers. Those who believed in the 'criminal type' were thwarted by the forging fraternity, many of whom came from good families and utilised their inner knowledge of society and the vulnerability of the bank manager class when faced by their betters. Typical of the well-bred forgers was Captain Henry Fane, a former officer of the Rifle Brigade, and a member of the Army and Navy Club. The club had the quaint habit of supplying blank cheques to those members who asked for them, and with the aid of such cheques Fane and his colleagues got away with a good deal of money, using the messenger boy gambit. Of an even more ingenious cast was Robert Hutchinson, Etonian and Leicestershire country gentleman who, as chairman of the local conservative association, organised a Budget Protest League against Lloyd George's soak-the-rich budget. One of those approached for a guinea subscription to this league was the local conservative candidate, Thomas Paget.

Armed with this cheque, Hutchinson called at Paget's house in London, and purloined a supply of headed notepaper. On this paper Hutchinson requested Lloyd's Bank, Leicester, to send a cheque-book to the Burlington Hotel, Eastbourne, into which a collaborator had booked under the name of the conservative candidate. On leaving the hotel, 'Paget' instructed the hotel to post his correspondence to 28 Upper George Street in the West End, which turned out to be a holding address for correspondence. Hutchinson made out a cheque for £975, which was duly cashed, though several of the nine £100 notes paid out by the bank eventually led back to Hutchinson's own bank account in Manchester.

The method adopted by Gerald Kennaway was cruder but no less effective—it involved stealing letters from pillar-boxes. Cheques contained in letters had their endorsements removed with acids, and Kennaway, a gentleman, had no difficulty in cashing them. Retribution was never far behind and he served several sentences in prison, in 1900, 1902, 1910 and 1916. Much of this was due to increased energy and perseverance on the part of the prosecution, and Sir Richard Muir, the prosecutor of Crippen, made himself a specialist in forgery cases. As the years went by, courts increased their sentences in cases of fraud, especially the so-called 'bucket shop' frauds. The names of small investors were uncovered from the files of various companies, and these—often country clergymen, a class never averse to financial dabbling—were circularised, fascinated by the prospect of fortnightly dividends. A company would be started with a formidable title and offices in a prestige thoroughfare in the City, and after sending out cheques for a few shillings the organisers of the frauds would disappear into obscurity, emerging soon afterwards with another company and another set of circulars. Even when caught, their sentences were light, and they thought a few months' imprisonment worth the risk. With years substituted for months, the 'bucket shop' frauds lapsed.

Society was not worried by the spate of minor frauds perpetrated on banks, which could afford to lose the money anyway, or on unimportant middle-class dabblers. Apprehension was felt only when society itself was involved, or worse, when frauds were carried out by people who were known and had been entertained socially on account of their money-making abilities. A man who could make millions was, by definition, a man worth cultivating.

One of the most spectacular of the grand masters of fraudulence was Ernest Terah Hooley, who in 1896-7 made £7 million profit, got rid of the lot, was made bankrupt to the tune of £1.5 million, and started again from scratch. His biggest and most dramatic coup was in 1896 when he bought the Dunlop Tyre Company for £3 million and refloated it a few months later for £5 million. This put him in line for a baronetcy, but whispers of his bankruptcy deterred the promoters. As soon as Hooley had got over the bankruptcy, he threw his energies into Siberian gold, and floated a £1 million company, but this was repudiated by the Russian Government and came to nothing.

From his house, Papworth Hall in Cambridgeshire, Hooley organised his empire, persuaded the Privy Council to make him

High Sheriff of Cambridgeshire, and disdainfully lent money to those members of the aristocracy who would creep low enough. He spent £250,000 on improving Papworth Hall, endowed the conservative party with large sums of money, and carried on his operations until 1912 when he found himself at the Old Bailey, charged with swindling a young Rochdale engineer of £2,000. Hooley was a challenge to the legal profession, but by 1912 his charisma had dispersed and he had outlived his period. When Hooley operated again in 1920 he was pounced upon, and made an example of for speculating in the Lancashire cotton boom.

Whitaker Wright reached his peak at the same time as Hooley. He broke into the London financial scene in 1889, promoted the West Australian Exploration and Finance Corporation in 1894, and the London and Globe Finance Corporation in 1895. These two companies floated venture after venture, and financed the Baker Street and Waterloo Railway, later known as the Bakerloo line. The West Australian venture proved immensely profitable and paid out millions in dividends. Whitaker Wright was accepted into aristocratic circles and the seal of respectability was given to his projects when the Marquis of Dufferin and Ava became chairman of the board of the London and Globe.

Whitaker Wright's home, Lea Park near Godalming, was perhaps one of the most spectacular private residences in Edwardian England. Bought in 1896 for £250,000, Wright spent £1 million on improvements, one of which was a conservatory beneath a large artificial lake. His architectural and landscaping visions transcended mere vulgarity. A marble fountain weighing sixty tons had to be hauled to its site by traction engines as it was too heavy for the railway to carry. A private theatre costing £15,000 was built inside the house and there were stables for fifty horses.

Behind this façade things were not as they seemed. In 1899 the Marquis of Dufferin declared that the London and Globe Finance Corporation possessed more than £500,000 in cash— actual figure £29,300. The crash was not far off. In 1901 an order was made winding up Whitaker Wright's companies, and the shareholders in the London and Globe, which had a capital of

£2 million, got nothing. Many were affected by the debâcle, and one firm of stockbrokers lost £365,000. Whitaker Wright still had friends in high places and it was considered that a prosecution would prove fruitless, though when he fled to France in 1903 it was decided to extradite him.

It was difficult to ascertain how many millions were involved in the crash, and Wright's habit of switching millions from one company to another made the case complex and arduous. Many lawyers privately confessed that they would never again officiate in a case where financial wizards were involved. Wright received, for that period, a fierce sentence of seven years, but committed suicide by taking cyanide in the lavatory at the Old Bailey. The verdict of suicide while of unsound mind would have been disputed by the envious. Whitaker Wright had made and lost millions, had the pick of mistresses and given yachts away as other men proffer drinks. In an age that worshipped wealth and conspicuous consumption, Wright was a subject for emulation; his death was seen as the departure of a god.

Murder Most Foul

Murder trials were very popular in Edwardian England, which saw a number of interesting cases. It also saw the beginning of the intriguing practice of forensic medicine, the supreme exponent of which was Sir Bernard Spilsbury. There were some picturesque advocates, such as Sir Edward Marshall Hall, who were as newsworthy as music hall stars and whose appearances at the Old Bailey were watched by their admirers. Marshall Hall defended Robert Wood in what was known as the Camden Town murder, and among those attending the trial were the actress Gertie Millar; Lady Tree, wife of the celebrated actor-manager; the playwright Pinero; the actor Henry Irving and the novelist Hall Caine.

This 1907 murder trial, though not one of the classic cases, featured Sir Charles Mathews for the Crown, and public saw it as a battle of the giants. By and large, there was not much interest in the accused, an artist who had once been praised by William Morris, and little sympathy with the victim, a prostitute.

Emily Dimmock, known as Phyllis, was found naked on her bed, her throat cut from ear to ear so savagely that the head was only attached to the body by a few muscles. The question was whether the artistic Wood could have done this deed to the girl whom he described as 'a crushed rose—that had not lost all its fragrance, and had been thrown aside. She seemed a girl who might have seen better days, who might have made a good wife in other circumstances'.[1]

Emily Dimmock was living with a man named Shaw, whose name she had taken, and the case revolved around a postcard sent to her from 'Alice' inviting 'Mrs Shaw' to meet 'her' at the Rising Sun public house, depicted in a sketch of a rising sun. The postcard was reproduced in a Sunday newspaper where it was seen by Ruby Young, a model who had been seduced by a medical man; she had turned prostitute and was on affectionate terms with Wood. She recognised the handwriting and style as belonging to him, and sent him the newspaper clipping. In great distress, Wood admitted to her that he had met Emily Dimmock at the Rising Sun, the Friday before she was murdered, that a boy had been touting picture postcards and he had bought one, and sent it to her. He had seen her on the Monday, had been with his brother on the Tuesday, and on the Wednesday had been walking alone. Wednesday had been the night of the murder. He persuaded Ruby Young to give him an alibi, to tell the police if they came to her that she had spent every Monday and Wednesday with him. He protested that there was nothing between Emily and himself, that he had signed the letter 'Alice' at Emily's request because 'the guv'nor might cut up rough', and that he liked Emily's company because she was intelligent (and had, though he did not tell Miss Young, a kink about prostitutes).

Ruby Young was frightened, and put the matter in a hypothetical way to a woman friend, who saw through the fabrication and introduced her to a journalist. He obtained the full story and introduced Ruby to a police inspector. It was not long before Wood was arrested, and he was recognised by a bookseller as having been with Emily as late as 10.30 pm at the Eagle public house on the evening of the murder. It seemed as though it was all up with Wood. However, his employers pooh-poohed the idea that the gentle, foolish youth was a murderer, and were willing to back him with expensive counsel. Counsel considered the evidence was all circumstantial and applied for bail, whereupon the arresting inspector disclosed that Wood had been recognised as a man leaving the murder house at 5 am on the morning of the murder. The witness was a carman who said that the man he saw had a peculiarity in the way he walked. This was denied by everyone who knew Wood—except Ruby Young, seemingly intent on slipping the noose around the neck of her lover.

The evidence of the carman was ruthlessly broken down by the defence. He agreed with the defence that it was a drizzly, foggy morning (which it was not), and that but for the street lamps it would have been impossible to identify anyone who left the house. The defence had a lighting-chart from the electric lighting company stating that the current had been switched off at 4.37 am, fifteen minutes before the witness had seen the alleged murderer pass beneath its glare. Nevertheless the collapse of one of the key prosecution witnesses did not prevent Wood being committed for trial, and at this point Marshall Hall was brought in.

For a year or two, partly due to a feud with Lord Northcliffe of the *Daily Mail*, Marshall Hall's stock had been low, but had picked up slightly in 1906. He had unsuccessfully defended a gamekeeper charged with stealing 20,000 pheasant eggs; he had prosecuted a mad woman for killing a child in a nursing home; and had been involved in a curious matrimonial case where a husband had pursued, in a tug, the liner in which his wife was travelling, to make sure that she was not joined by her lover. When Marshall Hall was offered the Camden Town murder case he realised this could restore his reputation, and he made the most of the opportunity, swaying public feeling on to Wood's side. A huge mob, solidly behind Wood, waited outside the court, which was surrounded by dozens of police. In the streets were fifty mounted policemen ready for riot and crowd control.

During the closing stages of the trial the judge veered from his animosity towards Marshall Hall and Wood, and in his summing up he indicated to the jury that he did not consider the prosecution's case strong enough. His statement that the jury was not bound to act on his view was inconsequential, for they too had swung round in favour of Wood, who was acquitted.

The Camden Town murder had the two vital ingredients—violence and sex—and no one was particularly worried that somewhere a prostitute murderer was on the rampage. A few sensationalists did not hesitate to point out that it might be Jack the Ripper repeating his performance in another subfusc area of London. The lynching of Ruby Young, who in the public's view deserved the same treatment as Emily Dimmock, was narrowly averted. All prostitutes were fair game to a hysterical mob.

The appeal of such cases as the Camden Town murder key in with the psychoanalyst's view that murder is a reenactment of the 'primal scene' of infancy, representing parental sexual intercourse; the victim is the parent, and the clues are 'symbolic representations of mysterious nocturnal sounds, stains, incomprehensible adult jokes'.[2] Even forgetting such an interpretation, it is not surprising that the Farrow murder case, though perhaps historically more significant than the Camden Town murder, proved less popular to the general public.

In 1905 an elderly couple named Farrow were found murdered in a small chandler's shop in High Street, Deptford. They lived over the shop and, according to gossip, there were large sums of money in the house (in fact, there was never more than £6 or so). A boy employed in the shop arrived one morning and found the shutters still closed. He peered through the letter-box, saw a chair upturned and called for help. Mr Farrow was dead in the kitchen, his head smashed, and his wife was dying upstairs in bed, also with head injuries. Two masks made from black stockings were discovered, plus an empty cash-box. Two milkmen declared that they had seen two men leave the shop at 7.15 am, and a man and a woman saw Mr Farrow come to the front door, look up and down the street, then go back. They observed with perfunctory interest that the old man was terribly injured about the head and face. The police assumed that Mr Farrow had regained consciousness long enough to go to the door, open it, look up and down the street, and return to the kitchen to die.

One of the first men on the scene was the chief of the CID, Sir Melville Macnaghten, who was excited by the appearance of a fingerprint on the cash-box. It was a blurred print, but it was a clue. The fingerprint section, now three years old, had something to go on, though there was momentary dismay when a young detective sergeant admitted that he had moved the box beneath the bed, fearing the ambulance men taking the body of Mrs Farrow downstairs would trip over it. The fingerprint, however, did not belong to the sergeant, nor to the couple.

Deptford was one of the lowest quarters of early twentieth-century London, and there were plenty of candidates for murder. Two brothers named Stratton seemed to merit especial investigation and a net was cast for them; this feeling was confirmed when the girl friend of one of the brothers contributed some evidence. The elder brother was easy to find, but it was decided to get them both together. As they enjoyed football, a cup-tie at the Crystal Palace seemed a logical Saturday afternoon venue. The brothers did not turn up. Instructions were issued to the police that either brother should be arrested if seen, and soon both were under lock and key with their fingerprints taken.

It was the first murder case in which fingerprinting was in evidence, and there was considerable delight when it was found that there were eleven points of resemblance between the print on the cash-box and the right thumb-print of the elder brother. (Today this would not be enough.) The whole system of fingerprinting had to be explained to the jurymen, who had a bonus by having their fingerprints taken and a lecture by the police. The defence called an expert, but as he had first offered his services to the prosecution his evidence was declared suspect. Representing the accused was Mr Rooth, later a London magistrate; he dismissed the whole concept of fingerprints contemptuously, saying that it savoured more of the French courts and was decidedly not suitable to 'the English mind'. The judge was more cautious, but commented on the 'extraordinary resemblance' between the photographs of the print on the box and the print from Stratton's thumb. The jury had little doubt abut the matter, and the Strattons were duly convicted and hanged.

In a letter to the criminologist William Roughhead, Henry James requested him to 'go back to the dear old human and sociable murders and adulteries and forgeries in which we are so agreeably at home'.[3] The Farrow murder was neither human nor sociable, nor did it have any tincture of adultery. The Crippen case had all three. There was also a vast difference in techniques between 1905 and 1910. The Crippen case produced a new hero for the masses—a real-life Sherlock Holmes in the person of Sir Bernard Spilsbury.

It is generally believed that the Crippen case was cut and dried, and that he richly deserved to be hanged for a cold-blooded and dastardly crime. Most people are a bit foggy about the actual circumstances of the case, and only know that Crippen was brought to retribution by the use of the new-fangled wireless telegraph.

Hawley Harvey Crippen was born in Michigan in 1862, came to England when he was twenty-one to pick up some medical knowledge, and returned to America, where he obtained a diploma in homeopathy and then one in ophthalmics, modest credentials that enabled him to call himself 'doctor'. He operated in fringe medicine in alliance with patent medicine companies, and married twice, his first wife dying in 1890 or 1891. During a stay in New York he met Cora Turner, real name Kunigunde Mackamotski, a seventeen-year-old girl of uncertain morals who had been the mistress of a stove manufacturer. She fancied that she had a voice worth cultivating, and Crippen paid for operatic lessons.

In 1900 his company sent him to England as its British representative. Later in the year he was joined in his rooms off the Tottenham Court Road by his wife, a bejewelled, vulgar,

Crippen, the most notorious murderer of the age

cheerful woman. Mrs Crippen set her sights on the English music hall, then in all its glory, and although she got one or two minor engagements she did not consider her talents were appreciated. When her husband was recalled for six months to America, she lowered her sights and entertained at 'smoking concerts' where cheap coarseness was much appreciated. While her husband was away she met Bruce Miller, an American music-hall performer, and was in all probability his mistress. On his return, Crippen took her away from the disreputable rooms in Guilford Street, and installed her in Store Street, Bloomsbury, loading her with expensive clothes which he could ill afford, as he moved from one area of fringe medicine to another. One firm with which he was involved was the Yale Tooth Specialists, where he employed the typist Ethel le Neve, a delicate, ailing and respectable girl.

In 1905 the Crippens moved to 39 Hilldrop Crescent in Camden Town, a large gloomy house in a district that had gone to seed, the idea being that they should take in lodgers so as to eke out Crippen's small income. Their domestic life was squalid in the extreme and, except when they were entertaining— for Mrs Crippen, under her stage name Belle Elmore, still had theatrical connections—they lived in the kitchen. They kept no maid, a circumstance that appalled their friends, for Crippen was technically a member of the middle classes.

Crippen took Ethel le Neve as his mistress, making guilty love to her in a series of hotel rooms. By 1909 the situation was deteriorating. The lodgers were always men with an eye for a buxom wench; Mrs Crippen, fretful and quarrelsome, knew about the two-year liaison with Ethel le Neve, and threatened to leave her husband, taking with her their joint savings amounting to £600. On 15 December she gave notice of withdrawal to the bank. A month later Crippen ordered five grains of hyoscin hydrobromide—a quantity so large that it had to be obtained from the wholesalers—and this he collected on 19 January 1910.

On 31 January the Crippens gave a little dinner-party. This was the last time Mrs Crippen was seen alive. Crippen gave out that she had gone to America and died on the voyage. Ethel le Neve moved into 39 Hilldrop Crescent (later renamed Filleted Plaice by a callous public), took the name of Crippen, and employed a French maid. She also decked herself out in Mrs Crippen's finery, and was indiscreet enough to go with her lover to a ball wearing one of his wife's brooches—a circumstance that was noted by acquaintances of the Crippens, though it was several months before the suspicions were told to the police. When they interviewed Crippen he changed his story, saying his wife had left him for another man, leaving her belongings behind. The police searched the house and, apparently satisfied, went away. Before completely dropping the matter, an Inspector Dew paid a visit to Crippen's consulting-room to ask a few supplementary questions, only to be told that the doctor had gone abroad. And so had Miss le Neve.

The police returned to the house, the garden was dug up, and a loose brick in the cellar encouraged them to concentrate their efforts there. Buried in quicklime under the floor were small pieces of flesh wrapped in an old pyjama coat, marked with the retailer's name. The specialists got to work. One piece of flesh was from the abdomen and had an operation scar. The flesh was therefore human. Analysis showed that it contained 2/7 of a grain of hyoscin.

The search was on for Crippen, and E. R. Henry, commissioner of police, offered a reward of £250. The response was incredible but largely irrelevant. The only lead came from Captain Kendall, of the liner *Montrose* bound from Antwerp to Canada, who had seen with puritanical disquiet 'Master Robinson' squeezing the hand of 'Mr Robinson'. He had sent a message by wireless to the owners who had contacted Scotland Yard. Inspector Dew travelled on the *Laurentic*, a faster vessel. In the guise of a pilot, he boarded the *Montrose*, and it was as he thought—the insignificant, polite, dapper, bespectacled Mr Robinson was Dr Crippen, wanted, as the reward poster put it, for, 'murder and mutilation'.

Without any further evidence, the presence of hyoscin and the abdominal scar would probably have sent Crippen to the gallows. The police thought so, and after Crippen had been brought back Dew was inclined to be languid, so much so that the prosecutor, Muir, suggested that Dew was suffering from sleeping sickness. The police bestirred themselves to find the final nail for the Crippen coffin. This centred around the pyjama jacket. If it had been bought before the Crippens moved to Hilldrop Crescent, it was possible, barely possible, that the remains had been put in the cellar by a previous tenant, Crippen maintained that he had bought the jacket several years earlier, but a buyer from Jones Brothers, the retailers, asserted that the material was not acquired until 1908 and that three pairs were supplied to Crippen in 1909. The jury was out for half an hour, their verdict was guilty, and the appeal failed. Crippen, the epitome of the little man who used the women's method of murder, was hanged.

Miss le Neve, tried as an accessory after the fact, was acquitted. Throughout the trial Crippen had done his best to protect his mistress. Marshall Hall, who was not involved in the case though he took an intense interest in it, maintained that Crippen would have made good his escape if he had fled alone, and Lord Birkenhead declared that Crippen 'was, at least, a brave man, and a true lover'. Marshall Hall had nearly been drawn into defending him, but Crippen's refusal to deviate from a suicidal line of defence would have afforded him no scope for his own astounding theory that the death of Mrs Crippen was due to an accident, that the hyoscin had been procured not to kill the woman but to reduce her sexual demands on Crippen, or render her unconscious so that he could take Miss le Neve to his house and have sex with her.

The drug was a comparatively new one, though in the form of henbane it was well-known in folk medicine. In small doses it produced drowsiness and sleep, and had the properties of affecting the memory centres. A person taking it would not know that he or she had done so, or realise that he or she had been unconscious. It was possible that Crippen had been drugging his wife for some time, gradually increasing the dosages as her resistance built up. That he bought a large quantity in one go does not indicate that he had never bought the drug before, either in its natural form as henbane—an easily obtained plant of the nightshade variety—or treated. A methodical, careful man, it was out of character for Crippen to betray himself by buying such a large quantity of hyoscin if his intention was to murder his wife, rather than put her into a state of oblivion while he dallied with his mistress.

Whether the prosecution felt any uncertainty about the verdict is a moot point. After the execution Muir made the cryptic remark that 'full justice has not yet been done'. This can only refer to either a belief that Ethel le Neve was an accomplice and should have shared Crippen's fate, or that Marshall Hall's tentative line of defence was right. One commentator on the case said that either Miss le Neve had no character at all, or plenty. The question remains open as to whether she was the instigator of it all, and whether Crippen was not the monster of legend but a puppet manipulated by a deceptively innocent typist.

The public, who dearly loved a villain to look like a villain, were well served by Frederick Seddon, the Holloway superintendent of the London & Manchester Insurance Company.

In 1910 Seddon sublet part of his house to Miss Eliza Barrow and her entourage—an adopted son and some people named Hook. Miss Barrow was forty-nine, crusty, suspicious, difficult to live with, and a miser, distrusting banks and keeping hundreds of pounds in gold and notes in a box beneath her pillow. She had £1,600 in gilt-edged securities, and owned a shop and a public house. Her total assets amounted to about £4,000. Seddon wheedled his way into her confidence, and advised her to transfer her securities to him in return for just over £3 a week. On 1 September 1911, Miss Barrow became ill and the doctor sent her to bed. On the night of 13 September she died, with Seddon sitting outside the door, not bothering to send for a doctor, a fact he admitted when he was brought to trial. Without going to see the body, the doctor granted Seddon a death certificate stating that Miss Barrow had died from epidemic diarrhoea. Seddon went to the local undertaker and bargained for the cheapest funeral possible—£4 less his 12s 6d commission— then returned to the house and took the contents of her money box, leaving £10 from an estimated £800. On the evening of the funeral, Seddon and his wife went to a music hall.

The only known relatives of Miss Barrow did not hear of the death for several days, and when they went to Seddon's house they found that he and his wife had gone away on holiday. Suspicious, the relatives went to the police, and in November the body was exhumed and found to contain arsenic. It was proved that the Seddons had bought fly papers, from which it was assumed that Seddon had obtained the arsenic. Mrs Seddon had changed with local tradesmen many of the Bank of England notes belonging to Miss Barrow and been misguided enough to endorse them with a false name and address. The public and the jury did not need anything else; they were already determined

Crowds waiting outside the Old Bailey for the outcome of the Seddon trial

that Seddon was guilty because he looked it, having close-set eyes and an air of utter callousness. The fact that he and his wife had visited a music hall on the night of the funeral was as significant as evidence that was purely circumstantial; Seddon had also made a psychological bloomer in taking his commission on the £4 funeral. He was hanged in April 1912, protesting his innocence.

A good deal of apprehension was felt by the public over a number of unsolved murders. They were not particularly worried that the police were baffled by the prostitute murders— Emily Dimmock, of the Camden Town case; Dora Kiernicke, whose nude body was found in January 1904 in a room in Whitefield Street, Tottenham Court Road; or Esther Praager, of 3 Bernard Street, Russell Square, also killed in the nude, though she had been strangled whereas Miss Kiernicke had had her throat cut.

The murder of Mrs Luard, in a summer-house near her home

at Ightham Knoll, near Sevenoaks, was another matter. For she was a lady, the wife of Major-General C. E. Luard. She had been shot, and robbery had apparently been the motive, for four valuable rings had been torn from her fingers and her purse had been stolen. The case was interesting because Scotland Yard accused the local police of walking over all the clues and not calling them in until it was too late. They were also scathing about the opinion of a Dr T. A. Mansfield, who was brought in initially, and who, observing that there were two bullet wounds in the head, suggested that the dead woman had shot herself simultaneously with two revolvers, neither of which was found. A theory was put forward that the murder had been done by a tramp, but there were also rumours that Mrs Luard was involved in an eternal triangle situation (though she was about sixty and her husband seventy), and a number of anonymous letters and postcards were sent to the members of the jury at the coroner's inquest. Although General Luard was a quarter of an hour's walk from the summer-house when the shooting occurred, this did not save him from calumny, but even those who roundly dismissed the idea of the general shooting his wife must have had misgivings when they heard that he had killed himself by leaping under a train.

Public anxiety was also roused by an outbreak of seaside and railway murders. Yarmouth had witnessed two within twelve years, both involving women strangled with boot-laces. In January 1914, a strangled seven-year-old boy was pushed under the seat of a train bound for Broad Street from Chalk Farm; on this line the stations were only two minutes apart. In 1904 the body of a thirty-five-year-old female book-keeper was found gagged and mutilated in the mile-long tunnel between Victoria and Brighton.

The Edwardian public liked to read about these things. But in novels and detective fiction the murderer was always brought to book. In so many things, why did not life emulate the good taste of fiction?

Notes to this chapter are on page 295.

CHAPTER NINE

PRELUDE TO WAR

AFTER 1910 there was no question for most people that war was coming. The apparatus of war was all about. Maggie Benson, the sickly sister of the Benson family of authors, wrote a letter on the train to Cornwall: 'We have just crossed into Cornwall by the great harbour at Devonport, with battleships and torpedoes lying in it, looking like great ugly noxious beasts . . .'[1] Few could avoid seeing the portents. As early as 1908 the once-popular society preacher, Stopford Brooke, who had, at a time when such things were of consequence, created a furore by leaving the Church of England to become a Unitarian, realised the implications of a world war: 'But war, such as it is now, is not only a crime, it is the worst of follies. And it ought to be impossible. If it is not soon rendered so, the whole fabric of civilization will be expunged, and Europe will go back to savage conditions'.[2]

The death wish consumed Britain. Sir Edward Grey was aimlessly procrastinating, waiting for conditions to settle down; King George V was timid, incapable of the intimate diplomacy of his father; Asquith was an effete bystander from another age, waiting for the stab in the back. There were troubles with strikes, suffragettes and the Irish, as well as distrust and antagonism between and within the services. It appeared to some that a war would solve these difficulties; to others that war would be categorically welcome, as it was to the notorious Frank Harris, quondam friend of Oscar Wilde. England, Harris considered, was effete, puritanical and poisonous (if only because W. H. Smith's book stalls had refused to sell the *English Review* which contained one of his short stories). D. H. Lawrence was of much the same mind, for similar reasons. 'We ought to be grateful to Germany', he wrote shortly after the outbreak of war, 'that she still has the power to burst the bound hide of the cabbage'. Rupert Brooke was 'extraordinarily happy' at the prospect of conflict.

In August 1911, Lloyd George wrote to Churchill: 'I have been reading the FO papers. They are full of menace. The thunderclouds are gathering. I am not at all satisfied that we are prepared, or that we are preparing'. The Admiralty was 'so cocksure, *insouciant* and apathetic, so far as one can judge from all that one sees and hears'.[3] The replacement of Sir John Fisher as the key man in the remodelled navy had perhaps not been so politically convenient after all.

Supporters of Haldane's 'model army' were also over-sanguine. Despite a study of the Russo-Japanese war, few experts had realised the devastating effect of small-arms fire employed in defence or the implications of the machine-gun. The British Expeditionary Force was perhaps the best disciplined of all the contemporary armies; its riflemen were beyond compare, and could fire up to eighteen rounds a minute. There was a plentiful supply of small-arms ammunition. Employed in the role of a strike force, the BEF would have been unequalled. As a subsidiary to the big, lumbering French army it was astonishingly ill-equipped, with little heavy artillery and inadequate medium artillery; worse still, it was short of artillery ammunition. Although it was known that communication would play a major part in modern war, telephones were in very short supply. Despite the fact that Britain led the world in heavy motor transport, the mentality of the army was still geared to the horse and the mule. Close-support weapons, particularly mortars and hand grenades, were lacking; hand grenades had been used to great effect in the siege of Port Arthur by the Japanese in 1904, and were to prove invaluable in trench warfare.

The British Army was not prepared for the kind of war it was going to fight. Kitchener knew it, but few others did. In the year before the war the number of men in the army actually went down. The Royal Navy was less efficient than it might have been; though the dreadnoughts and battle-cruisers were handsome, they were rarely what was needed in the conditions imposed on them. The aeronautical side was ill-developed, while too much money and attention had been devoted to airships. Fortunately the French air force was stronger, as was their aircraft engine technology, devolving from their supremacy in motor-car manufacture.

The British politicians were not alone in being unable to foresee the kind of war it was going to be, nor did they have a monopoly in sloppy statesmanship. George V was weak, but so was the Tsar. When the Tsar was forced to order mobilisation, he specified that it was to be against Austria-Hungary alone. This effort to restrict the conflict was unsuccessful, for his ministers overruled him, making the mobilisation general and thereby implicating Germany.

Would it have been possible to avert the war? It is an academic point, for war would have broken out somewhere, if not in 1914 then in 1915 or 1916. All the elements had been drawn together to make conflict inevitable. If vacillating is immoral, there were plenty of culprits, but in retrospect none of the nations involved was totally culpable, with the exception of Serbia. Austria-Hungary not unnaturally wished to keep Serbia in their fold; the Russians wanted to protect their minorities, who by a quirk of borders lived in Serbia, and Germany was anxious that Austria-Hungary should not have a lump knocked off her as this would diminish her credibility as a leading power. Austria-Hungary was the one ally upon which Germany could depend; Italy was an ally in name only. The alliance between France and Russia meant that any involvement of Russia in conflict with Germany would necessarily bring in France. Had the Tsar had his way and mobilised only against Austria-Hungary, then the situation might have cooled, with the Germans able to gain prestige as the benevolent responsible nation anxious to lower the temperature.

The assassination at Sarajevo on 28 June 1914 of the Austrian Archduke Franz Ferdinand by Bosnian-Serb students Princip and Cabrinović, who thought to solve Austro-Hungarian repression by the murder of figureheads, was only really significant as a spark to a fuse. Five weeks were to elapse between the assassination and the outbreak of war.

To the average Briton, no country was so uninteresting as Serbia. A little perfunctory indignation had been roused on her behalf in 1909 when *Punch* published a cartoon in which Europa, intervening between Austria and Serbia, was saying to the former: 'I think I can persuade my young friend here to be reasonable, and I am sure you can afford to be generous', to which Austria retorted, 'I don't remember to have asked your opinion, madam. But—if he's prepared to lick my boots, I'll then consider whether I'll allow him to go on living.' The climate of opinion represented by *Punch* had one basic quality— the willingness to patronise, to forget that the indignities forced upon Serbia by Austria were paralleled throughout the British Empire. The British press could always tap a vein of easy sentiment by sympathising with a small nation menaced by a hostile neighbour. But in 1914 the fate of Serbia caused few hackles to rise.

Belgium was different. On the map of Europe, she looked tiny and vulnerable, and somehow cosy. Britain identified with her. On 1 August 1914 Germany and Russia were at war; on 3 August Germany and France were at war, and Germany marched into Belgium. At midnight on 4 August Britain and Germany were at war, Germany having declined to pull her troops back from Belgium. In retrospect there does not seem to have been any military advantage to Germany in invading Belgium. It was a psychological blunder of the first magnitude. It may be that the German mind considered that Britain would not go to war where there were no pickings for her. Unquestionably, Germany considered that British diplomacy was Machiavellian and cunning, and that altruism rarely entered into British calculations.

Furthermore, Germany had already been assured by George V that Britain had no intention of warring with her. And it was only natural to mistake British confusion and muddle for disinterest.

War was inevitable. But Britain's participation was not. Why, asked the Germans, should the British be concerned about the insignificant boundaries of Europe when they themselves had shuffled the map of the world about in such a robust manner? It must be admitted that the Germans had a point. Their record was good. Their colonial policy in Africa was reasonably enlightened, and the assimilation into the German confederation of such disparate states as Baden, Saxony and Wurtemberg had been accomplished in a civilised manner. Nor was there any atrocity or repression in Alsace-Lorraine, won from France after the Franco-Prussian War of 1870. They could have pointed out that their colonial administration was a good deal better than that of poor little Belgium, whose overseas empire, the Congo, was harshly run as a private preserve of King Leopold.

'To Hell with Servia' Horatio Bottomley had exploded in his paper *John Bull*. To Hell with Belgium? But the atmosphere was too charged for this. In the hours before war was declared, Winston Churchill wrote that it was like waiting for the results of an election.

The French had no qualms about a continental war, and were contemptuous of British hesitation and uncertainty. There were solid reasons for a war with Germany. In eastern France there were large deposits of iron but little coal, but in western Germany there was coal but little iron. France had recently leapt into a leading place in the technological race with her achievements in motor manufacture and aeronautics. If she succeeded in winning mineral resources from Germany and dulling the impact of German technology there was no reason why France should not overtake Britain, well-known to be on the decline. The economy demanded war, either now or in the near future. Unlike Britain, France had invested heavily in her army. In the preceding ten years she and Russia had spent £842 million on their military machines, considerably more than Germany and Austria (£682

million). The pace was killing. Current expenditure on arma-
ments could not be maintained without bankruptcy.

France felt no indignation about Belgium. The treaty
guaranteeing Belgium neutrality had long been obsolete, and,
unknown to the sentimental British public, the French, British
and Belgium general staffs had assumed that France and Belgium
would form a single battlefield. Had the Germans not invaded
Belgium, thus putting themselves outside the pale so far as the
innocents went, the odds are that the French would have done so.
There were even plans for a landing of British troops on the
Belgian coast. There is room for speculation that France
deliberately leaked these plans to the Germans, encouraging them
to anticipate the situation and thereby guarantee British
intervention.

The extraordinary euphoria aroused by the war reflected
relief. The age of apprehension was over, and the issues were
now clear-cut. In *The World Crisis* 1911–18, Winston Churchill
quotes Dryden to demonstrate the mood; it is difficult to make
Dryden appear saccharine and soppy, but somehow Churchill
managed it:

> Men met each other with erected look,
> The steps were higher that they took,
> Friends to congratulate their friends made haste,
> And long-inveterate foes saluted as they passed.

At the outbreak of war, D. H. Lawrence descended from one
of his rural fastnesses into Barrow-in-Furness. 'All went mad',
he declared, with 'soldiers kissing on Barrow Station, and a
woman shouting defiantly to her sweetheart'.[4] Big business had
not wanted war. 'Money was a frightened and trembling thing.
Money shivered at the prospect'.[5] The newspapers had realised
that warmongering was totally different from actually going to
war. On 4 August, the last day of peace, the *Daily News* had put
in a plea for neutrality: 'if we remained neutral we should
be . . . able to trade with all the belligerents . . . We should be
able to capture the bulk of their trade in neutral markets'. Most
sternly anti-war had been the *Manchester Guardian*: 'We care as
little for Belgrade as Belgrade does for Manchester.'

Lloyd George had not wanted war. Even a German invasion of Belgium might be overlooked if they merely 'trespassed' on a corner of it to gain access to France, then evacuated it and paid compensation. To Lloyd George, however, war was less important than keeping the Liberal party together. Churchill wanted war, and so did the leader of the Conservative opposition, Bonar Law, on account of 'the honour and security of the United Kingdom'. In the best summing-up of the situation, Lloyd George wrote that 'the nations backed their machines over the precipice'.

Release was found for the masses by gathering 30,000 strong outside Buckingham Palace singing *God Save the King*, and smashing the windows of the German Embassy. Others were not so sanguine. Wrote Max Beerbohm: 'What a world! What a period to have been born into! It is very epical and all that; but the horror and sadness and absurdity of it all . . . But so far as one can foresee, the thing is not so much a purge as an additional poison'.[6] Only when the reality of war was brought home by the massive casualty lists did the euphoria succumb and Beerbohm's comment that it was not so much purge as poison make sense. 'The British nation surging forward in its ancient valour'— Winston Churchill again—moved more sluggishly as the cream of its young men were wiped out and bitterness took the place of gaiety.

Notes to this chapter are on page 295.

EPILOGUE

THE EDWARDIAN period can be seen as the first truly modern age, when the seeds of problems that bedevil us today were sown. Some have seen it as an overblown epilogue to the nineteenth century. There was certainly some overlap. Victorian manners and mores did not disappear with the death of the old queen, and, indeed, persisted throughout the war and into the 1920s. In many ways Victorian attitudes wore better; the Edwardian flower was forced too rapidly, an opulent and vulgar bloom that faded quickly, fostered on thin soil.

The Edwardians gathered in the fruit of Victorian energy and invention. Aids to industry and commerce, such as the telephone, the typewriter, and the electric motor, revolutionised life. There was also a spin off on the domestic front. A variety of labour-saving devices, such as the vacuum cleaner and the gas cooker, were assimilated into the home, and no longer were servants an essential part of middle-class life.

People had more time for entertainment, diversion and sport. Today's entertainment industry devolves from the Edwardian preoccupation with the pleasure principle. Women released from their homes occupied themselves with a variety of interests. There were not only bridge parties but women's leagues, and those well-brought-up women who fifty years earlier would have

The Edwardian preoccupation with the pleasure principle is well illustrated in this engraving

been condemned to a life of afternoon calls and needlework could opt for an outlet amongst the suffragettes—or they could even go out to work. The typewriter and the telephone offered increased opportunities for office-workers and made young women independent, heroines to the young writers of the time, such as H. G. Wells.

Edwardian women were more to be commended than their men folk. They brought a breath of life into the dull languid world of business, and in the newly-formed suburbs they

Edwardian women were everywhere, though their intrusion into men's preserves was not perhaps as idyllic as in this illustration

formulated a culture involving the gramophone, intellectual word games, cheap editions of the classics, and the new art. They bullied and cajoled their men into the great outdoor sport of the age, cycling, and the lanes of the home counties echoed to the ting-a-ling of their bicycle bells, occasionally punctuated by the shriek of a lady cyclist who had come face to face with the new-fangled motor car.

In a different category were the grand ladies, scorning the passage of time and living in the past, deploring the vulgarities of Edward VII and his court, looking askance at the shopocracy and the Jewish moneylenders accepted into society and basking in its calculated approval. There was a schism between the grand ladies of the old school and the fashionable society ladies, many of whom at some time seem to have been actresses and whose fate so often revolved around marriage to an American or to an aristocrat, or failing marriage, an alliance. Doll-like, brittle, with dresses and gowns costing hundreds of pounds apiece, and provoking underwear now named lingerie, these society ladies pervaded Ascot and Henley, motor car and balloon rallies, court and county ball, proving what money could buy.

No age was more conscious of money. Wealth was the criterion of merit. Financial wizards were welcomed into society, and only when they were sent to prison did their friends deplore their crooked behaviour. The preoccupation with money, no matter how it was obtained, extended to those classes formerly immune to the appeal of Mammon. Country clergymen eagerly fell victim to get-rich-quick schemes operated by the so-called 'bucket shops'.

A seven-roomed flat in the best suburbs could be rented for £50 a year, Scotch salmon was 2s per lb, and a Jermyn Street tailor would make a suit for six guineas. Champagne, sold on draught, was only 6d a glass in West End bars; postage was a penny; and income tax a shilling in the pound. £10,000 a year was a 'snug fortune'; one could keep a small house in town, a modest house in the country, and indulge in a little hunting. In London a fashionable bachelor could live exceedingly well on £500 a year.

The anomalies were evident. In 1903 it was reckoned that 21s 8d was the minimum living wage for a family of five. In 1914 nearly a quarter of the male wage earners earned less than 25s a week. Women in the sweated industries were lucky to earn more than 5s a week. Admittedly a six-roomed villa in subfusc Edmonton could be rented for 10s a week, but for the poor that was a fortune.

Bitterness between the haves and the have-nots underlay the whole period, and it is not surprising that this occasionally erupted in violence. Had the Liberal party not gained office and inaugurated the first feeble welfare state, the nation would probably have exploded, and only the outbreak of war prevented a full confrontation between capital and labour, a circumstance that was postponed until the 1926 General Strike. The assimilation of militant trade unionists into Parliament, where their

The contrast between haves and the have-nots was everywhere in evidence, no more so than in the City where street hawkers, bootblacks, billposters, and newspaper sellers rubbed shoulders with the richest in the land

claws were smartly trimmed, also did much to rob labour of its threat.

The ineptitude of management and government in coping with the upsurge of the poor has never been forgotten. The inability to come to terms arose from a refusal to recognise that things had changed. The poor were still poor, but they wanted to know why. They were served with greater information. They knew that the purchasing power of the pound was getting less and less, and also that dividends were increasing. The conclusion they drew was correct: the rich were only concerned with getting richer, preferably with no exertion, preferring to ignore the economic and industrial progress of France and Germany and investing in money-making schemes in the Empire, such as South African gold, rather than revitalising British industry by putting in new machinery, thus increasing productivity, and raising wages to a viable level. The moribund state of British industry was a result of laziness at the top, and greed.

Engaged in an orgy of spending, it is not surprising that the well-off preferred to suppress their anxieties and apprehensions. Had they devoted more attention to a cold study of the problems facing Britain rather than to yachting, motoring and sport, these problems might have been solved. It was not idle apprehension, however; the problems were real. Prestige-laden as was the Royal Navy, it could not be denied that there were things about it that were not as they should be, that the expensive dreadnought programme had been effectively countered by the Germans, and that control by the Admiralty was haphazard and disputed. The problems of capital and labour were only too real—no one could ignore the waves of strikes that every so often paralysed a section of industry.

The activities of the suffragettes also caused alarm. To the better off these were more dismaying than the machinations of the kaiser or the unruly workers. There had always been troubles with Europe and the lower orders had always to be watched and kept in check. That womenfolk, even those of breeding and education, should indulge in violence and destructive acts—this was frightening and difficult to combat, particularly as no one knew where the suffragettes would strike next. The Edwardians reacted instinctively to the threats to a life that was becoming increasingly complex and difficult to manage. The Victorians had made the internal combustion engine and the electric motor viable; nineteenth-century America had perfected a host of industrial marvels from the sewing machine to the telephone, and technical advances in the communication media, principally the newspaper, provided too much data for the consumer to assimilate.

The newspaper proprietors made certain that readers' half-hidden anxieties were prodded and probed. Every irritant was magnified by Northcliffe and his contemporaries; and international events that would have been dismissed with a nod by Lord Palmerston were gloated over and presented in frightening terms. The British newspaper magnates had learned of the power of the press from America, where the Hearst newspapers had been instrumental in starting a war with Spain over Cuba.

*There was escape—into the countryside and to the seaside. It was a boom period for
hotel and boarding-house keepers. Ramsgate was very popular among Londoners*

British newspapers did not quite manage a war, but not for want of trying.

Instant communication produces instant knowledge, and when the lower and lower-middle classes had their prejudices played upon first of all by the *Daily Mirror*, and then, in 1911, by the *Daily Herald* (started by the London Society of Compositors as a strike sheet) there was sufficient ill-feeling and half-understood information on all sides to guarantee apprehension or even panic. The newly informed classes were acquainted with the trials and tribulations of the government, not realising that the vehemence between Conservatives and Liberals was a component of a highly sophisticated game. Timid readers of the *Daily Herald* on 25 January 1911 reacted like scalded cats to the motto on the front page:

> Like the rolling on of ocean
> > In the eventide of fear—
> 'Tis the People marching on.

It was easy to escape from pressures and anxieties. The rich had their motor-cars, the middle classes had their beloved bicycles and the young men their motor cycles. The increasing network of tramways made the countryside available to Londoners, motor buses became extremely popular, while the railways ran seaside excursions. Pleasure weekends were spent at the coast; there was a boarding-house boom, and Margate, Southend and Brighton echoed with the revelry of clerks out on a spree. For those with rural tastes the Edwardian age was an ideal one to live in, for, with the departure of farm workers to the towns, country cottages could be bought for a song by weekenders.

Life was more complicated, and so was commerce and business. Despite the eight-per-cent unemployment figure, there was a constant demand for white-collar workers, and with the coming of the welfare state the government needed a host of clerks to man the newly-formed labour exchanges and to unravel the mysteries of national insurance. Few would have guessed that there was industrial stagnation as London spread and new prestige

The dream of the future. Or was it a nightmare?

office blocks arose, and there was no shortage of money for vast metropolitan enterprises such as the continuation of the Thames Embankment towards Chelsea and the driving of Kingsway through the slums of Drury Lane. Hectic and noisy, the new London seemed to indicate that there was a master mind at work, creating a great new capital for the Empire.

The redevelopment of London was deceptive. Planners preferred not to think of slums and slum clearance, and as Lutyens and others designed country houses for those who could afford them—it was the last time a sizeable country house could be economically built—the poor lived in squalor, a squalor made more profound by the fact that many charitable organisations of Victorian times had disappeared, and there were few to sponsor working-men's dwellings.

Muddle and go-as-you-please resulted in an untidy and meandering London. Ribbon-building extended along the roads made civilised by the coming of the tram. The motor car and the motor bus did not come neatly and methodically, but were crammed into the dusty London streets alongside horse-drawn buses, lumbering waggons, coal carts, and the assortment of

personalised horse-drawn vehicles. The Underground railway
was a stop-go project, only made viable by the introduction of
the electric engine. Businesses and shops were drawn as if by a
magnet to the Piccadilly and Oxford Street areas, creating
traffic problems that are with us still. London was a mess, and no
one cared. There were palliatives but no remedies; the attempt
to capitalise on magic Oxford Street failed—New Oxford Street
never caught on.

Much the same was true in the provinces—a dashing new
building here, a new road there, and, above all, a suburbia brought
into being by better road communications—a wasteful and bitty
suburbia undisturbed by town planning acts and left much to itself
for more than forty years. We are the inheritors of Edwardian
laissez faire, in housing, in roads, in dispute between capital and
labour, management and workers, and of Edwardian unwilling-
ness to replenish the life blood of British industry.

The 1914–18 war solved many problems. Although it created
more unemployment no one, except the Germans, could be
blamed any more. It brought new life to industry, and the
munitions and arms factories moved into top gear with a
fluency that would have gratified the giants of the Industrial
Revolution. The war helped to solve the suffrage problem; the
four years did more for feminine self-sufficiency than half a
century of vociferous agitation. The troubles of the Irish
drifted into a lower key, and the domestic wrangles between
Liberals and Conservatives became dull and vacuous. The
politicians no longer had to wait and see. The event they had dimly
foreseen had happened, and it was not so bad as they had thought.

NOTES AND REFERENCES

Death of a Great Queen (PAGE 13)

1 Gladstone, Mary. *Diaries and Letters* (1930), 454
2 Strachey, Lytton. *Queen Victoria* (1921), 269
3 St Helier, Lady. *Memories of Fifty Years* (1910), 352
4 Beerbohm, Max. *Letters to Reggie Turner* (1964), 124
5 Ward, Mrs E. M. *Memories of Ninety Years* (1922), 84
6 Bowley, A. L. *The Change and Distribution of the National Income* (1920), 21
7 Lane, Margaret. *Edgar Wallace* (1936), 173
8 Escott, T. H. S. *London Society in the New Reign* (1904), 90
9 Sitwell, Osbert. *Left Hand, Right Hand!* (1945), 241

King and Queen (PAGE 27)

1 Lane, Margaret. *Edgar Wallace* (1936), 195
2 Fitzroy, Sir Almeric. *Memoirs* (1926), 99-100
3 Athlone, Princess Alice, Countess of. *For My Grandchildren* (1966)
4 Paget, Lady Walburga. *Embassies of Other Days* (1923), 152-5
5 Young, Kenneth. *Arthur James Balfour* (1963), 236
6 Redesdale, Lord. *Memories* (1915), 185
7 One of His Majesty's Servants. *Private Life of the King* (1901), 89
8 Redesdale, Lord. *Memories* (1915), 187
9 Gore, John. *King George V* (1941), 117
10 Hearnshaw, F. J. C. *Edwardian England* (1933), 62
11 Conan Doyle, A. *Memories and Adventures* (1924), 331
12 Playne, C. E. *Society at War* (1931), 115

The Men at the Top (PAGE 42)

1 Escott, T. H. S. *London Society in the New Reign* (1904), 75
2 Raymond, E. T. *Uncensored Celebrities* (1918), 118
3 *The Free Trader* (31 July 1903)
4 Owen, Frank. *Tempestuous Journey* (1954), 142
5 Raymond, E. T. *Uncensored Celebrities* (1918), 87
6 Owen, Frank. *Tempestuous Journey* (1954), 143
7 Buchan, John. *Memory Hold the Door* (1940), 161
8 Raymond, E. T. *Uncensored Celebrities* (1918), 82
9 Magnus, Philip. *King Edward VII* (1964) 412
10 Maurice, Sir Frederick. *Haldane* (1937), 165

London—The Great Sprawl (PAGE 57)

1 Burke, T. *Nights in Town* (c 1915), 75

Society in Jeopardy (PAGE 71)

1 Esher, Lord. *Journal and Letters* (1934), 383
2 Conan Doyle, A. *Memories and Adventures* (1924), 266
3 Wells, H. G. *Experiment in Autobiography* (1934), 635
4 Sitwell, Osbert. *Left Hand, Right Hand!* (1945), 182
5 Bennett, Arnold. *Journals 1898-1910* (1932), 274
6 Cardigan, Countess of. *My Recollections* (1911), 174
7 Nevill, Lady Dorothy. *Reminiscences* (1906), 121
8 Escott, T. H. S. *London Society in the New Reign* (1904), 102
9 Cunnington, C. Willett. *English Women's Clothing in the Present Century* (1952)
10 Escott, T. H. S. *London Society in the New Reign* (1904), 125

Suburban Life (PAGE 84)

1 Nowell-Smith, Simon, ed. *Edwardian England* (1964), 365
2 Hobhouse, L. T. *Democracy and Reaction* (1904), 70
3 *Magazine of Art* (1903), 276
4 *Magazine of Art* (1903), 325
5 *Magazine of Art* (1903), 379
6 Gaunt, William. *The Aesthetic Adventure* (1945), 182
7 Bentley, E. C. 'The Inoffensive Captain', *Strand Magazine* (1914)
8 Blackwood, Algernon. *Secret Worship* (1908)
9 Benson, E. F. *The Room in the Tower* (1912)
10 Swan, Tom. *Edward Carpenter* (1905), 24
11 Benson, A. C. *Diary* (1926), 252
12 Greenwall, Harry J. *Northcliffe* (1957), 94

The Condition of the People (PAGE 103)

1 Masterman, C. F. G. *The Condition of the People* (1909), 15
2 Bosanquet, Helen. *Poor Law Report* (1909), 145
3 Bosanquet, Helen. *Poor Law Report* (1909), 148
4 Bosanquet, Helen. *Poor Law Report* (1909), 149
5 Bosanquet, Helen. *Poor Law Report* (1909), 172
6 Bosanquet, Helen. *Poor Law Report* (1909), 180
7 Rowntree, Seebohm. *Poverty* (1903), 103
8 London, Jack. *The People of the Abyss* (1902)
9 Owen, Frank. *Tempestuous Journey* (1954), 171

The Rural Exodus (PAGE 118)

1 Haggard, H. Rider. *Rural Britain* (1902), II, 542
2 Haggard, H. Rider. *Rural Britain* (1902), II, 542
3 Carpenter, Edward. *My Days and Dreams* (1916), 282
4 Lyttelton, Rev Hon E. *Memories and Hopes* (1925), 194
5 Green, Peter. *Kenneth Grahame* (1959), 294
6 Benson, A. C. *Diary* (1926), 166

The Coming of the Motor Car (PAGE 128)

1 Northcliffe, Lord, et al. *Motors and Motor Driving* (1906), 61
2 Northcliffe, Lord, et al. *Motors and Motor Driving* (1906), 307
3 Peel, Mrs C. S. *100 Wonderful Years* (1920), 119
4 Blumenfeld, R. D. *Diary*

Eugenics and Birth Control (PAGE 143)

1 Ussher, R. *Neo-Malthusianism* (1897), 93
2 Schuster, Edgar. *Eugenics* (1913), 75
3 Ellis, Havelock. *Man and Woman* (1914), 529

Edwardian Love and Romance (PAGE 155)

1 Aldington, Richard. *Portrait of a Genius But* (1950), 137
2 Wells, H. G. *Experiment in Autobiography* (1934), 438
3 Wells, H. G. *Experiment in Autobiography* (1934), 478

The Feminists (PAGE 166)

1 Wells, H. G. *Experiment in Autobiography* (1934), 483–4
2 Pankhurst, E. S. *The Suffragette Movement* (1935) 209
3 Pankhurst, E. S. *The Suffragette Movement* (1935), 332
4 Wells, H. G. *Experiment in Autobiography* (1934), 485

The War Lords (PAGE 186)

1 Fisher, Lord. *Memories* (1919), 274
2 Fisher, Lord. *Records* (1925), 174
3 Nowell-Smith, Simon, ed. *Edwardian England* (1964), 520
4 Wolseley, Lord and Lady. *Letters* (1922), 380
5 Raymond, E. T. *Portraits of the New Century* (1928), 289
6 Esher, Lord. *Journal and Letters* (1934), I, 401
7 Fitzroy, Sir Almeric. *Memoirs* (1926), I, 212
8 Maurice, Sir Frederick. *Haldane* (1937), 134
9 Magnus, Philip. *King Edward VII* (1964), 331
10 Raymond, E. T. *Portraits of the New Century* (1928), 164

The American Threat (PAGE 203)

1 Adams, W. S. A. *Edwardian Heritage* (1949), 74
2 Woodward, W. E. *A New American History* (1938), 571
3 Bennett, Arnold. *Journals 1898–1910* (1932), 73
4 Roosevelt, Theodore. *Edited Correspondence* (1922), I, 200
5 Morton, A. L. *A People's History of England* (1948), 476
6 Nevill, Lady Dorothy. *Leaves from the Note Books* (1910), 31
7 Young, Kenneth. *Arthur James Balfour* (1963), 277

The Sporting Life (PAGE 217)

1 Ribblesdale, Lord. *Impressions and Memories* (1927), xxii
2 Laver, James, ed. *Edwardian Promenade* (1958), 33

Showbiz (PAGE 230)

1 Sitwell, Osbert. *The Scarlet Tree* (1946), 290
2 Pearson, Hesketh. *Bernard Shaw* (1948), 240

Murder Most Foul (PAGE 262)

1 Marjoribanks, Edward. *Sir Edward Marshall Hall* (1929), 250.
2 Symons, Julian. *Bloody Murder* (1972), 14
3 Roughhead, William. *Tales of the Criminous* (1956), 254

Prelude to War (PAGE 275)

1 Benson, A. C. *Life and Letters of Maggie Benson* (1917), 381
2 Jacks, L. P. *Life and Letters of Stopford Brooke* (1917), II, 653
3 Owen, Frank. *Tempestuous Journey* (1954), 212
4 Aldington, Richard. *Portrait of a Genius But* (1950), 267
5 Beerbohm, Max. *Letters to Reggie Turner* (1964), 176

BIBLIOGRAPHY

Adams, W. S. *Edwardian Heritage* (1949)

Alden, P. *The Unemployed* (1905)

Anon. *Private Life of the King* (1901)

Bailey, L. *Edwardian Scrapbook 1900–1914* (1957)

Baker, H. T. *The Territorial Force* (1909)

Beaton, Cecil. *The Glass of Fashion* (1954)

Bennett, Arnold. *Journals 1896–1910* (1932)

Beveridge, W. H. *Unemployment* (1909)

Bosanquet, Helen. *The Standard of Life* (1906)

Bosanquet, Helen. *The Poor Law Report* (1909)

Bowley, A. L. *The Change and Distribution of the National Income* (1920)

Briggs, Asa. *Seebohm Rowntree* (1961)

Bryce, Lord. *Hindrances to Good Citizenship* (1909)

Burke, T. *Nights in Town* (1915)

Campbell, Lady Colin. *Etiquette* (1911)

Carter, E. F. *Edwardian Cars* (1955)

Cecil, Robert. *Life in Edwardian England* (1969)

Clegg, H. A. *A History of British Trade Unions* (1964)

Cole, G. D. H. *World of Labour* (1913)

Cornwallis West, G. *Edwardian Hey-Days* (1930)

Cowles, Virginia. *Edward VII and his Circle* (1956)

Cowles, Virginia. *1913: The Defiant Swan Song* (1967)

Cunnington, C. Willett. *English Women's Clothing in the Present Century* (1952)

Cust, Sir Lionel. *King Edward VII and his Court* (1930)

Davies, Maud F. *Life in an English Village* (1909)

Dickinson, G. Lowes. *The International Anarchy ,1904–14* (1926)

Dilnot, G. *Scotland Yard* (1926)

Doyle, A. Conan. *Memories and Adventures* (1924)

Edes, Mary, ed. *Age of Extravagance* (1955)

Ensor, R. C. K. *England 1870–1914* (1936)

Escott, T. H. S. *Society in the New Reign* (1904)

Esher, Lord. *Journal and Letters* (1934)

Farrer, J. A. *England under Edward VII* (1922)

Fisher, Lord. *Memories* (1919)

Fitzroy, Sir Almeric. *Memoirs* (1926)

Frere, J. A. *The British Monarchy at Home* (1963)

Fulford, R. *Votes for Women* (1957)

George, W. L. *Women and Tomorrow* (1913)

Gilman, C. P. *Woman and Economics* (1905)

Gladstone, Mary. *Diaries and Letters* (1930)

Gooch, G. P. ed. *British Documents on the Origin of the War* (1928)

Gretton, R. H. *Modern History of the English People 1880–1922* (1912–29)

Grey, Viscount. *Twenty-Five Years* (1928)

Haggard, H. Rider. *Rural England* (1902)

Halévy, E. *The Rule of Democracy* (1952)

Heath, F. G. *British Rural Life and Labour* (1911)

Hearnshaw, F. J. C. *Edwardian England 1901–10* (1933)

Hobhouse, L. T. *Democracy and Reaction* (1904)

Hobson, J. A. *Psychology of Jingoism* (1901)

Hobson, J. A. *The Social Problem* (1901)

Hobson, J. A. *The Industrial System* (1909)

Humphreys, A. W. *History of Labour Representation* (1912)

Hynes, S. *The Edwardian Turn of Mind* (1968)

Jones, L. E. *An Edwardian Youth* (1956)

Kennedy, R. *Book of the Motor Car* (1913)

Lane, Margaret. *Edgar Wallace* (1936)

Laver, James. *Edwardian Promenade* (1958)

Lee, Sidney. *King Edward VII* (1925–7)

Liddell, A. G. C. *Notes from the Life of an Ordinary Mortal* (1911)

London, Jack. *People of the Abyss* (1903)

Maccoby, S. *English Radicalism 1886–1914* (1953)

MacDonald, Ramsay. *Socialism and Society* (1905)

Magnus, Philip. *Kitchener* (1958)

Magnus, Philip. *Edward VII* (1964)

Mann, H. H. *Life in an Agricultural Village* (1905)

Masterman,·C. F. G. *In Peril of Change* (1908)

Masterman, C. F. G. *Condition of England* (1909)

Maurice, Sir Frederick. *Haldane* (1937)

Minney, R. J. *The Edwardian Age* (1964)

Money, L. G. C. *Riches and Poverty* (1905)
Morton, A. L. *A People's History of England* (1938)
Muirhead, J. H. *Service of the State* (1908)
Nevill, Lady Dorothy. *Reminiscenses* (1906)
Newnham-Davis, Lt-Col. *Dinners and Diners* (1910)
Nicolson, Harold. *King George V* (1952)
Northcliffe, Lord, ed. *Motors and Motor-Driving* (1906)
Nowell-Smith, Simon, ed. *Edwardian England* 1901–1914 (1964)
Owen, Frank. *Tempestuous Journey* (1954)
Pankhurst, E. S. *The Suffragette Movement* (1935)
Peel, Mrs C. S. *How to Keep House* (1902)
Peel, Mrs C. S. *Life's Enchanted Cup* (1933)
Petrie, Sir Charles. *Drift to World War* 1900–14 (1968)
Playne, C. E. *Society at War* (1931)
Ponsonby, Sir Frederick. *Recollections of Three Reigns* (1951)
Pope, W. MacQueen. *The Melodies Linger On* (1950)
Priestley, J. B. *The Edwardians* (1972)
Prothero, R. E. *English Farming Past and Present* (1912)
Purdom, C. B. *The Garden City* (1913)
Raymond, E. T. *Uncensored Celebrities* (1918)
Raymond, E. T. *Portraits of the New Century* (1928)
Reeves, Mrs Pember. *Round About a Pound a Week* (1913)
Rowntree, B. S. *Poverty* (1901)
Russell, G. W. E. *Prime Ministers and Some Others* (1918)
Spender, J. A. and Asquith, Cyril. *Herbert Henry Asquith* (1932)
St Helier, Lady. *Memories of Fifty Years* (1910)
Strachey, Ray. *The Cause* (1928)
Street, G. S. *People and Questions* (1910)
Tweedsmuir, Susan. *The Edwardian Lady* (1966)
Wallas, G. *Human Nature in Politics* (1908)
Warwick, Frances, Countess of. *Afterthoughts* (1931)
Webb, S. and B. *English Poor Law Policy* (1910)
Wells, H. G. *Anticipations* (1901)
Wells, H. G. *A Modern Utopia* (1905)
Wells, H. G. *First and Last Things* (1908)
Wells, H. G. *Experiment in Autobiography* (1934)
Young, A. B. F. *The Complete Motorist* (1904)
Young, K. *Arthur James Balfour* (1963)

The following newspapers, magazines and reference books of the period also provide interesting material:
Cassell's Magazine; Daily Herald; Daily Mail; Daily Mirror; Daily Telegraph; Girls' Own Annual; Illustrated London News; The King; National Review; News of the

World; Nineteenth Century; Pall Mall Magazine; Pearson's Magazine; Punch; Quarterly Review; Queen; Reynold's Newspaper; Sphere; Strand; Tatler; The Times; Woman at Home; Woman's World.

Annual Register; Daily Mail Year Book; Whitaker's Almanack

INDEX